Fitness Training
in Football
– a Scientific Approach

Jens Bangsbo

August Krogh Institute,
University of Copenhagen
Denmark

1

tos:
ational player
B...ing training
(ga... Brøndby
IF, D...
later ...

© 1994 Jens Bangsbo.

Publisher: HO+Storm, Bagsværd.
Translation: Ylva Hellsten,
Paul Balsom, Tine Bak, Matt Rogers,
Sophie Musgrove, Jens Bangsbo.
English edition:
Jens Bangsbo, Ylva Hellsten.
Photos: Per Kjærbye.
Artist: Helge Torn.
ISBN: 87-983350-7-3

Printed in Denmark

Foreword

I have known Jens Bangsbo for many years, both as a player and an exercise physiologist, and have greatly benefited from the information provided by him. He possesses the ability to combine experience as a player with scientific knowledge, and to apply new scientific findings to football training in a way that is understandable to coaches and players.

„Fitness training in football - a scientific approach" covers all the physical aspects of football, and presents information on fitness training and preparation for matches that has not previously been available to coaches. Exercises are well described and it is easy to perform the suggested training. The training is efficient and allows the players to develop their fitness level and technical skills at the same time.

In the past, Danish players have been characterized as being technically skilful but physically inferior. In the recent years, however, the players' fitness level has greatly improved, and part of the present success for Danish football, both at a club and national team level, can be attributed to the application of the principles and exercises presented in this book.

The book has proven invaluable for me as a coach, and I strongly recommend it to anyone who wants to improve individual and team performance.

Richard Møller Nielsen,

coach of the Danish National team,
coach of the year 1992 (World Soccer).

Preface

Through the years I have participated in many fitness training sessions, which I afterwards have realized were of little value. This was either due to the training being of limited relevance to football, or due to the improvement gained from the training soon being lost again since the particular aspect of training was not maintained. It is important that the fitness training is specific and efficient, especially because this training often is both physically and mentally demanding.

Results from scientific studies can help to obtain a better understanding of the demands and the limitations of physical performance in football. Such knowledge combined with practical experience provides a good basis for planning optimal programmes for fitness training. A few years ago I attempted to take this approach in two books about fitness training in football. I was pleased that the books created interest among coaches and that Scandinavian Football Associations selected them to be compulsory teaching material. This encouraged me to update and edit the material into one book, and to translate it into English. My hope is that the book will help to bridge the gap between science and practice, and that it will improve preparation for matches and fitness training in football.

I would like to take the opportunity to thank the coaches and the players, including the players in the Danish National team, for their great effort in the numerous studies performed. Furthermore, I want to extend my gratitude to all the individuals that have collaborated with me in the studies. Also, I want to thank Paul Balsom, Karolinska Institute, Sweden, for constructive discussions; John Brewer, Lilleshare, England, and Mary Nevill, Loughborough University, England, for comments on the manuscript; and especially Ylva Hellsten, August Krogh Institute, Denmark, for help with editing of the book. Finally, I would like to acknowledge the financial support and encouragement from the Danish Football Association, the Danish Sports Research Council (Idrættens Forskningsråd), and the Danish Elite Sports Organization (Team Denmark).

Football is not science –
but science may improve the level of football.

Jens Bangsbo, January, 1994

Content

Introduction

Anyone who observes a football match can recognize that football is a physically demanding sport. But how much does a player actually work during a match? What happens in the body when playing football? How do the players cope with the physical requirements? How should the players prepare for a match? In recent years scientific studies have provided a substantial amount of information in regard to these issues. This book combines scientific results with practical experience in order to give the reader an understanding of the basic principles of match preparation and evaluation of players.

The first chapter explains how the body functions during exercise, with a particular focus on how it responds during a football match. After watching a football game the observer is left with a general impression combined with recollections of specific situations. The amount of information that can be obtained through observation is limited however, and is influenced by subjective evaluations, even for the most experienced coach. In one chapter, an analysis of the physical demands of football is given, which is based on objective and systematic recordings as well as physiological measurements performed during games.

There are several reasons as to why performance testing can be beneficial in football, but a test is only effective if it is specific to the game. The chapter »Performance Testing« describes new tests which are relevant for football and designed to objectively assess a player's level of fitness.

In order to cope with the physical demands and to maintain the technical standard throughout a match, it is important that the players have a high level of fitness. Playing matches regularly helps maintain the fitness level of a player, but additional fitness training is required. The training should be specific to football, with an emphasis on performing exercises with a ball. Involving the ball during practice ensures that the muscles used in football are trained and also elevates the motivation of the players. It furthermore allows for efficient use of often limited training time, as technical skills and tactical knowledge are also practiced.

In two chapters, principles of fitness training are discussed in general terms, with practical suggestions on how to organize and conduct training. Considerations are made for all types of players, from recreational players, who train a couple of times a week, to full-time professionals. Fitness training should be based on the fitness level and the specific competencies of the actual group, as well as of the individual player. Furthermore, in order to cover all aspects of training in football it is important that fitness training is well integrated into the overall training programme.

The following chapters describe the three main areas of fitness training: aerobic, anaerobic, and specific muscle training. This terminology may not be familiar to the reader, but the terms are thoroughly explained and only used for the purpose of separating the different training forms. Within each of the chapters a number of training drills and exercises are given to illustrate the training principles.

The different components of fitness training should not be given the same priority all year around. The chapter »Planning the Season« describes how fitness training may be varied throughout the year as well as during the week. At the end of the book two chapters cover the importance of food and fluid intake for a football player. In recent years carbohydrate loading has been shown to improve the performance in endurance sports. Does that also apply to football? A recent study of top-class players gives an answer to that question. In addition, dietary recommendations to accommodate nutritional requirements for training and matches are provided. During a match a player should drink regularly to avoid dehydration and the associated detrimental effects on physical performance. Advice is given for how much, when, and what to drink before, during, and after a match.

The aims of this book are to help the reader understand and utilize fitness testing and training principles, as well as to provide guidelines for achieving effective match preparation. By combining this knowledge with experience about a specific group of players, a well-structured training can be attained, thus benefiting both the coach and the players.

Basic Physiology
of Football

*When kicking a
ball the working muscles
must generate energy.
How is this energy produced?*

Figure BP 1

The figure illustrates how oxygen (O_2) from the atmosphere is transported to a muscle. Air containing oxygen is inhaled through the mouth and passes via the trachea to the lungs where the oxygen diffuses into the blood. When the heart beats, blood carrying oxygen is transported to the muscle. The oxygen is used by the muscle for production of energy, and the by-product carbon dioxide (CO_2) is transported via the blood back to the lungs and removed from the body during exhalation.

Basic Physiology
of Football

This chapter describes how the body functions in football. It discusses the most important physiological responses to exercise, and the adaptations that occur as a result of training.

Oxygen transport

When breathing in (inhaling), air which contains approximately 21% oxygen (O_2) flows into the lungs. Some of the oxygen in the lungs diffuses into the blood via a complex network of air sacs, and is then transported to the muscles and different organs of the body. The oxygen transport system consists of heart, blood vessels, and blood (see Fig. BP 1). The right half of the heart pumps blood low in oxygen to the lungs for replenishment with oxygen. The oxygenated blood then flows to the left half of the heart. When the heart muscle contracts (heart beat), the blood is then pumped to all parts of the body via blood vessels. When the blood arrives at a muscle it flows into smaller blood vessels (capillaries) where some of the oxygen and nutrients in the blood, such as carbohydrate and fat, are liberated for use by the muscle fibres. Within the muscle, the nutrients are broken down chemically in a process that requires oxygen, resulting in the release of energy. One of the by-products of this energy production is carbon dioxide (CO_2), which is transported by the blood to the lungs where it is then removed during breathing out (exhaling).

The different components of oxygen transport are described in detail below.

Ventilation (breathing)

Air is drawn into the lungs through the contraction of a large dome-shaped sheet of muscle above the stomach (diaphragm). When the diaphragm relaxes shortly after, the air within the lungs is exhaled. This movement of air in and out of the lungs is called ventilation, and the rate of ventilation can be determined by measuring the amount of air that is exhaled in one minute.

In a resting state ventilation is around five litres of air per minute (l/min). During exercise, ventilation increases due to the increased demand for oxygen in the muscles and can rise to 100 l/min for untrained individuals. For extremely well-trained athletes it may exceed 200 l/min. Maximum ventilation can be increased by training, e.g. the average maximum ventilation of a group of Danish players increased from approximately 142 to 148 l/min after four weeks of intensive training (see Fig. BP 2).

There are certain factors which may affect ventilation. For example, if the amount of oxygen in the air is reduced the body tries to compensate for this by inhaling more air. This is illustrated by the findings in a study with the players on the 1986 Danish World Cup team. They performed a given sub-maximal bout of exercise at sea level and at an altitude simulating that of Mexico City (about 2300 metres above sea level), where the air contains less oxygen. It was observed that the ventilation of 105 l/min at this altitude was 15 l/min higher than at sea level.

Circulation

The function of the heart is to pump blood around the body. Cardiac output (cardiac = heart) is the total amount of blood that the heart pumps out per minute. The amount of blood which is pumped out per heart beat is called

Figure BP 2

The figure shows the ventilation and heart rate during maximal-intensity exercise for a group of Danish players before and after a four-week training period. The training increased the maximum ventilation, whereas there was no change in the maximum heart rate.

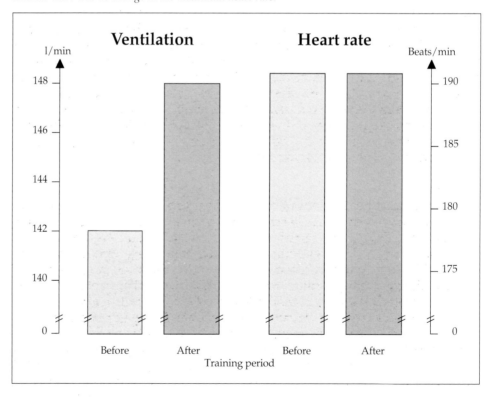

stroke volume. Heart rate refers to the number of times the heart beats per minute. The following relationship exists between these three variables:

Cardiac output = Stroke volume x heart rate

In a resting state, roughly 80 millilitres (ml) of blood is pumped per heart beat (stroke volume) and a normal resting heart rate is about 60 beats per minute (beats/min). Thus, at rest the heart pumps out approximately five litres (80 ml x 60 beats/min) of blood per minute (cardiac output).

Cardiac output
Cardiac output increases during exercise as a result of an increase in the oxygen demand of the active muscles. A rise in cardiac output from 5 l/min at rest to 25 l/min during maximal-intensity exercise is often observed.
The increase in cardiac output during exercise is accompanied by a redistribution of blood flow. Blood supply to the less active parts of the body, such as the liver and the kidneys, is decreased. Most of the blood is directed to the active muscles which have the greatest need for oxygen.
Fitness training improves the capacity of the heart to pump out blood – maximum cardiac output is increased. Very well-trained individuals can have a cardiac output of up to 40 l/min. The higher cardiac output after training allows for an increased blood supply and, thus, oxygen delivery to the active muscles during high-intensity exercise.

Stroke volume
The greater amount of blood that is pumped out by the heart during exercise is partly the result of an increase in stroke volume. During maximal-intensity exercise when cardiac output can be 25 l/min, the stroke volume may be 125 ml in comparison to 80 ml at rest. Endurance training enables the heart to hold more blood and its muscular structure becomes stronger. Consequently, the heart is able to pump out more blood per heart beat and an increase in stroke volume is the reason for the higher maximum cardiac output observed after a training period. Values of 200 ml of blood per heart beat have been measured for top-class endurance athletes.

Heart rate
At rest the heart beats about 60 times per minute. Well-trained endurance athletes have a lower resting heart rate which, in extreme cases, can be below 30 beats/min. During exercise the heart rate rises which results in an increase in cardiac output. The maximum heart rate for young women and men around 20 years of age is about 200 beats/min. However, there is a large range within a given age group. In a study of a group of boys and girls aged 16 to 19, a range in maximum heart rate from 180 to 230 beats/min was found. In order to make use of heart rate measurements during training it is necessary to determine the maximum heart rate for each player. For example, a heart rate of 170 beats/min recorded during a training game could reflect a very high exercise intensity for a player with a maximum heart rate of 180 beats/min (exercising at a level corresponding to 94% of maximum heart

rate). However, for a player with a maximum heart rate of 230 beats/min the exercise would be less demanding, as 170 beats/min would correspond to only 74% of maximum heart rate.

Maximum heart rate decreases as age increases. A 20-year-old individual with a maximum heart rate of 200 beats/min might have a heart rate of only 170 beats/min when 60 years old.

Heart rate during exercise is influenced by both the environment and by training. In the study of the Danish players competing in the 1986 World Cup, the average heart rate of the players during a standard bout of exercise performed at an altitude corresponding to that of Mexico City was 12 beats/min higher than at sea level. Thus, for the same exercise the heart had to work harder at a high altitude compared to at sea level.

Endurance training causes an increase in stroke volume, thus the heart does not have to beat so often in order to pump out the same amount of blood. Therefore, the heart rate will be lower at a given exercise intensity after a period of training (see Fig. BP 3). Training does not, however, affect the maximum heart rate. For example, the average heart rate for a group of

Figure BP 3
The figure illustrates how training affects heart rate. Before and after a period of training a player's heart rate was recorded at three different running speeds. After the training, the heart rate was lower for the two lower running speeds, whereas the heart rate was unchanged during the maximal running. For comparison, values for an untrained person with the same maximum heart rate as the player are also shown.

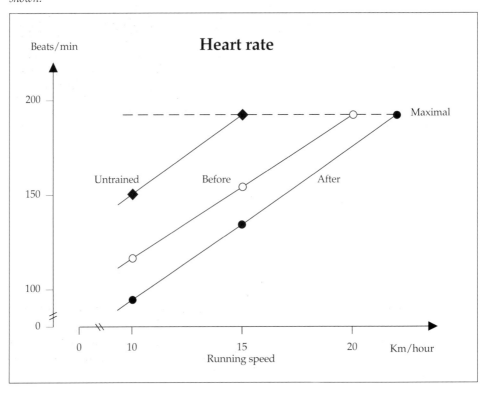

In order to prepare for the 1986 World Cup in Mexico, the Danish players trained wearing equipment which lowered the oxygen content of the air breathed.

Danish players during maximal-intensity exercise was 191 beats/min both before and after a period of intensive training (see Fig. BP 2 – page 18). Thus, an increase in maximum cardiac output as a result of training is not caused by the heart beating more frequently, but by an increase in the amount of blood pumped out into the circulation per heart beat.

Blood

The volume of blood in an average adult is approximately five litres. About 40-45% of the blood consists of red blood cells. The remaining portion of the blood is a fluid called plasma. The red colour of the blood is due to the protein hemoglobin which is found in the blood cells. Hemoglobin binds oxygen and is important for the transport of oxygen from the lungs to all parts of the body where the oxygen is to be used. The concentration of hemoglobin (the amount of hemoglobin per litre of blood) is not changed by training, but the total blood volume can increase. Blood volume has been found to increase from five to seven litres with many years of endurance training. An increase in blood volume enhances the capacity to supply oxygen to the muscles.

In the plasma, protein, fat, and carbohydrate are transported. Furthermore, plasma removes substances such as lactate, which have been released from different tissues. During exercise, blood also has an important role in the transport of heat, generated in the active muscles, to the skin where it is liberated to the surroundings. By an increase in blood flow to the skin during exercise overheating may be avoided (see page 34).

Energy production

Energy production with oxygen (aerobic)

Energy is needed in order for the muscles to function. This energy may be derived from the chemical breakdown of different substrates with the utilization of oxygen. Because oxygen is used, the process is termed aerobic energy production (aero = air). As a by-product of this process carbon dioxide is produced (see Fig. BP 4).

The amount of oxygen that the body uses per minute is termed oxygen uptake. At rest the oxygen uptake is about 0.3 l/min. During exercise the oxygen uptake is higher than at rest and increases with increasing exercise intensity. However, the capacity to transport and utilize oxygen is limited. The largest amount of oxygen that can be used per minute by the body is termed maximum oxygen uptake. For healthy individuals, the maximum oxygen uptake is within the range of 2 to 7 l/min. More energy, and thus oxygen, is needed to move a heavier body. To make comparisons between individuals of different sizes, the value for maximum oxygen uptake may be divided by the body weight. By this calculation, an individual who weighs 80

Figure BP 4

The figure shows how energy is produced in the muscles through aerobic and anaerobic processes. For aerobic energy production, oxygen (O_2) is utilized in processes in which fat and carbohydrate (glycogen) are used. Anaerobic energy production does not require oxygen and proceeds either through the breakdown of high-energy phosphates stored in the muscle, or by the use of carbohydrate (glycogen) with the formation of lactate.

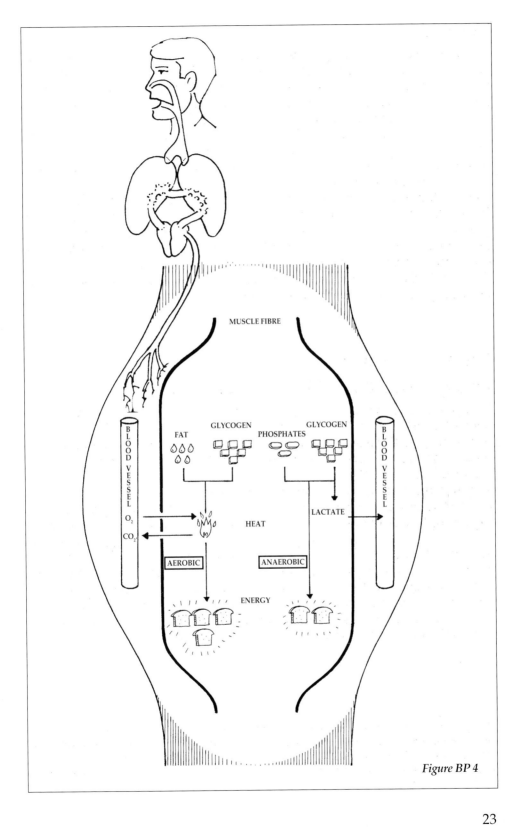

Figure BP 4

23

Figure BP 5

The figure shows two players with the same maximum oxygen uptake (4 l/min), but with different body weights. Thus, the two players have a different maximum oxygen uptake when expressed per kg body weight (67 vs. 50 ml/min/kg), and the demand will be greater for the heavier player if the two players run at the same speed.

kg and who has a maximal oxygen uptake of 4 l/min will get a value of 50 ml/min/kg. Another individual with the same absolute maximum oxygen uptake, but with a body weight of 60 kg, will have a value of 67 ml/min/kg (see Fig. BP 5).

Figure BP 6 shows the average maximum oxygen uptake (expressed as ml/min/kg) for 82 top-class Danish male players and for 20 Danish female national team players. Values from other Danish elite athletes are included for comparison. The maximum oxygen uptake of the Danish players is similar to values obtained from other top-class players in Europe. Maximum oxygen uptake can be increased by training. After two months of intensive pre-season training, the maximum oxygen uptake of a group of Danish elite players increased from 57 to 62 ml/min/kg, without a change in body weight.

Figure BP 6
The figure illustrates the average maximum oxygen uptake expressed as ml oxygen/min/kg body weight for 20 female (on the left) and 82 male (on the right) top-class Danish football players. The results are compared with data for elite Danish handball players and long-distance runners, as well as with results for untrained individuals. The maximum oxygen uptake of the female and the male football players was higher than that of the untrained individuals, but considerably lower than that of the long-distance runners.

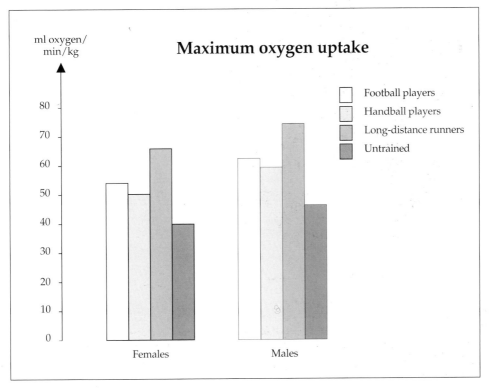

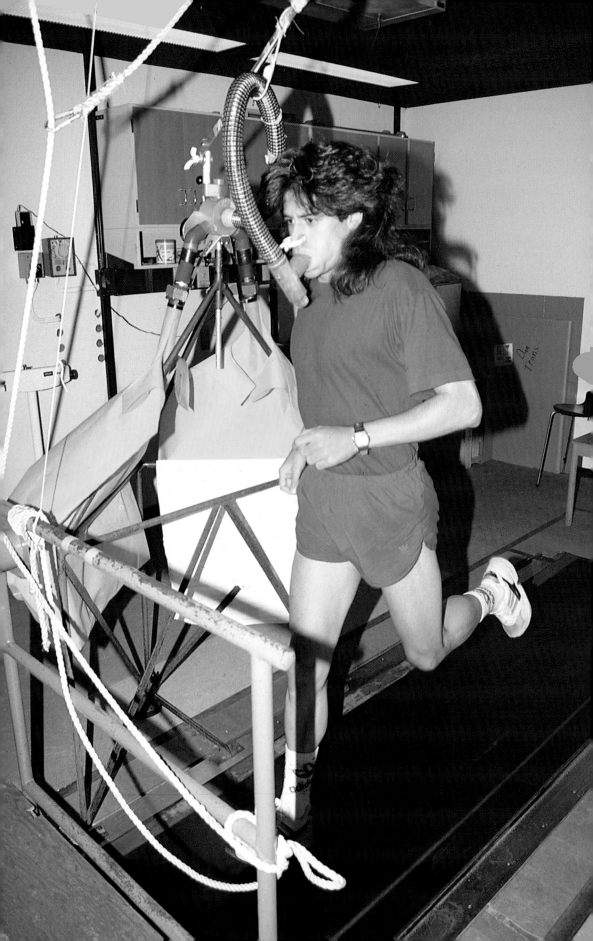

While it is relatively simple to measure a person's maximum oxygen uptake, it is more difficult to measure the endurance capacity, which is the person's potential to exercise for prolonged periods of time. There are several factors which determine endurance capacity but the most important is the extent to which fat can be used as a source of fuel. Different types of training can improve this capacity (see page 103).

Energy production without oxygen (anaerobic)

The transport of oxygen to the muscles is not always sufficient to enable energy demands to be met entirely by aerobic energy production. This applies especially at the beginning of exercise where there are rapid changes in energy demand and during high-intensity exercise. In such cases the muscles also produce energy through processes which do not require oxygen. These are called anaerobic energy processes (an = non, aero = air).

Small energy stores (high-energy phosphates) present in the muscles can rapidly make energy available through anaerobic processes (see Fig. BP 4). Energy can also be produced at a high rate from the anaerobic breakdown of carbohydrate (glycogen), where a substance called lactate is formed as an end product. During high-intensity exercise, lasting longer than a few seconds, a large amount of lactate is produced.

Lactate

Some of the produced lactate in active muscles is released into the blood, while the remainder accumulates within the muscles and can be used as a fuel to produce energy in the presence of oxygen (see Fig. BP 7 – page 28). As the intensity of exercise is increased, more lactate is produced, leading to a higher and higher muscle and blood lactate concentration.

Lactate released from the muscles is transported in the blood to the heart. Here, the blood from the muscles is mixed with blood from less active areas of the body, which has a lower lactate concentration (see Fig. BP 7). Thus, the lactate concentration in the blood leaving the heart is lower than that of the blood flowing directly from the active muscles to the heart. As the heart pumps blood around the body, it is possible to measure raised lactate concentrations in blood taken from the arm, even if it is the leg muscles that have produced the lactate. However, the lactate concentration in blood taken from the arm or fingertip gives only limited information about the amount of lactate produced, as the lactate in mixed blood has been diluted and because some lactate is used as a fuel by the exercising muscles and other tissues (see Fig. BP 7). Figure BP 8 shows two players with the same blood lactate concentration. From this picture one might wrongly conclude that the two

A player's maximum oxygen uptake can be determined by collecting exhaled air in bags during running until exhaustion on a motor driven treadmill. The volume of air in the bags is measured and the content of O_2 and CO_2 in the air is determined.

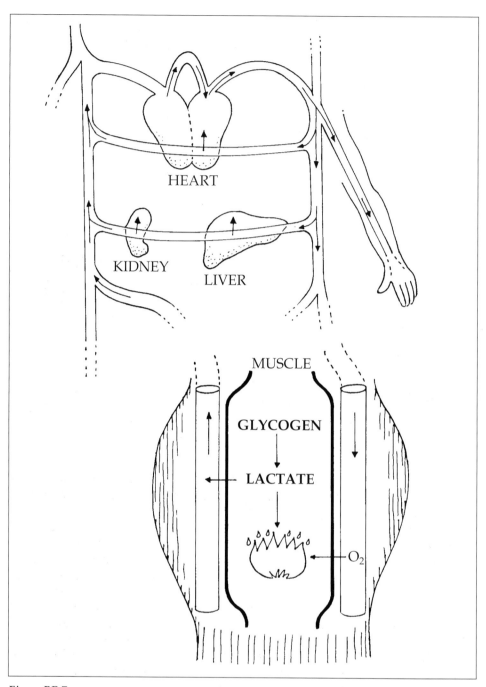

Figure BP 7
The figure illustrates the fate of lactate produced in the muscles. Some of the lactate remains in the muscle where it either accumulates or is used as a substrate for aerobic energy production. Lactate released into the blood is transported to the heart, which pumps it around the body, and various tissues, such as the heart, liver, and kidneys, absorb lactate from the blood. A small proportion of the lactate is transported to the arms. It is therefore possible to measure elevated lactate concentrations in blood sampled from the arm, even though exercise has been performed with the legs.

During high-intensity exercise the active muscles produce lactate.

players had produced the same amount of lactate. This is not correct however, as player B produced more lactate but also had a higher removal rate of lactate than player A.

There is another consideration to be made when using blood lactate concentration as an estimation of lactate production. During high-intensity exercise of short duration (i.e. 2-10 seconds) there is a large production of lactate which is not released into the blood. In a study it was demonstrated that with a 10 second period of maximal exercise the muscle lactate concentration was increased from 1 to 18 millimoles* (mmol)/kg of muscle. However, the blood lactate concentration did not increase above 5 mmol per litre (mmol/l) of blood. It is clear that blood lactate concentration only gives an indication that lactate has been formed, and that the production of lactate during high-intensity exercise can only be accurately determined by measuring lactate concentration directly in the exercising muscles.

*The unit »millimoles« (mmol) indicates a certain quantity of a substance. This unit is practical to use within the disciplines of chemistry because it allows substances to be compared. In a resting state the lactate concentration in both muscles and blood is around 1 mmol (per kilogram of muscle and per litre of blood, respectively) which corresponds to an absolute quantity of 90 milligrams.

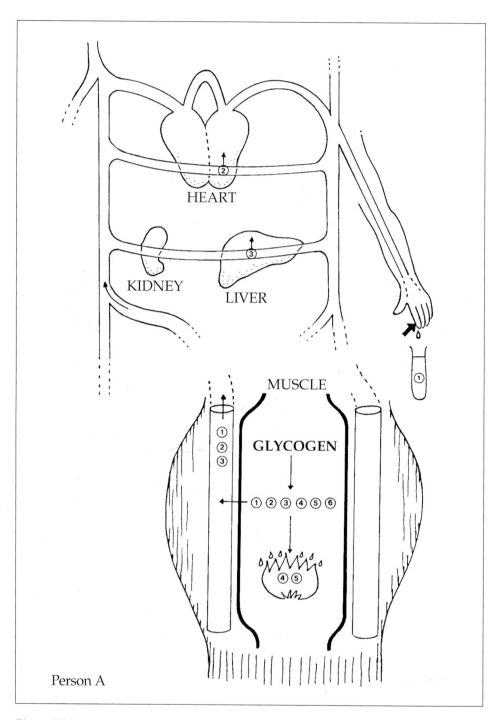

Figure BP 8
The figure schematically illustrates an example of the fate of lactate after exercise for two individuals. Person A produced less lactate (six units) than person B (nine units) during exercise. The lactate that remained in the muscle for A and B was three and four units, respectively, but as B utilized the lactate within the muscle more efficiently, both individuals accumulated one unit of lactate in the muscle ⑥.

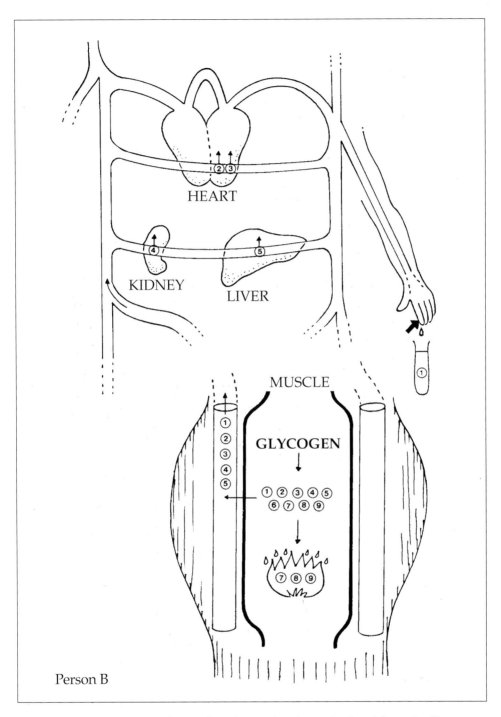

HEART

KIDNEY   LIVER

MUSCLE

GLYCOGEN

Person B

Person A released three units of lactate from the muscle, whereas B released five units. However, as person B was better at removing lactate from the blood, one unit of lactate was found in the blood taken from the hand in both individuals, even though the lactate production for A and B was different. This example illustrates that blood lactate concentrations do not always reflect the production of lactate in the muscles.

Energy stores (substrates)

Carbohydrate, fat, and protein are the major energy nutrients of the body. Energy production is based mainly on the combustion of these substrates, but they are not fuels which can be used interchangeably. For instance, only carbohydrate can be used as a fuel for anaerobic energy production.

During exercise, carbohydrate and fat are the main sources of fuel, whereas the contribution from protein is small. During low intensity exercise the proportion of energy derived from carbohydrates versus fat is equal. As exercise intensity increases, the amount of carbohydrate used will increase (see Fig. BP 9), and at very high intensities carbohydrate is utilized almost exclusively.

Carbohydrate and fat are essential components of the energy producing processes in the muscles and it is, therefore, important that they are stored in the body. Most of the carbohydrate (about 300 grams) is stored in the muscles as glycogen. The liver can also store glycogen (about 75 grams), and a small amount of carbohydrate is found in the blood as glucose (about 5 grams).

Figure BP 9
The figure shows the energy production and utilization of fat and carbohydrate during exercise at different intensities. At rest and during low-intensity exercise, approximately equal amounts of fat and carbohydrate are used for energy production. As the exercise intensity increases, more carbohydrate is used, and during high-intensity exercise, energy is derived almost entirely through the use of carbohydrate.

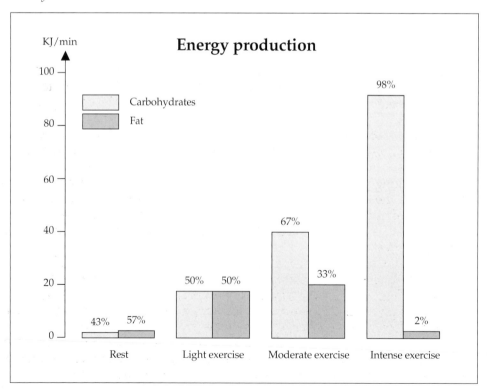

Muscle glycogen is used at a rapid rate during high intensity activities in football.

Thus, there is about 400 grams of carbohydrate available for use by the active muscles. This is a small amount compared to the 5-20 kg of fat stored in adipose tissue situated under the skin, around the abdominal cavity, and in the muscles.

As exercise progresses, the muscles will increase the use of fat as a fuel, and the liver will release more glucose into the blood, which is then taken up by the muscles. In this way the muscle glycogen stores can be reserved. However, with long periods of exercise the muscle carbohydrate stores may be depleted as the contribution from fat and liver glucose may be insufficient. Depletion of carbohydrate reserves makes it necessary to decrease the exercise intensity or even stop: a condition referred to by marathon runners as »hitting the wall«.

The size of the muscle glycogen stores may also be limiting for performance in football. The distance run by football players during a match has been estimated from video analysis, and the results have been related to the decrease of glycogen in the muscles. Although the muscle glycogen concentrations before the match varied among the players, the glycogen levels were similar at the end of a game. The players with the highest initial glycogen stores covered the most distance, thus indicating that the amount of muscle glycogen influences performance during a match (see also page 302).

The utilization of the different sources of fuels during exercise is dependent on training status. For the same exercise intensity, a trained individual will use more fat than an untrained individual, thereby sparing carbohydrate. Training also enables larger amounts of carbohydrate to be stored in the muscles. A trained person is therefore able to perform more exercise in a set amount of time. In football this means that well-trained players have the potential to perform frequent and long periods of high-intensity exercise during a match.

Temperature regulation

The transfer of heat from the body to its surroundings, or vice versa, can occur in four different ways – by *convection, conduction, radiation*, and *evaporation* of water (see Fig. BP 10).

Circulating air causes heat to be released from, or absorbed by, the body, depending on the temperature of the air and of the body – this type of heat exchange is termed convection. Direct contact of the body with an object or a medium causes the transfer of heat via conduction, e.g. when swimming in cold water the body loses heat through conduction. When a body is exposed to sunlight it absorbs heat, whereas in a cold environment it releases heat; these are both forms of radiation. By regulating the blood flow to the skin, the body can, to some extent, control the temperature of the skin and regulate the loss of heat by these three methods.

The body may also lose heat through the evaporation of water. It is not possible for the body to absorb heat through evaporation. Most of the water that evaporates from the body is in the form of sweat, but evaporation of water also occurs during breathing. This method of heat loss is used by dogs to cool down. If it is hot, dogs breathe heavily in order to lose heat.

Exercise in a normal air temperature environment

During exercise heat is produced as a by-product of the energy producing processes. The major form of heat loss from the body during exercise is through the evaporation of sweat. Not all of the heat produced during exercise is removed, and the body temperature therefore rises. The higher the intensity of the exercise, the greater the increase in body temperature. During maximal exercise the body temperature may rise to around 41 °C, whereas the muscle temperature can increase to 43 °C.

An increase in muscle temperature improves the performance capacity of the muscles, but in order to avoid overheating it is important to lose some of the heat produced. The ability to lose heat by evaporation of sweat is increased

Figure BP 10
The figure illustrates the different ways that the body can absorb and release heat. Through the evaporation of sweat the body can only release heat, whereas through conduction, convection, and radiation heat can be both transferred to and from the body.

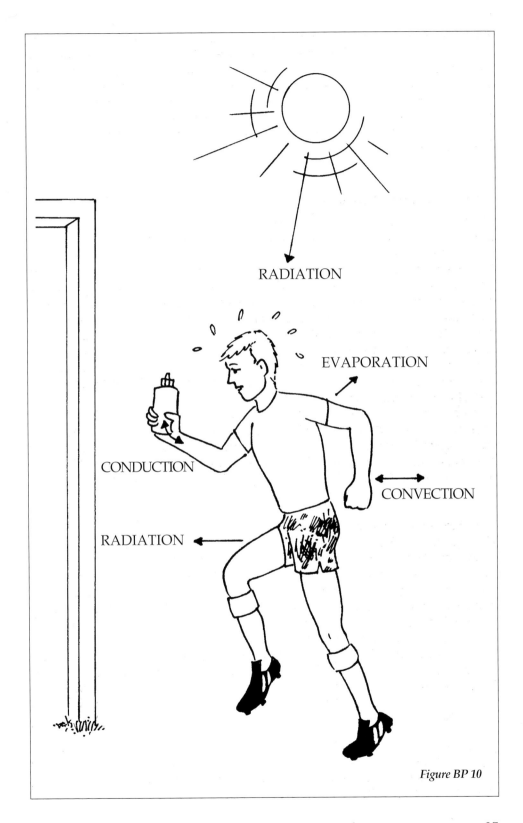

RADIATION

EVAPORATION

CONDUCTION

CONVECTION

RADIATION

Figure BP 10

35

During match-play a player produces a large amount of heat, which is released from the body through various processes, such as evaporation of sweat.

through training. Thus, during a standardized period of exercise, the body temperature of a well-trained individual will be lower than that of an untrained person. In general, body temperature increases to about 38 °C with exercise at an intensity corresponding to 50% of maximum oxygen uptake.

Exercise in a hot environment

During exercise in a hot environment the heat lost from the body through convection and radiation is very small, and in some cases heat may even be absorbed by the body, e.g. if the radiation from the sun is strong. Under these conditions the need for heat loss by evaporation of sweat greatly increases. If the body is not able to release a sufficient amount of heat the body temperature can rise dramatically, and performance may be impaired. It has been demonstrated that the distance covered by high-intensity running during a football match was reduced by 50% when the air temperature was 30 °C compared to 20 °C. When humidity is high, heat loss through evaporation of sweat is inhibited. Thus, on a hot and humid day it is more difficult for a player to lose heat, which may in turn have a negative effect on physical performance.

Muscle Function

The muscle and skeletal systems enable us to move. Therefore, a basic knowledge of muscle structure and function, as well as an understanding of the concepts of endurance and muscle strength is helpful for comprehending the limitations of physical performance in football.

Figures BP 11 and BP 12 (see page 38) show the muscles of the body which are most important for football.

Figure BP 11
The figure shows the muscles on the front of the body. The names of the muscle groups that are most specific to football are given.

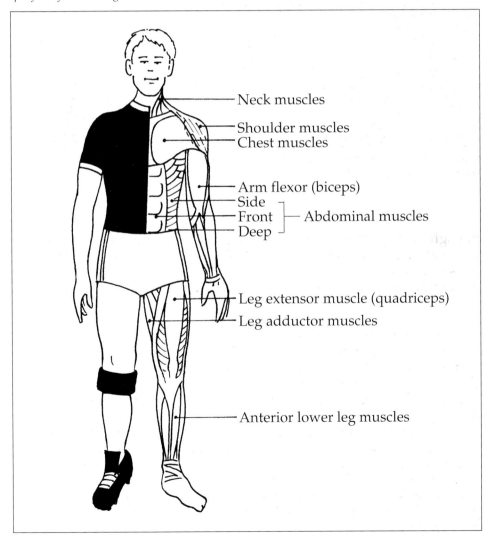

Neck muscles

Shoulder muscles
Chest muscles

Arm flexor (biceps)
Side
Front — Abdominal muscles
Deep

Leg extensor muscle (quadriceps)
Leg adductor muscles

Anterior lower leg muscles

Muscle structure

A muscle consists of muscle fibres that are surrounded by connective tissue, small blood vessels (capillaries), nerves, fat, and a fluid (see Fig. BP 13). Information about the composition of a human muscle can be obtained by analysis of a small piece of muscle (muscle biopsy) that has been surgically removed. The muscle is composed of different fibre types which can be identified by chemical staining of thin slices cut from a biopsy. In Fig. BP 13 the muscle fibres and the surrounding capillaries, which appear as spots, can be clearly seen. The capillaries supply the muscle fibres with nutrients and oxygen and remove by-products as well.

Figure BP 12
The figure shows the muscles on the back of the body. The names of the muscle groups that are most specific to football are given.

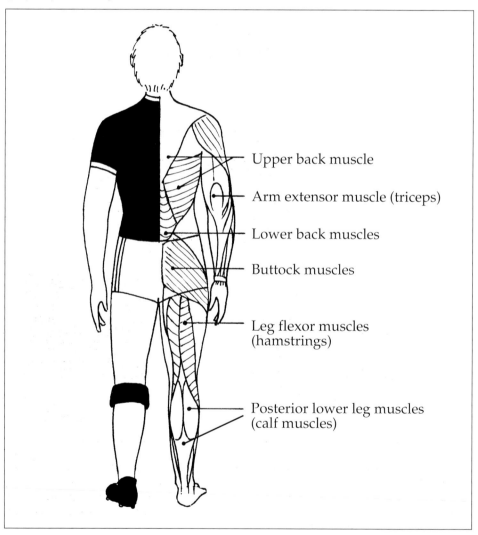

Upper back muscle

Arm extensor muscle (triceps)

Lower back muscles

Buttock muscles

Leg flexor muscles (hamstrings)

Posterior lower leg muscles (calf muscles)

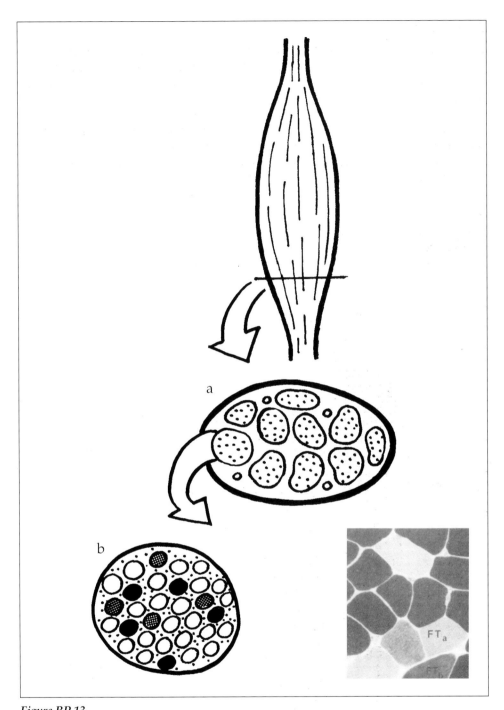

Figure BP 13
The figure shows a cross-sectional view of a muscle. The muscle consists of bundles of muscle fibres which are bound together by connective tissue. Nerves and large blood vessels are located between the bundles (a). If the cross-sectional view is enlarged, the individual fibres and the small blood vessels (capillaries), which surround the fibres, can be seen (b). Through the use of chemical methods it is possible to distinguish between different types of muscle fibres.

39

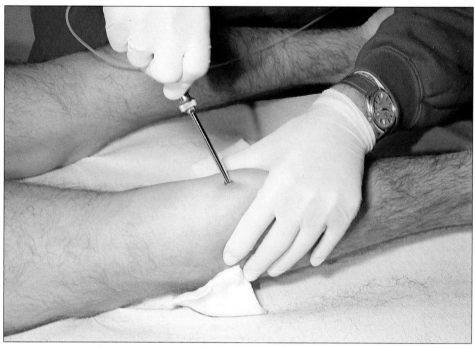

From a small piece of a muscle (biopsy), information about the levels of enzymes and structure of the muscle can be obtained.

Muscle fibres

There are two main muscle fibre types: slow-twitch fibres (ST, red fibres) and fast-twitch fibres (FT, white fibres). The ST-fibres produce tension relatively slowly, and are capable of working for several hours without becoming fatigued (see Fig. BP 14). This is because they produce energy mainly through oxygen-dependent pathways. FT-fibres can be divided into FTa- and FTb-fibres. The FTb-fibres develop tension much faster than ST-fibres, but they have a lower endurance capacity (see Fig. BP 14). The endurance capacity of the FTa-fibres lies between that of the ST- and FTb-fibres. Compared to the ST-fibres, the FT-fibres have a greater capacity to produce energy anaerobically.

Fibre type distribution, which is the proportion of the different fibre types, varies between muscles. A biopsy from the calf muscle of one player showed a distribution of 90% ST-fibres, 8% FTa-fibres, and 2% FTb-fibres, compared to 35%, 50%, and 15%, respectively, in a biopsy from a thigh muscle of the same leg. The fibre type distribution of a given muscle group also varies between elite athletes competing in different sports. For instance, elite long-

Figure BP 14
The figure illustrates some general characteristics of muscle fibres. The force developed and the speed by which force is produced by the fibres is shown in the upper part of the figure, and the fibres' capacity to exercise for prolonged periods of time is illustrated in the lower part. The FTb-fibres produce force very rapidly but fatigue quickly, whereas the ST-fibres generate force more slowly and have a higher endurance. The characteristics of the FTa-fibres lie between those of FTb- and ST-fibres.

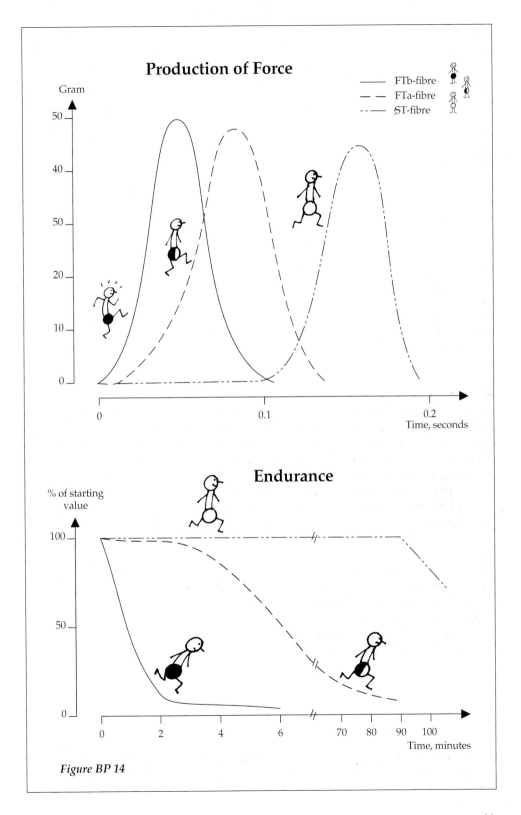

Figure BP 14

41

distance runners and cyclists, who possess a good endurance capacity, often have a large proportion of ST-fibres in the quadriceps muscles. On the other hand, sprinters must produce large amounts of energy in a very short time and these athletes usually have a high percentage of FT-fibres in their quadriceps muscles.

Why do elite athletes have fibre type distributions that meet the demands of their sport? Is it a result of the training, or is it a hereditary factor? Current research suggests that training results in only minor changes in the proportion of FT- and ST-fibres. However, changes from FTb-fibres to FTa-fibres seem to occur with endurance training. This can explain why few FTb-fibres are found in muscles from elite athletes competing in endurance sports.

Although FT-fibres may not be converted to ST-fibres, the endurance capacity of FT-fibres can be markedly improved with endurance training. Thus, the endurance capacity of a well-trained individual with a high percentage of FT-fibres can be greater than that of an untrained individual with a high proportion of ST-fibres.

Figure BP 15
The figure shows the fibre type composition of a calf muscle from Danish long-distance elite runners as well as from top-class and recreational football players. It should be noted that very few FTb-fibres were found in the muscle from the top-class players and the long-distance runners, whereas a relatively large number were found in the muscle from the recreational players.

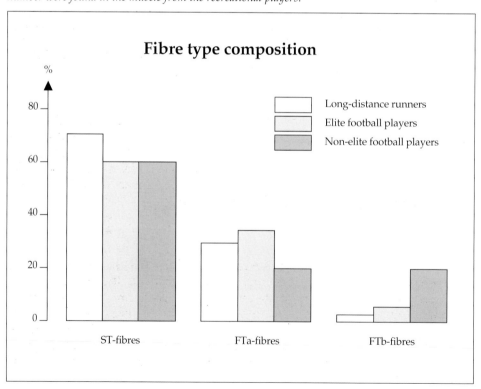

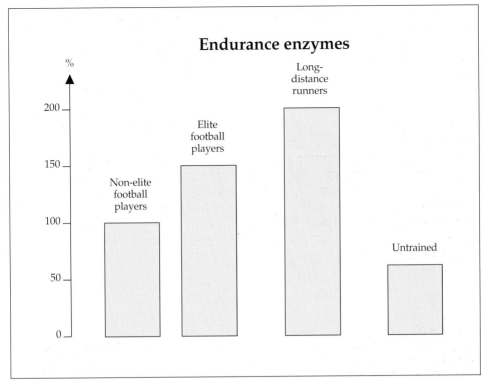

Figure BP 16
The figure shows the level of muscle endurance enzymes for recreational and top-class football players, as well as for elite long-distance runners and untrained individuals. The values are expressed in relation to the data for the recreational players (100%). The recreational players had a higher level of muscle endurance enzymes than the untrained individuals, whereas the levels in top-class players were between those of the recreational players and the long-distance runners.

Studies on football players have shown that the fibre type distribution for a given muscle varies among individuals. In contrast to recreational players however, top-class players have a low proportion of FTb-fibres in the leg muscles, a characteristic also seen in endurance trained athletes (see Fig. BP 15). An additional sign of a high endurance level of elite players is the finding of a large number of capillaries supplying the muscles.

Muscle enzymes
In the muscle fibres there are different types of proteins, of which some are called enzymes. Certain enzymes determine the ability of the muscle to work aerobically whereas others regulate the use of fat. These are called endurance enzymes. The level of endurance enzymes found in muscles of top-class football players is higher than in recreational players and untrained individuals (see Fig. BP 16). However, even higher levels of endurance enzymes have been found in elite marathon runners and professional racing cyclists (see Fig. BP 16).

Endurance enzymes are rapidly affected by inactivity. The level of these enzymes was found to be markedly decreased in a group of Danish elite players after only a three-week break from their ordinary training. After a four-week re-training period the level was still significantly lower than before the break. This illustrates that it takes more time to regain endurance than it does to lose it.

The link between nerves and muscles

Muscles are activated by nerves. Figure BP 17 illustrates schematically the basic pathways of communication between nerves and muscles. Impulses from the brain are sent to the spinal cord via nerve fibres, where they are transmitted by other nerve fibres to the muscles. When the impulses reach the muscle, the muscle fibres contract.

Figure BP 17
The figure illustrates how the brain and nervous system communicate with the muscles. Information is transmitted from the brain to the muscle via the nerves. A part of the muscle then contracts. The greater the number of impulses that are sent from the brain, the greater the number of muscle fibres that contract and, therefore, the higher the tension that is produced. The muscle can also transmit information to the nervous system which responds by sending impulses back to the muscle (a reflex).

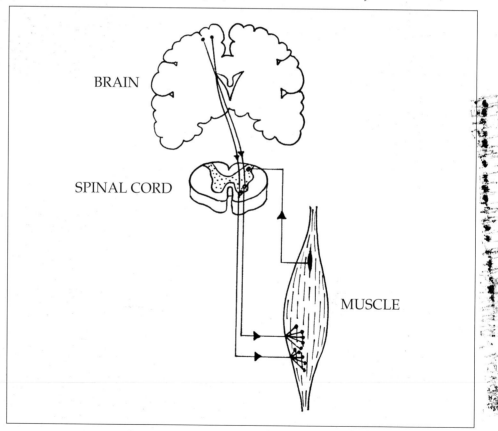

Even an easy task during a match may require full concentration.

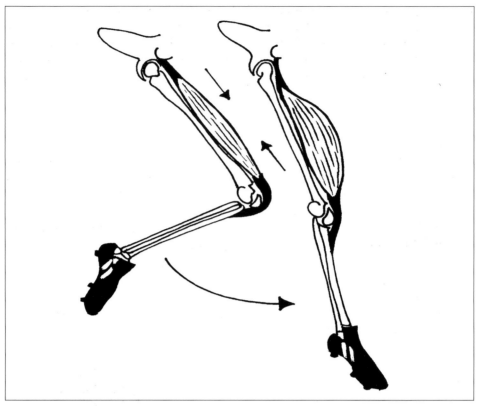

Figure BP 18
The figure illustrates how the lower leg is moved forward by contraction of the leg extensor muscle (quadriceps).

The function of the nervous system can be divided into two components: *automatic* and *voluntary*. If a given movement is repeated many times it can gradually become automatic. Movement patterns are »stored« in the brain, ready to be retrieved when needed. In football there are many examples of how a voluntary movement eventually becomes automatic, for example, a pass with the inside of the foot. When learning to perform a movement the player will need to concentrate, but with increasing confidence and skill the movement can be performed automatically during a match. Sometimes it may be necessary to make adjustments. After a movement has been voluntarily corrected through training, it may be »stored« in the brain again and used automatically. The main purpose of technical training is to improve coordination and to make movements automatic.

A muscle can also contract without signals from the brain – a so-called reflex, which occurs if a muscle is quickly stretched. After the muscle is stretched, nerve cells in the muscle communicate with nerve cells in the spinal cord (see Fig. BP 17 – page 44). These latter cells then send impulses back to the muscles causing the muscle to contract. The reflex of a quadriceps muscle can be evaluated by a quick strike just below the knee.

An example of a reflex action in football is landing after jumping to head the ball. Immediately after the feet contact the ground on landing the quadriceps muscles are stretched. This triggers a reflex that initiates muscle contraction in order to stop the stretching of the muscles and a simultaneous voluntary activation of the quadriceps muscles keeps the player from falling over when landing.

Types of muscle action

At each end of a muscle there are one or more tendons which connect the muscle to the skeletal system. When the muscle contracts the ends of the two tendons move towards each other, and the bones to which they are attached rotate around a skeletal joint (see Fig. BP 18). For example, if a glass of water is held with a stretched arm, the arm flexor muscle (biceps) must contract to enable the hand to move to the mouth (see Fig. BP 19).

Figure BP 19
When bringing a glass of water from a table to the mouth the arm is bent at the elbow joint through the contraction of the arm flexor muscle (biceps)

The muscles can contract in different ways. During an *isometric* contraction the muscle length does not change, e.g. in a tackle the muscles of the legs work isometrically at the moment of contact. A shortening of the muscle during activation is called a *concentric* contraction, e.g. the quadriceps muscle works concentrically when kicking a ball, as does biceps when lifting the glass (see Fig. BP 18 and BP 19). During the third type of contraction the muscle length increases, which is called an *eccentric* contraction, e.g. when stopping a high ball with the thigh the quadriceps muscle works eccentrically. Figure BP 20 illustrates the three types of muscle contractions using the example of landing after a header. Both concentric and eccentric contractions are defined as dynamic since they involve some form of external movement.

Figure BP 20
On landing after jumping the quadriceps muscles lengthen as they contract (eccentric work) in order to counteract the downward movement of the body, and thereby preventing the player from falling. At the point when the downward movement has been completely retarded the quadriceps muscles momentarily work isometrically. Then they work concentrically in order to straighten the legs.

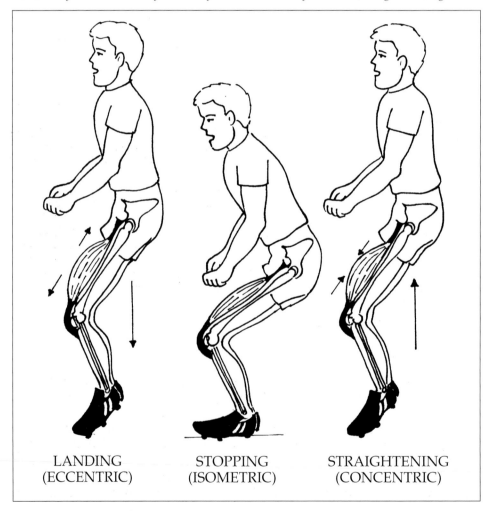

| LANDING | STOPPING | STRAIGHTENING |
| (ECCENTRIC) | (ISOMETRIC) | (CONCENTRIC) |

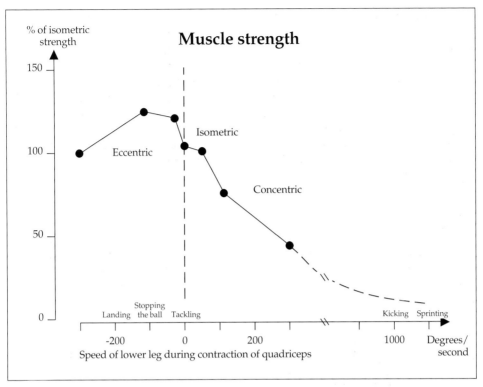

Figure BP 21

The figure shows the force exerted by the quadriceps muscle of a Danish elite player during different types and speeds of contraction. The force was measured with strength testing equipment where the speed of the lower leg was constant during the entire movement (isokinetic). The player was in a seated position (see picture page 51).

For the eccentric work, the leg started in a horizontal position and the player pushed against a motor-driven arm that moved the leg downward, i.e. the quadriceps muscle lengthened. Isometric work was performed by pressing the leg against the arm which was in a fixed position. For the concentric work, the player pushed on the arm with the moving leg from a 90° bent position to a horizontal position. The greatest strength was recorded during eccentric work. The force during the concentric work decreased as the speed of the contraction increased. Some average speeds of muscle contraction during typical football activities are presented at the bottom at the figure. When the speed is similar to that of a leg kicking a ball, the force production of the quadriceps muscle is about 10% of maximal isometric force.

Muscle strength

Muscle strength: The greatest force that the muscle can produce in a given position or in a given movement at a certain speed.

It is difficult to give a precise definition of muscle strength as strength is dependent on the type and speed of muscle action. This is illustrated in Fig. BP 21. In general, muscle strength is the greatest during an eccentric contraction. Isometric muscle strength is greater than concentric muscle strength, and concentric strength decreases with increasing speed of contraction. As an example, at a contraction speed similar to that occurring during a football kick, the quadriceps muscle is only able to produce approximately 10% of the force generated during a maximum isometric action.

The relationship between strength and speed of contraction for two top-class players is shown in Fig. BP 22. One of the players was considerably stronger at all movement speeds, but the decline in strength with increasing speed was similar for the players.

In a complex movement it is difficult to evaluate the force developed by the muscles involved, as the muscles work differently. For instance, when kicking a ball some muscles contract eccentrically, some isometrically, and others concentrically. Moreover, the speed of contraction varies during the movement. These factors may explain why studies have shown only small increases in kicking performance despite large increases in the strength of isolated muscle groups following a strength training period.

Muscle strength is related to the occurrence of injuries. In a study it was found that in a group of English players the individuals who had strong legs had fewer injuries than the weaker players. After an injury it is important to regain the muscle strength lost during the inactive period. In a study muscle

Figure BP 22
The figure shows the relationship between muscle strength and speed of muscle contraction for the player in Fig. BP 23 (A) and for another top-class player (B). The two curves show a similar pattern but player B was not able to produce as much force as player A.

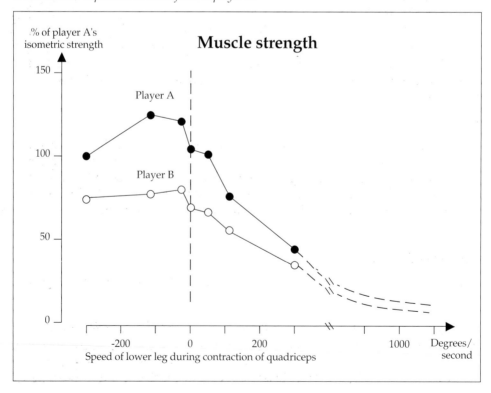

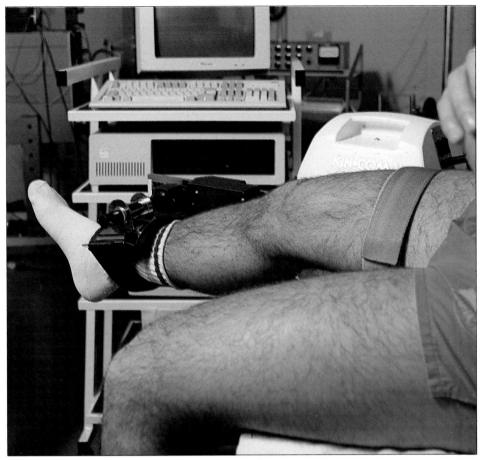

With special strength testing equipment it is possible to measure force exerted at different speeds of muscle contraction.

strength was evaluated during a period following an injury. For players that had had knee-surgery two years earlier, the average strength of the quadriceps muscle of the operated leg was only 75% of the strength of the muscle in the other leg. This indicates that the re-building process was not adequate and that the risk of these players becoming injured again was high.

Muscle endurance

Muscle endurance: The ability of the muscle to work for a prolonged period of time.

It is difficult to give a precise definition of muscle endurance since the time to muscle fatigue is dependent on the exercise intensity and the type of exercise, i.e. isometric or dynamic. When playing football most muscle groups are working dynamically, and particularly the calf muscles are heavily stressed.

51

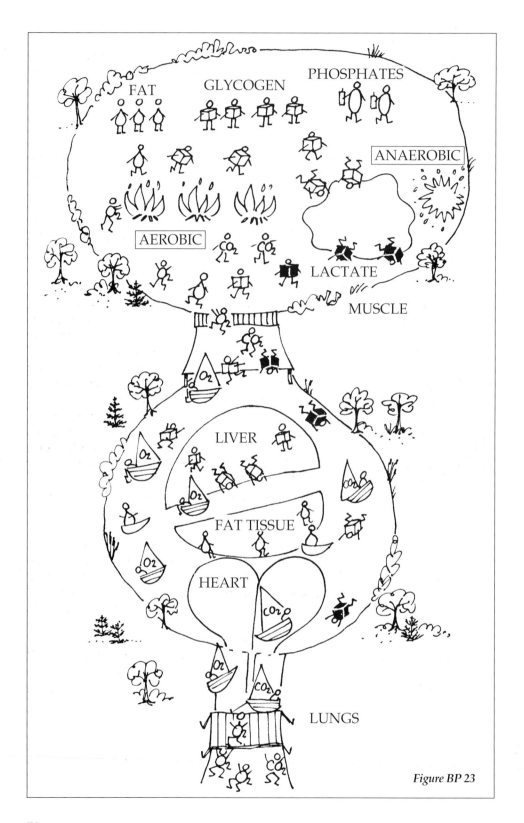

Figure BP 23

It is not surprising, therefore, that the calf muscles of top-class players have a high endurance capacity. In football, isometric endurance is of less importance than dynamic endurance because isometric muscle contractions rarely last more than a few seconds.

Summary

This chapter describes how the body functions at rest and during exercise, and discusses some of the physiological changes that occur after a period of physical training.

When inhaling, the lungs are filled with air, and some of the oxygen within the air diffuses into the blood where it is bound to hemoglobin and transported to all parts of the body (see Fig. BP 23). During exercise most of the absorbed oxygen is used by the active muscles for chemical processes which produce energy (*aerobic* energy production). Carbon dioxide is formed during these processes and is transported by the blood to the lungs, where it is then removed from the body. The blood also transports heat, which is generated by the active muscles during energy production. Most, but not all, of the heat is removed from the body, and body temperature rises during exercise.

Carbohydrate and fat are the primary fuels used for energy production in the muscles during exercise. These substrates are located in the muscles, but may also be taken up from the blood. The glucose in the blood is released from the liver whereas the fat originates from the various fat stores in the body.

The muscles can also produce energy without the use of oxygen, through the breakdown of energy-rich phosphates and through a process by which carbohydrate is broken down and lactate is formed (*anaerobic* energy production). Some of the lactate is released from the muscles to the blood and is thus dispersed throughout the body.

Muscles are activated via the nervous system. There are three types of muscle action during which the length of the muscle either shortens (*concentric*), lengthens (*eccentric*), or does not change (*isometric*).

Muscle strength is the greatest force that the muscle can produce in a given movement at a certain velocity. The highest muscle strength can be achieved during eccentric work. During concentric work there is an inverse relationship between the speed of muscle contraction and the tension produced, i.e. a muscle produces less strength the faster it contracts. Muscle endurance refers to the capacity of the muscle to exercise for prolonged periods of time. Both muscle strength and muscle endurance are dependent on the fibre type distribution and the training status of the muscle. Appropriate training will lead to an improvement in performance through adaptations within the muscle, such as an increase in the size of fibres, in the number of capillaries, and in the levels of certain enzymes.

Physical demands
of Football

Physical Demands
of Football

The demands of football can be divided into four components: technical, tactical, social/psychological, and physical. The ideal football player should have good tactical comprehension, be technically skilful, mentally strong, function well socially within the team, and have a high physical capacity. However, by performing exceptionally well in some of the areas, a player can compensate for weaknesses in other aspects of the game.

This chapter will focus on the physical demands of football, but will also include aspects of the technical, tactical, and psychological components where appropriate. The information is obtained from studies in which the time-motion characteristics of players during match-play have been analyzed, and in which physiological variables have been measured before, during, and immediately after a match.

Match analysis

The physical demands of football can be evaluated by analyzing the movement patterns of players during match-play. Due to variations in the activities of a player from match to match and different individual playing styles, many observations, on the same player and on different types of players, need to be made in order for data from time-motion analysis to be representative of the activities in football.

In recent years the movement patterns of Danish male football players from first and second division teams have been analyzed in several matches.

Method

A video camera was used to film each player during an entire game. The players' movements were later analyzed by identifying ten different categories:

1. Standing
2. Walking (4 km/h)
3. Jogging (8 km/h)
4. Low-speed running (12 km/h)
5. Moderate-speed running (16 km/h)
6. High-speed running (21 km/h)
7. Sprinting (30 km/h)
8. Backwards running (12 km/h)
9. Heading
10. Tackling

Figure PD 1

The figure shows the activities of a Danish top-class midfield player during a competitive match. The values are expressed both in minutes and in distance (kilometres) covered during the different activities. As an example, low-intensity running accounted for 13 minutes, thus corresponding to a distance of 2.5 kilometres (13 minutes x 12 km/h).

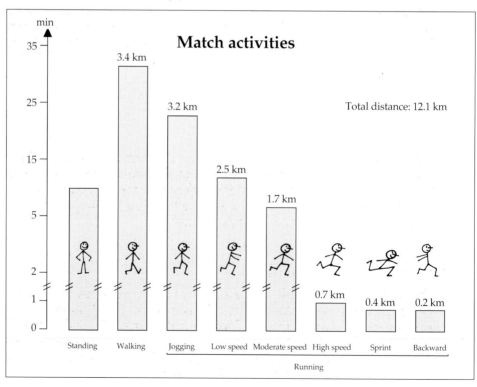

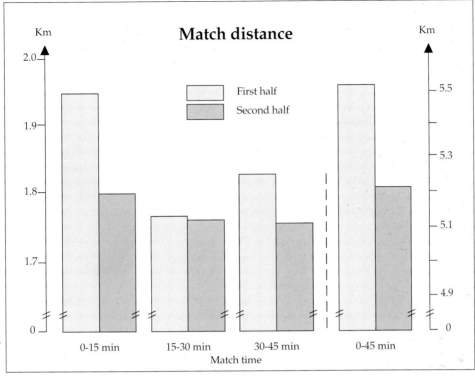

Figure PD 2
The figure shows distances covered in the first and second half of a match. To the left each half is divided into 15-minute intervals (0-15, 15-30, 30-45 min) and to the right the two halves (0-45 min) are compared. The players covered a longer distance (around 300 metres) during the first half compared to the second half. This was due to more distance being covered at the start and end of the first half compared to the corresponding intervals in the second half.

The average speed (indicated in brackets) for each category was determined from measurements of movement speeds from the video tapes, as well as from tests where the players simulated the different movement patterns over a given distance on a football field. In the discussion that follows, the categories 5, 6, and 7 are defined as high-intensity running.

Match-play activity profiles

Figure PD 1 shows an example of the activities of a first division midfield player during a competitive match. From 70 such analyses of outfield male players, the average distance covered during a match was estimated to be 10.8 kilometres with a range from 9 to 14 kilometres. In comparison, goalkeepers covered a distance of about 4 kilometres. Figure PD 2 shows the distances covered in 15-minute periods by the outfield players.

The activity profile of the Danish elite players is illustrated in Fig. PD 3. It can be seen that the players, on average, were standing still for 17% and walking for 40% of the total game time. During approximately 35% and 8% of the total time the players were running at a low and high speed, respectively. Sprinting accounted for about 0.6%, i.e. about 30 seconds. The relatively short duration of high-speed running for a player does not reflect the overall intensity of competitive matches. During periods of a match some players are running at high speed, while others are standing still or walking. For example, the forwards may exercise at a low intensity when their team is defending. It is also worthwhile to note that a game includes a considerable number of natural breaks, e.g. while the players are waiting for a free-kick to be taken. In the matches played in the 1992 European Championship the average amount of time in which the ball was actually in play was 57 minutes per game.

During a top-class match a player performs around 1100 changes in activities, e.g. switching from standing to moderate running to walking. Table PD 1 shows the number of activities performed (A) and the average duration of each activity (B) during a match for the players from the Danish league. The distance covered with the ball was between 0.5% and 3% of the total distance.

Figure PD 3
The figure shows the average values of different activities during matches for Danish elite players. The values are expressed both in percentage of playing time and in minutes.

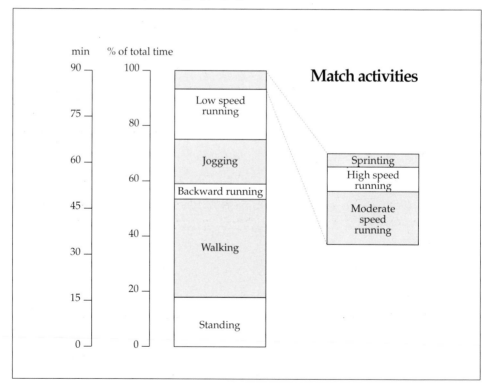

A. Activities

| | Standing | Walking | Low-intensity running | | | High-intensity running | | | Total |
			Jogging	Low speed	Backward	Moderate speed	High speed	Sprint	
All	122	329	253	251	26	120	57	19	1179
Division									
First	143	339	302	250	35	140	66	23	1300
Second	90	315	175	250	12	89	42	11	984
Position									
Defender	158	354	268	210	37	106	41	16	1192
Midfield player	97	317	257	277	30	127	58	17	1190
Forward	125	330	229	231	5	120	69	24	1140

B. Mean time for activities (seconds)

| | Standing | Walking | Low-intensity running | | | High-intensity running | | | Total |
			Jogging	Low speed	Backward	Moderate speed	High speed	Sprint	
Alle	7.8	6.7	3.5	3.5	3.6	2.5	2.1	2.0	4.5
Division									
First	7.2	6.0	3.3	2.8	2.5	2.3	2.0	1.8	4.2
Second	7.9	7.6	3.7	2.9	5.0	2.5	2.0	2.2	5.5
Position									
Defender	7.4	6.4	3.2	2.9	2.4	2.7	2.4	2.0	4.5
Midfield player	8.0	6.4	3.7	4.0	2.6	2.3	2.0	2.1	4.5
Forward	7.7	7.4	3.2	3.3	7.5	2.5	2.0	1.7	4.7

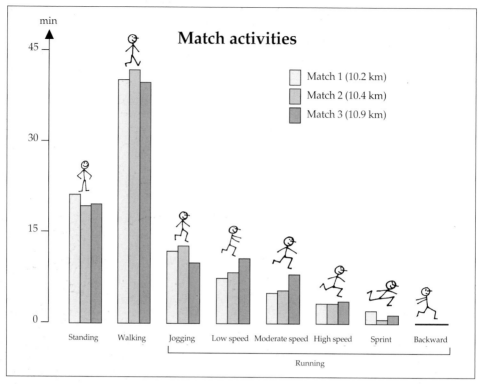

Figure PD 4
The figure shows the activity profile of an elite player during three successive home matches. For this player there was only a small variation from match to match.

The midfield players and forwards had possession of the ball for longer periods than the defenders. Analysis of the players of the Danish team in the 1992 European Championship showed that the average time that the players were in possession of the ball was 1.3 minutes, with a range from 0.3 to 3.1 minutes. On average, a player dribbled 30 times during a game and the time per dribble was 2.9 seconds.

Match to match variations

The distance that a player covers during a match is dependent on several factors, such as the opposing team, the importance of the game, motivation, and team tactics. Nevertheless, it has been found that the total distance covered by most players varies less than 1 km from match to match, with the largest variation being 1.7 km. Figure PD 4 gives an example of a player that covered approximately the same distance and had the same type of movement activity profile in three successive home matches.

*The time a player is in possession of the ball
is limited to a few minutes per game.*

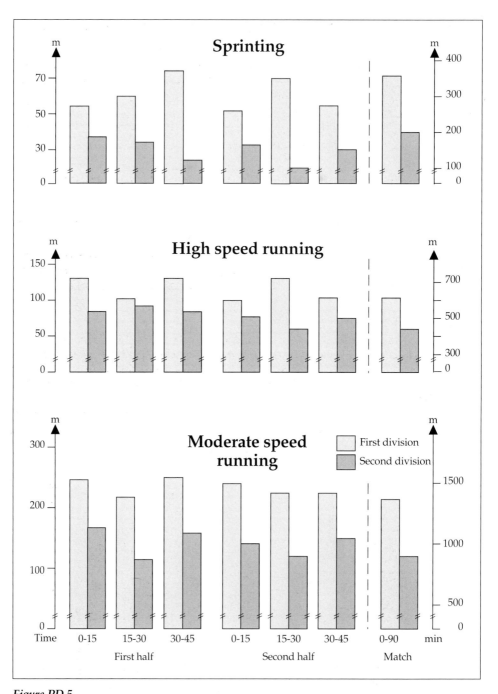

Figure PD 5
The figure shows the distance covered by Danish first and second division players during a match within the three categories of high-intensity running. To the left each half of the game has been divided into 15-minute intervals (0-15, 15-30, 30-45 min), and to the right the values for the entire match are given (0-90 min). The first division players performed considerably more high-intensity running than those from the second division. For both the first and second division players the high-intensity running was evenly distributed throughout the match.

Comparison between first and second division players

The mean distance covered during a match was similar for the first and second division players. However, the first division players performed high-intensity running more frequently (see Fig. PD 5), and ran less at low speed. The results suggest that the higher the level of football, the more high-intensity running is performed. Figure PD 5 also shows that there was no appreciable variation in high-intensity running throughout a match for either the first or second division players

Differences between defenders, midfield players, and forwards

A player's work-rate during a match is primarily related to fitness level and tactical role in the team.

In a study of Danish elite players, five were defenders (two sweepers, one central defender and two full-backs), ten were midfield players, and three were forwards. Figure PD 6 shows the average distances covered by the

Figure PD 6
The figure illustrates distances covered by defenders, midfield players, and forwards during top-class competitive matches. To the left each half of the game has been divided into 15-minute intervals (0-15, 15-30, 30-45 min), and to the right values for the whole game are shown (0-90 min). Apart from the last 15 minutes of the match the midfield players covered considerably more distance than the other two groups of players.

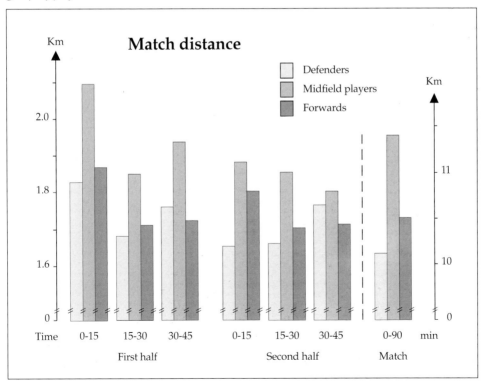

players in each position. It can be seen that the defenders and the forwards covered approximately the same distance, but the distance was significantly less than covered by the midfield players. Why do midfield players run more during a game? It could be that this position requires more running, or that the players selected to play in midfield have a higher fitness level than the other players. Both suggestions are plausible since it has been shown that midfield players in general have a higher level of fitness. There was no apparent difference between the three groups of players with regard to the distance covered by high-intensity running, so the midfield players performed more low-speed running than the defenders and forwards. Table PD 1 (see page 61) shows that the midfield players not only ran at low speed more frequently, but also for a longer duration each time, thus reflecting the tactical role of the midfield players to link the defence and the attack.

Figure PD 7
The figure shows the average number of headers (to the left) and tackles (to the right) performed by defenders, midfield players, and forwards during top-class competitive matches. Values are presented for the first and second halves. The noticeable differences are that the forwards had more headers than the other groups of players during the first half, and that the defenders made the most tackles.

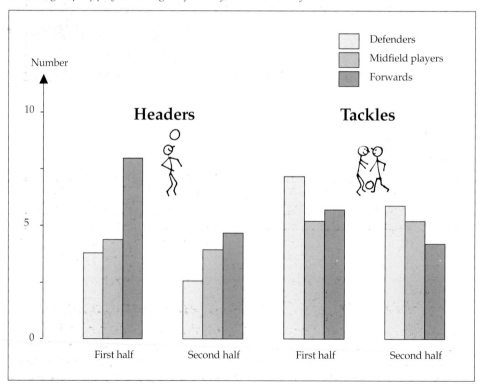

Players frequently perform energy demanding activities during a match.

Other match activities

For the observed Danish top-class players the average number of headers and tackles during a match was 8 and 11, respectively. Figure PD 7 shows the values for defenders, midfield players, and forwards. In the 1992 European Championship, the mean number of passes per player in a game was 35 and the number of interceptions was 15. The average number of shots at goal per player was 1.1 per match, while one goal was scored at every 12 attempts.

Physical capacity and distance covered during a match

In addition to match-analysis, ten of the Danish elite players performed a long-term intermittent exercise test until they were exhausted. The pattern of running during the test was similar to that of match-play. Thus, the distance covered during the test gave an indication of each player's football-specific

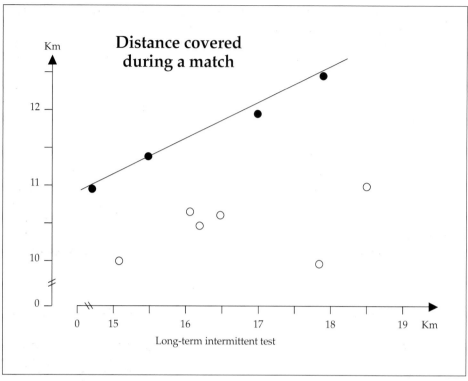

Figure PD 8
The figure shows the relationship between the distance covered in a football-specific long-term intermittent exercise test performed to exhaustion, and the greatest distance covered in one out of at least three matches. Relative to the test result, four of the players (●) covered considerably more distance during the match than the other six players (○).

endurance capacity. In Fig. PD 8, the test result is compared to the longest distance covered during three competitive matches. The figure shows that in relation to endurance capacity, four of the players (indicated with a filled circle) covered significantly more distance during a match than the other six players. Apparently, the latter six players did not fully utilize their physical capacity during the matches. Part of the explanation may be tactical limitations. For example, one of the players who covered the shortest distance during a match, but who had a good test result, was a central defender whose role as a marker probably affected the distance covered during the match. The degree of motivation may also influence the physical performance during a match, and the shorter distance covered by the six players may have reflected an inability of these individuals to mentally push themselves enough.

The comparison between the distance covered during a match and the performance in the intermittent exercise test revealed that the majority of the tested players could have run more during the matches. It would probably have been advantageous for the team if they had done so. However, all activities during a match should have a purpose, and it is important to recognize that frequent rest periods are needed in order for a player to be able to repeatedly perform high-intensity exercise. It should also be emphasized that a player's average work-rate during an entire game does not always need to match his or her physical capacity. For example, if the result of the match is decided at an early stage, the exercise intensity for the rest of the match can be reduced. This does not seem to explain the difference in performance between the observed players, however, since only in one match was the result decided by more than one goal.

The opportunities to improvise in football are numerous. The ability to surprise an opponent may be of major importance for the success of a team. This element is lost if a player is running at the same tempo all the time. The finding of more high-speed running by the first division players compared to the second division players suggests that it is important to be able to perform high-intensity exercise during a match. This is supported by observations of matches at an international level, which are characterised by periods of exercise at a low intensity alternated with periods at a very high intensity.

The activities of individual players during matches were assessed through computer analysis of video recordings.

Summary

The following conclusions are based on the observations of Danish elite players:

1. Top-class players stand or walk for more than half a match.
2. Top-class players run further during the first half of a match than during the second half, but the distance covered by high-speed running is the same.
3. Top-class players perform more high-intensity running than non-elite players.
4. Midfield players perform more low-speed running than defenders and forwards, but the amount of high-speed running is the same for the three groups.
5. Some players do not fully utilize their physical capacity during a match.

These findings are representative for football in general, since the activity profile of the Danish top-class players resembles those of elite players from Sweden, Germany, Australia, and England. The activity profile of an English top-class midfield player is shown in Fig. PD 9 for comparison.

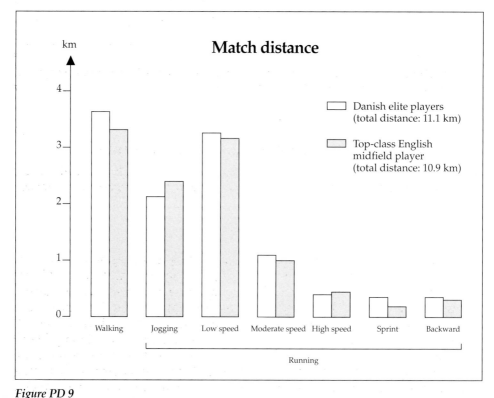

Figure PD 9
The figure shows the activities of a English Premier League midfield player during a competitive match. The values are expressed in distance (kilometres) covered during the different activities and compared with values for Danish elite players.

70

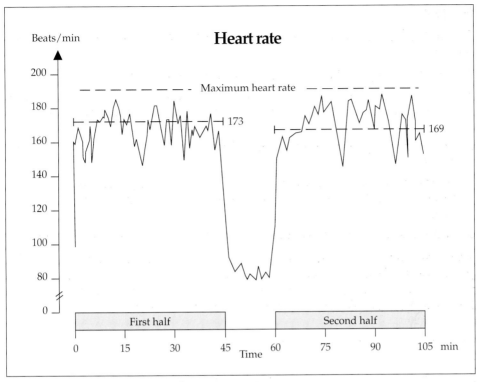

Figure PD 10
The figure shows the heart rate of a player during a match. The maximum heart rate for the player and the average values for first and second half are also given.

Physiological measurements during match-play

Various physiological measurements, such as heart rate, blood lactate, body temperature, and fluid loss, have been obtained in connection with matches.

Heart rate

Modern telemetric equipment has made it possible to continuously monitor heart rate during a match without restricting a player's movements. Figure PD 10 shows an example of a Danish male top-class player's heart rate during a competitive match. The heart rate was between 150 and 190 (maximum heart rate) beats/min for most of the match with levels falling below 150 beats/min only for short periods. The heart rate values shown in Fig. PD 10 are characteristic of those found during a match although exceptions are found among players such as goalkeepers and sweepers that mainly have a defensive role. Based on heart rate measurements, the mean relative exercise intensity of a match can be estimated to approximately 70% of the maximum oxygen uptake. These recordings show that football places high demands on the heart and the oxygen transporting system.

71

Blood lactate

The blood lactate concentration of a player during a match can vary greatly, as illustrated in Fig. PD 11. Similarly, blood samples taken at the same time from several players on a team can have a large range of lactate concentrations. In Fig. PD 12 the average and maximum blood lactate concentrations for different groups of Danish and Swedish players are presented. The values are from samples taken during half-time or immediately after a match. On average, the lactate concentration was relatively high and similar to those found for German elite players. Individual values were occasionally as high as levels observed after intense exhaustive exercise.

What causes the large variations in blood lactate concentration?

Variations in the blood lactate concentration can be explained by differences in the activities of the players just before the blood sampling. This was clearly demonstrated in a study with a top-class Danish team. During a non-competitive match each player was filmed for five minutes prior to a blood

Figure PD 11
The figure shows blood lactate concentrations for a player before, during, and after a match. The values varied greatly during the match ranging from 3 to 10 mmol/l.

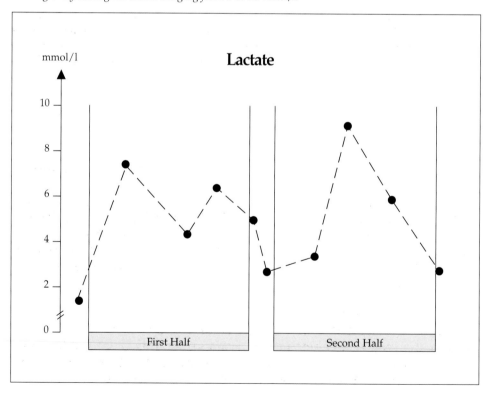

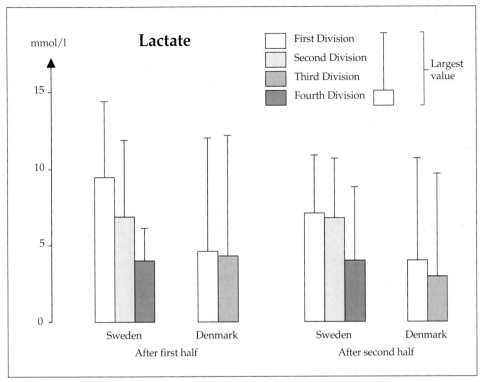

Figure PD 12
The figure shows average and maximum blood lactate concentrations of different groups of Danish and Swedish players. The blood samples were taken at half-time (on the left), and after the match (on the right). The Swedish first division players had considerably higher values than players from the lower divisions and than the Danish first division players. Lactate concentrations higher than 9 mmol/l have been found in all divisions, except for the players from the Swedish fourth division.

sample being taken. There was a large variation in blood lactate concentration between players, and a strong relation was found between lactate concentration and the activity profiles during the period before each sampling. This is evident from the examples given in Figs. PD 13 and PD 14 (see page 74). The more high-intensity exercise performed during the five minutes prior to the sampling, the higher the heart rate and lactate concentration. If values from competitive matches were also included, the relationship was even stronger (see Fig. PD 14).

What can be concluded from blood lactate measurements?
Based on findings of low blood lactate concentrations in players at half-time and after matches, the conclusion in some studies has been that football players only produce small amounts of lactate during a match. However, this

conclusion is incorrect. If towards the end of the first half, or the end of the match, players had a low activity level, it does not mean that their exercise intensity and blood lactate levels were low for the whole match. For example, as shown in Fig. PD 13 one player had a relatively low blood lactate concentration (4 mmol/l) after the match, but at one point during the match his concentration was 10 mmol/l, indicating that during the game he had performed high-intensity exercise and had had a high lactate production.

It is worthwhile to re-emphasize that the blood lactate concentration underrates the production of lactate (see page 29). The high blood lactate concentrations found on several occasions during a match clearly demonstrate the importance of the lactate producing energy system during periods of a match.

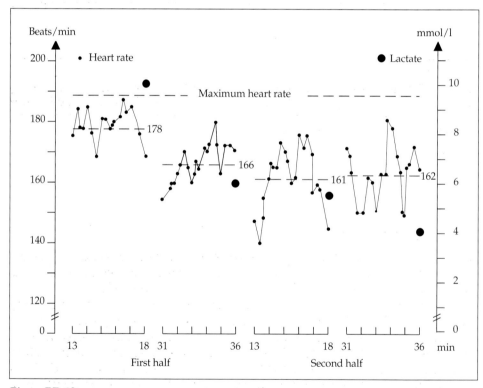

Figure PD 13
The figure shows blood lactate concentrations and heart rates for a player during a non-competitive match. Heart rate was recorded during a five-minute period before the blood sample was taken. The dotted-lines represent mean heart rate for each five-minute period. The results indicate that the higher the heart rate is during a period prior to blood sampling, the higher the lactate concentration in the blood.

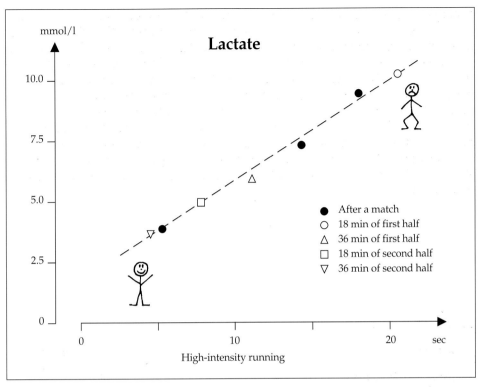

Figure PD 14
The figure illustrates the relationship between lactate concentration in blood samples taken during match-play and duration of high-intensity running, performed during a five-minute period before the sample was taken. The values are from the same player as in Fig. PD 13. It is clear that more high-intensity running results in higher lactate concentrations.

Body temperature

It is possible to get an idea of a player's exercise intensity and energy production during a match by measuring body temperature immediately after the match, provided the surrounding temperature is not too high.

Players from the Swedish first division were found to have an average body temperature of 39.5 °C after a match. The average values for players from the second, third, and fourth divisions were lower than those of the first division players – 39.2, 39.0, and 39.1 °C, respectively. This difference in temperature indicates that the exercise intensity was the highest for the first division players. In several first division matches, played in an air temperature of around 22 °C, body temperatures above 40 °C were found. One reason for such high temperatures towards the end of the match is a loss of fluid, as this inhibits heat transfer from the body. Nevertheless, the major cause for the rise in body temperature is the high energy production during a match.

75

Loss of body fluid

During a match a player's body weight will decrease due to the evaporation of sweat (see page 34). The magnitude of this weight reduction is dependent on both weather conditions and the player's work-rate. A top-class player typically loses between 1 and 3 kg during a match, but a reduction of 4-5 kg may occur in extreme circumstances. During the 1986 World Cup in Mexico, the Danish players lost on average 2.5 litres of sweat per match. Such a loss of body fluid inhibits performance (see page 321).

Muscular strength and coordination (technique)

Through analysis of match-play activities it is possible to evaluate muscular strength and coordination (technique) in football.

Speed in football is related to the explosive strength of the leg muscles, the ability to coordinate movements, and the ability to perceive a given situation (i.e. the ability to see, understand and evaluate). A player needs to be able to quickly change direction, for example, in order to evade a tackle or try to get away from a marking defender. It is not surprising, therefore, that the ability of professional football players to rapidly change direction has been found to be markedly better than that of other athletes.

Football also requires a high level of strength in the muscles of the upper body.

It is advantageous for a player to be able to make a long pass as this enhances the possibility of exposing the defensive line of the opponents. Similarly, the power of a shot or the speed of a pass are important as a ball travelling at high speed will give the goalkeeper or defender less time to react. The to kick ability to kick is dependent on strength and coordination of the leg and hip muscles. For some players a high muscular strength of the upper body may also be useful. A study has shown that the length of a throw-in is closely related to strength of the chest muscles. Similarly, heading requires strong arm, neck, chest, and abdominal muscles, in combination with an ability to coordinate the involved muscle groups.

When tackling, the body should function as a rigid unit. This is achieved by good isometric strength in the chest, abdomen, and back musculature. Tackling also requires good strength, both in the supporting and the tackling leg, which first must produce force dynamically and then work in a fixed position (isometrically). When passing and controlling a ball the body is supported on only one leg, except for when the ball is controlled by the chest or with the head. In order to maintain balance good coordination of the muscle groups is required.

A player does not appear to lose strength during a match, as it has been shown that a player is just as strong towards the end of the match as in the beginning.

Summary

Recordings of activities and physiological measurements during matches can be used to evaluate the demands of football.

The aerobic energy system provides by far the greatest amount of energy used during a match. Heart rate and body temperature measurements indicate that a top-class player exercises at an average intensity of approximately 70% of maximum oxygen uptake. Such a high exercise intensity maintained for 90 minutes places high demands on the oxygen transport system and the endurance capacity of the muscles. For a player of average size, the energy consumption during a match is roughly 5.0 megajoules* (MJ), i.e. 1150 kilocalories (kcal).

Anaerobic energy production is important because it is needed for periods of high-intensity exercise. During a match, a top-class player performs about 20 sprints that on average last less than three seconds. The energy production for these sprints is derived primarily from the anaerobic breakdown of high-energy phosphates, which are re-generated during a subsequent rest period. During periods of high-intensity exercise, energy is also provided by the anaerobic lactate producing processes, as is indicated by high blood lactate concentrations during match-play.

Well-developed coordination and a relatively high strength level in certain muscle groups, in particular the leg muscles, are advantageous for a football player.

*1 MJ = 230 kcal

Performance
Testing

Performance Testing

Performance tests for football players can be designed to cover the technical, tactical, psychological, and fitness components of the game.

Reasons for testing

Testing should be done with a purpose, so clear objectives should be defined before selecting a test. There are several good reasons for testing players:

- To study the effect of a training programme.
- To motivate players to train harder.
- To give players objective feedback.
- To make players more aware of the objectives of the training.
- To evaluate whether a player is ready to play a competitive match.
- To plan short- and long-term training programmes.

In order to fulfil these purposes, it is important that the test used is relevant to football and resembles the conditions during match-play. However, due to the many aspects of the game, one should be aware that a test cannot predict how a player will perform during a match.

Fitness tests

This chapter will focus on how to evaluate fitness. Playing a match is the best overall test for a player, but it is difficult to isolate the physical components and to obtain an objective measure of performance during a match. Instead, selected components can be evaluated on the training field when the player is performing defined football activities.

In this chapter some tests which are specific to football are described. In the tests the players perform intermittent exercise as in football, and the tests can be carried out on a football field with the players wearing football shoes. The tests also have the advantage that they can be completed in a short amount of time.

When a test is performed outdoors, variables such as the condition of the field and the weather may affect the test result. If an outdoor test is to be repeated, one should therefore try to ensure that the field and weather conditions are as similar as possible for the tests. To eliminate a variation in conditions the testing can be performed indoors, although some specificity to match-play is thereby lost.

General requirements

In order for a fitness test to be reliable, certain factors have to be considered before beginning the testing:

1. The players should be well rested.

2. The players should be thoroughly warmed up.

3. The players should be given clear instructions on how to perform the test.

4. The players should have performed the test on at least one occasion, on a separate day, before a test result can be considered valid.

5. Test equipment should be in good working order and the test areas should be accurately marked.

6. The players should be aware of the aim of the test.

Being well rested before a test means that the players should not have performed intensive exercise during the day prior to testing or on the day of the test. The first time a test is performed the test result can not be considered reliable, as the players, even with good instructions, will be unaccustomed to the demands of the test. The players will be thinking about which tactics that can be used to achieve the best test result.

Sprint test

On average, a player sprints less than a total of one minute during a match (see page 60). However, these sprints are very important because high-speed running is usually performed when there is a need for it. The result of a match may be decided because a player is able to run faster than an opponent in a given situation. Speed in football is based on several factors. Firstly, the ability to quickly see, perceive and analyze a situation, and then to take appropriate action. Secondly, the ability to rapidly produce energy, which among other things is dependent on training status and fibre type distribution in the muscles (see page 40). Thirdly, how fatigued the muscles are before sprinting. The need to sprint during a game is not predictable, so a player should be able to recover quickly from high-intensity exercise. In football, sprints are generally shorter than 40 metres and often include changes in direction, e.g. a forward who quickly changes direction in order to get away from an opponent. In the test described below these factors have been considered.

It is important to be fast in football.

Description

1. Course

The running course is illustrated in Fig. PT 1.

2. Performing the test

A lap consists of a sprint from A to B along the marked lines, followed by 25 seconds of low-intensity running from B to C. The test consists of seven laps and the duration of each sprint is recorded.

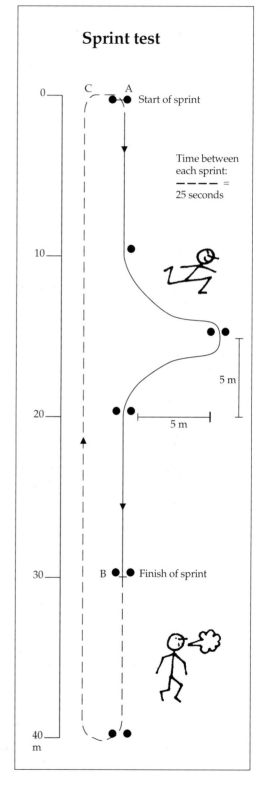

Sprint test

Start of sprint

Time between each sprint:
= 25 seconds

5 m

5 m

B — Finish of sprint

Figure PT 1

The figure illustrates the dimensions of the sprint test area and the running course. The distance between A and B is 34.2 metres and the distance between B and C is 50 metres. A player sprints from A to B and then jogs from B to C within 25 seconds.

Test results
The seven sprint times for a player, e.g.

Sprint no.	1	2	3	4	5	6	7
Time (sec)	6.73	6.88	fall	7.14	7.35	7.50	7.65

can be combined to form three test results.

a. Best time
The best time is the fastest of the seven sprint times. In the above example this is 6.73 seconds.

b. Mean time
The mean time is calculated as the average of the seven sprint times. If the player falls or stumbles, the time for this trial is omitted and replaced by the mean time for the previous and the subsequent sprint.* In the example the time for the third sprint is calculated as the mean of the time for sprint 2 and sprint 4, i.e. $(6.88 + 7.14)/2 = 7.01$ seconds. The mean time of the seven sprints is then calculated as $(6.73+6.88+7.01+7.14+7.35+7.50+7.65)/7 = 7.18$ seconds. The mean time expresses a player's ability to perform several sprints within a short period of time during match-play.

c. Fatigue time
The fatigue time is the difference between the slowest and the fastest time. In the example, the time for the first sprint is subtracted from the time of the seventh sprint. Thus, the fatigue time is 0.92 seconds. A high fatigue time suggests a poor ability to recover from a sprint. Hence, this time indicates how a player's performance is affected by preceding bouts of high-intensity exercise during match-play.
Scheme PT 1 shows test results from a group of top-class Danish players.

Scheme PT 1

	Best time	Mean time	Fatigue time
Result (sec)	6.80	7.10	0.64
Range (sec)	6.53-7.01	6.83-7.31	0.15-0.92

*If a player falls or stumbles in the first sprint, the test should be stopped and then re-started when the player has recovered. If a player falls during the seventh sprint, the time is calculated as the time for the sixth sprint plus the difference between the fifth and the sixth sprint. If a player falls more than once, the test result should not be used.

The mean blood lactate concentration immediately after the seventh sprint was 11 mmol/l with a range from 9-14 mmol/l. The results show that a considerable amount of lactate is produced during these short sprints (approximately seven seconds).

Organization
When performing the test, Scheme PT 2 may be used.

Name/ Sprint	Sprint time (sec)							Best time	Mean time	Fatigue time
	1	2	3	4	5	6	7			

Scheme PT 2

Hints for the coach
The following procedure can be used when the test is introduced:

1. The players may perform a couple of trials with 80-90% effort between A and B, and then jog from B to C.
2. The players should be given time to learn how to run through the gates in the best technical way.
3. The players should get a feel for the speed required to run from B to C in 25 seconds.

Emphasize that:

a) The run from A to B is all-out, i.e. run performed in the shortest possible time.
b) When running from B to C, the player must be at C (the starting point) between 20 and 24 seconds after the end of the sprint. The route illustrated must be followed.

It is a good idea to use the course for a warm-up prior to testing to get reliable test results and to avoid injuries.

A player performing the sprint test.

Test leaders
Two test leaders should be used: One at the starting point (A) and the other one at the finish of the sprint (B – see Fig. PT 1).

The test leader at A starts the test by shouting »2-1-Go«. The counting is coordinated with the following arm movements: On »2« the arm is raised vertically, on »1« it is moved to an angle of about 45° between the arm and the horizontal, and on »Go« it is moved to the horizontal. This is a signal for the test leader at B to start the stop-watch. When the player passes the finishing line, the test leader at B stops the stop-watch and records the time. At the same time the test leader at A starts a stop-watch and verbally helps the player to be ready for the next sprint after 25 seconds.

Equipment
Two stop-watches, at least four posts (or cones), a tape measure, Scheme PT 2, and a pen (or pencil in wet weather).

Testing a team
Only one player can be tested at a time. A test lasts approximately:

$7 \times 7\,s + 6 \times 25\,s = 199$ seconds, i.e. 3 minutes and 19 seconds

If a small break (e.g. one minute) is allowed between each player, testing of 16 players will take approximately one hour. It is important that the players keep warm while they are waiting to perform the test.

Intermittent endurance test

The intermittent endurance test has been designed to evaluate a player's endurance capacity in football. It includes a combination of exercises that reflect the intermittent activity profile of a game.

Description

1. Course

The test area is shown in Fig. PT 2a. The dimensions of the test area correspond to the penalty area of a football field and one lap is 160 m.

2. Performing the test

The players follow the course shown in Fig. PT 2b. The test starts with high-intensity running for 15 seconds, followed by 10 seconds of jogging (see the figure text), and continues in this way until forty periods of high-intensity running (10 minutes) and thirty-nine periods of jogging (6.5 minutes) have been completed.

Test result

The test result is the distance covered during the forty periods of high-intensity running. The players should be instructed to cover as much distance as possible during these periods. To calculate the total high-intensity running distance, the number of laps completed is multiplied by 160 (m). The distance covered during the last lap is then added. This distance is obtained by determining the position on the course where the player finished on Fig. PT 2a and then using Scheme PT 3. For example, if a player finishes at position 27 on the course (see Fig. PT 2a) the corresponding distance can be found to be 100 m in Scheme PT 3. If the player had also completed 11 laps, the test result would be 11 x 160 m + 100 m = 1860 m.

Scheme PT 3

Position	1	2	3	4	5	6	7	8	9	10
Distance (m)	3	6	8	12	16	20	24	28	32	35
Position	11	12	13	14	15	16	17	18	19	20
Distance (m)	37	40	43	46	48	51	54	57	59	62
Position	21	22	23	24	25	26	27	28	29	30
Distance (m)	65	70	76	82	88	94	100	105	111	117
Position	31	32	33	34	35	36	37	38	39	40
Distance (m)	123	129	135	137	140	143	145	148	151	154
Position	41									
Distance (m)	157									

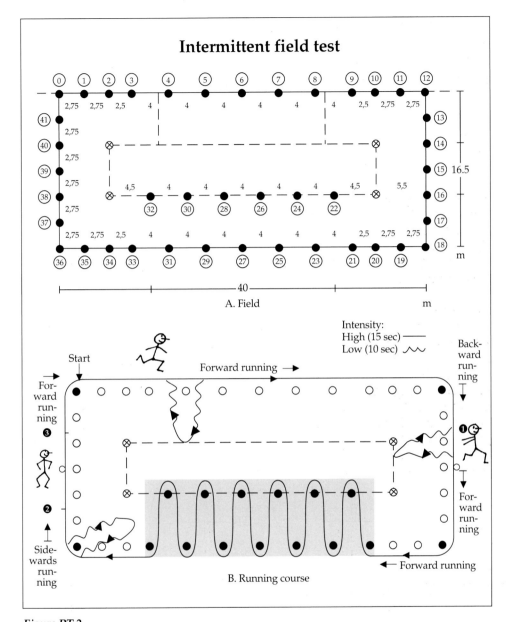

Intermittent field test

A. Field

B. Running course

Intensity:
High (15 sec) ——
Low (10 sec) 〰〰

Figure PT 2
The upper half of the figure shows the dimension of the test area for the intermittent endurance test (A) and the lower half shows the running course (B). The test area is of the same size as a penalty area. A part of the 6-yard (5.5 m) box can be used as a side line for the central area. It is advantageous if the markers indicated by (●) are higher than 160 centimetres (posts).

The symbol ❶ indicates backward running, ❷ indicates sideward running facing away from the centre, and ❸ indicates sideward running facing towards the centre. One lap is 160 metres. A player runs at high speed along the outlined course for 15 seconds. In the subsequent 10-second recovery period the player jogs to the central area and back to the last cone/post passed on the course. If the player is inside the shaded area (see figure) when the signal for the recovery period is given, the player should continue to the next post and then jog back to the post last passed. The player should wait at the cone or the post until the signal is given for the next 15 seconds of high-intensity running.

The test results for 41 Danish top-class players, divided into three groups according to position in the team, are presented in Scheme PT 4. It appears that the midfield players performed the best, although comparisons between positions may not be valid due to the relatively small number of players in each group.

	Total	Defenders	Midfield players	Forwards
Numbers of players	41	17	14	10
Averange running distance (m)	1926	1937	1968	1837
Range (m)	1688-2126	1721-2126	1759-2108	1688-2014

Scheme PT 4

Immediately after the players had completed the test, a fingertip blood sample was taken to measure the concentration of lactate. The average concentration was 8.5 mmol/l with a range from 5 to 13 mmol/l, which corresponds well with lactate concentrations found after intense periods of match-play (see page 72). Thus, the test appears to simulate the demanding periods of a football match.

A relationship was found between the result of the intermittent endurance test and the longest distance covered during several matches (match-distance). For example, one player who ran 1720 m during the test covered a total distance of 10.7 km during a match, while another player had a test result of 1940 m and a match-distance of 12.6 km. It appears that the better the test result, the greater is the distance that can be covered during a match (see Fig. PT 3). However, the actual distance covered during a match is influenced by many factors, such as a player's tactical strategy and motivation, and not just endurance capacity.

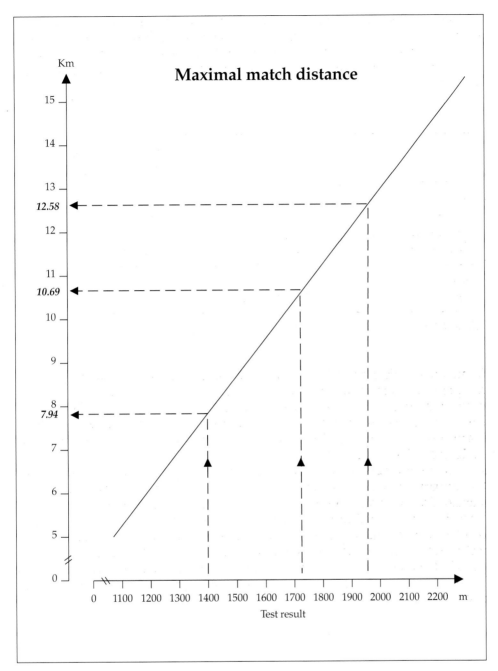

Figure PT 3
The figure illustrates the relationship between the performance in the intermittent endurance test (see Fig. PT 2 – page 89) and the greatest distance that a player can cover during a match (match-distance). A test score can be converted to match-distance by locating the test result on the horizontal axis, moving vertically up to meet the line, and then horizontally to the match-distance on the vertical axis. For example, if the distance covered during the field test is 1400 m, the corresponding match-distance is estimated to be 7.94 km. The results of two players from the intermittent endurance test and their match-distance are also shown on the figure.

In Scheme PT 5 a number of test results have been transformed into estimated maximal running distances during a match. Thus, the scheme may be used to find the potential distance that a player can cover during a match based on the test result. The procedure is as follows:

Find the test result (to the nearest 100 m) in the left hand column. Move horizontally to the column which is closest to the actual test result (to the nearest 10 m), and read the maximum match-distance (in km).

The use of Scheme PT 5 is illustrated by the shaded example. A player covered 1768 m in the test, which corresponds to a potential match-distance of 11.12 km.

	0	10	20	30	40	50	60	70	80	90
1200	6.22	6.31	6.39	6.48	6.56	6.65	6.74	6.80	6.91	6.99
1300	7.08	7.17	7.25	7.34	7.42	7.51	7.60	7.68	7.77	7.85
1400	7.94	8.03	8.11	8.20	8.28	8.37	8.46	8.54	8.63	8.71
1500	8.80	8.89	8.97	9.06	9.14	9.23	9.32	9.40	9.49	9.57
1600	9.66	9.75	9.83	9.92	10.00	10.09	10.18	10.26	10.35	10.43
1700	10.52	10.61	10.69	10.78	10.86	10.95	11.04	11.12	11.21	11.29
1800	11.38	11.47	11.55	11.64	11.72	11.81	11.90	11.98	12.07	12.15
1900	12.24	12.33	12.41	12.50	12.58	12.67	12.76	12.84	12.93	13.01
2000	13.10	13.19	13.27	13.36	13.44	13.53	13.62	13.70	13.79	13.87
2100	13.96	14.05	14.13	14.22	14.30	14.39	14.48	14.56	14.65	14.73
2200	14.82	14.91	14.99	15.08	15.16	15.25	15.34	15.42	14.51	14.59
2300	15.68	15.77	15.85	15.94	16.02	16.11	16.20	16.28	16.37	16.45

Scheme PT 5

Organization
The Schemes PT 6 – PT 8 below may be used when performing the test.

Test scheme *Scheme PT 6*

Name	Start time	Finish time	Rounds	Finish position
	0:00	16:30		

After the test the results can be converted into running distances by using Scheme PT 7.

Test distance *Scheme PT 7*

Name	Rounds		Addition	Total
Example	11	x 160 m	+ 100 m	= 1860 m
		x 160 m	+ m	= m
		x 160 m	+ m	= m
		x 160 m	+ m	= m
		x 160 m	+ m	= m
		x 160 m	+ m	= m
		x 160 m	+ m	= m

Time schedule

In the intermittent endurance test players perform high-intensity exercise for 15 seconds, followed by 10 seconds of jogging. Each player starts with the high-intensity exercise period. The time schedule shown in Scheme PT 8 can be used.

High-intensity (min:sec)	Low-intensity (min:sec)	High-intensity (min:sec)	Low-intensity (min:sec)
0:00	0:15	4:35	4:50
0:25	0:40	5:00 - from here on values	
0:50	1:05	are continued in the same manner	
1:15	1:30	as given in the beginning, i.e the	
1:40	1:55	following times will be:	5:15
2:05	2:20	5:25	5:40
2:30	2:45	Values are continued until:	
2:55	3:10	15:00	15:15
3:20	3:35	15:25	15:40
3:45	4:00	15:50	16:05
4:10	4:25	16:15	16:30
Values are continued in the two next columns			(finish)

Hints for the coach

The following procedure can be used when the test is introduced:

1. The players may initially complete two or three laps of the course without stopping for the 10-second jogging periods in order to get accustomed to the different types of running.
2. A signal can then be used (e.g. a whistle) to cue the players to jog to the central area and back to the cone which was last passed. This may be done first outside, then inside the shaded area (see Fig. PT 2b).
3. The signals can be made for the 10- and 15-second periods so that the players can judge the duration of both the high-intensity running and the jogging.

Emphasize that:

a) After the signal that indicates the end of the 15-second high-intensity running a player must not pass another cone.
b) At the end of the 10-second period, when waiting at a cone, the players must not start the high-intensity running until the signal is given.

Players performing the intermittent endurance test.

When repeating the test the players should be reasonably acquainted with the protocol, but the course can be used for warm-up to again practice the different types of running.

The coach should allow plenty of time to set up the course the first time this test is performed. In order for the coach to become familiar with the testing procedure it is a good idea to test only a few players before testing the whole team. Initially the test may appear complicated, but when the components are understood it is possible to quickly organize and accurately perform the test.

Test leaders

The test requires two leaders. One of them uses a whistle to signal the 15- and 10-second intervals (see Scheme PT 8). The other records the number of completed laps and the finishing position of each player.

It is helpful to use a tape on which audio signals are recorded every 15 and 10 seconds. During the test, the leader who gives the signal can listen to and follow the signals of the tape. Another possibility is to play the tape loud enough so that the players can hear the audio signals directly. In this case, the test requires only one test leader who records the number of completed laps and the finishing position of each player.

Equipment

A stop-watch, a whistle, 42 posts/cones (or another kind of marker), a tape measure, Schemes PT 6 and PT 8, and a pen (or pencil in wet weather).

Testing a team

When a team is tested the players may start the test at 25-second intervals. In Scheme PT 9, the starting and finishing times for 16 players are indicated.

Scheme PT 9

Player	Start (min:sec)	Finish (min:sec)	Player	Start (min:sec)	Finish (min:sec)
1	0:00	16:30	9	3:20	19:50
2	0:25	16:55	10	3:45	20:15
3	0.50	17:20	11	4:10	20:40
4	1:15	17:45	12	4:35	21:05
5	1:40	18:10	13	5:00	21:30
6	2:05	18:35	14	5:25	21:55
7	2:30	19:00	15	5:50	22:20
8	2:55	19:25	16	6:15	22:45

Testing 16 players will take approximately 23 minutes. The best time for passing is when two players are standing at the same cone at the end of a rest period. Running together in groups should be avoided. If one wishes to have fewer players on the course at a given time, the players can be started at greater intervals (e.g. every 50 seconds). When testing a whole team, it can be helpful to have an extra test leader who guides the players and records their finishing positions.

Yo-Yo intermittent tests

Recently two tests of relevance for football have been developed: the *Yo-Yo intermittent endurance test* and the *Yo-Yo intermittent recovery test*. In the Yo-Yo intermittent tests the players perform repeated 20-m shuttle runs interspersed with a short recovery period during which the players jog. The time allowed for a shuttle, which is progressively decreased, is dictated by audio bleeps from a tape. The aim of the test is to complete as many shuttles as possible. The test ends when the player is no longer able to maintain the required speed.

The aim of the Yo-Yo intermittent *endurance* test is to evaluate a player's ability to repeatedly perform intense exercise after prolonged intermittent exercise. A situation that resembles the last part of a football match. In the test the players have a 5-second rest period between each shuttle and the total duration is between 10 and 20 minutes.

The aim of the Yo-Yo intermittent *recovery* test is to examine a player's ability to recover from intense exercise. This ability is important in football as it influences a player's potential to perform high-intensity exercise during a game. In this test the running speeds are higher than during the endurance test and there is a 10-second jogging period between each shuttle. The total duration of the test is between three and 15 minutes.

Both tests have a level for elite-trained players and one for recreational players. Thus any player, independent of training status, can be evaluated. Another advantage is that a whole squad (up to 30 players) can be tested at a time. The tests have been proven useful and are now used by several European top-class teams.

More information about the tests can be obtained by contacting HO+Storm, Brudelysvej 26, 2880 Bagsværd, Denmark (Fax number: Int-45-44984666).

When to test

The time for when a test is to be performed depends on the aim. If the coach wishes to observe the effect of a change in training, testing should be conducted before and after the period of altered training. Testing can also be useful after a period of a restricted amount of fitness training or after a pre-season period. Moreover, testing can be performed before and after a period without regular training, e.g. a holiday.

It may be suitable to test intermittent endurance performance four to six times per year:

Test 1: At the start of the preparation (re-building period – see page 275) for the season.

Test 2: Two to three weeks prior to the start of the season.

Test 3: Early in the season. The fitness level of some players may decrease during the season as a result of a reduced amount of fitness training (see page 284). The test should be carried out sufficiently early to ensure that there is enough time to implement revised training programmes before the end of the half-season or season, if necessary.

In countries where there is a mid-season break :

Test 4: At the start of the preparation (re-building period) for the second half of the season.

Test 5: Two to three weeks prior to the start of the second half of the season.

Test 6: During the second half of the season. The same circumstances apply here as early in the season described under Test 3.

In countries where there is no mid-season break:

Test 4 and 5 may be performed sometime in the middle of the season.

Players from a Danish top-class team performing the Yo-Yo intermittent recovery test two weeks before a European Cup quarter-final.

In addition to regular testing of a team, there may be cases where individual players need to be tested. For example, it may be useful to test a player during a rehabilitation programme in order to guide the player in the training and to determine when the player is ready to play competitive matches again. This can be evaluated by comparing post-injury test results with those recorded prior to the injury. The field tests described in this chapter are particularly effective since they include movements similar to those which occur during a match. If the player is not fully recovered or experiences some form of pain during the tests, this should be reflected in the test result.

Summary

There are a number of good reasons for using fitness tests, such as motivating a player to train harder and determining whether a player has recovered from an injury. However, in order to fulfil these purposes the tests need to be relevant for football. A football player should have a high endurance capacity and should be able to quickly recover after a sprint. These performance components can be tested by the described tests. Testing should be performed at times of the year when the results are most useful, e.g. when changes in the training programme occur.

Fitness
Training

102

Fitness Training

Football is a physically demanding sport characterized by frequent strenuous activities such as high-intensity running, tackling, turning, and jumping. It has been shown that a top-class male football player makes approximately 1100 changes in exercise intensity and covers a distance of about 11 km during a match (see page 59). Fitness training can help a player endure the physical demands of football and maintain the technical abilities throughout a match. Every football player, regardless of standard of play, can benefit from a fitness training programme.

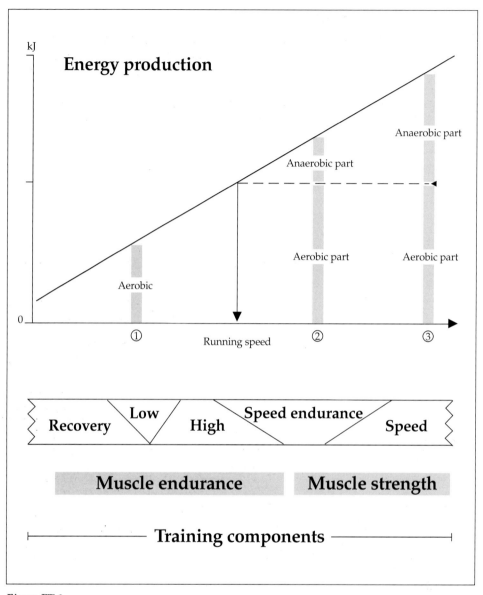

Figure FT 1

The figure shows energy production at different running speeds. At low running speeds (e.g. the speed indicated by ① most of the energy is produced aerobically. At the speed indicated by the vertical arrow, the limit of energy production from the aerobic system is reached (maximum oxygen uptake – indicated by the dotted-line) and at higher speeds the remaining energy is produced anaerobically. The figure shows two running speeds ② and ③ with the same aerobic energy production (i.e. maximal) but with a different anaerobic energy production.

At the bottom of the figure the various components of fitness training are positioned according to energy production during training.

Recovery = recovery training, low = aerobic low-intensity training, high = aerobic high-intensity training, speed endurance = speed endurance training, speed = speed training, muscle endurance = muscle endurance training, muscle strength = muscle strength training.

Types of fitness training

At low exercise intensities*, the muscles produce energy almost entirely from aerobic processes. During high-intensity exercise the aerobic energy production is limited and a major part of the energy used is supplied by anaerobic processes (see Fig. FT 1).

Based on the energy pathway that is dominant, fitness training in football can be divided into a number of components (see Figs. FT 1 and FT 2).

Fitness training in football

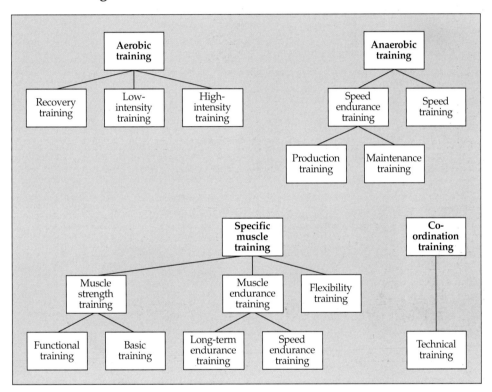

Figure FT 2
Components of fitness training in football.

* **Exercise Intensity:** Work performed per unit time. For example, if player A runs 1 km in four minutes and player B runs the same distance in eight minutes, then player A has exercised with an intensity twice as high as that of player B.

During a match or a training session, a player's exercise intensity varies frequently. In some periods energy is provided almost exclusively via the aerobic system, while at other times a large proportion of the energy is produced via the anaerobic systems. Figure FT 3 shows examples of how the exercise intensity can vary during games and drills within aerobic and anaerobic training. Some overlapping exists between the two categories of training, e.g. the exercise intensity during aerobic high intensity training may, in short periods, become as high as during anaerobic speed endurance training.

The separate components within fitness training are briefly described below.

Aerobic training

Aerobic training can be divided into *aerobic high-intensity training*, *aerobic low-intensity training*, and *recovery training* (see Fig. FT 1).

Figure FT 3
Examples of the exercise intensities (expressed in relation to maximal intensity (100%)) of a player during games within aerobic and anaerobic training. Some overlapping exists between the categories of training, e.g. the exercise intensity during Aerobic$_{HI}$ training may in short periods become as high as during Anaerobic speed endurance training.
The exercise intensity eliciting maximum oxygen uptake and maximal exercise intensity of the player are represented by the lower and the higher horizontal dotted-line, respectively.

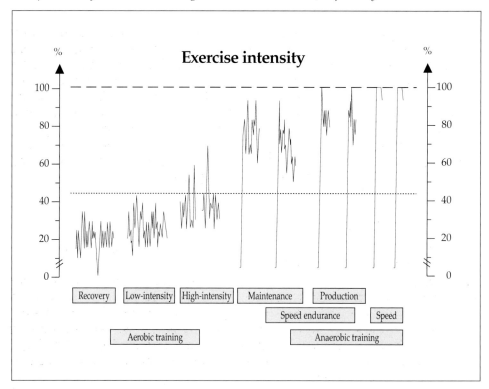

Playing football is a demanding form of exercise. It is here illustrated by the players of the Danish National team before over-time in the 1993 Artemio Franchi Cup (the European Champions vs. the South American Champions) match against Argentina. Fitness training is necessary to cope with the demands of football.

A football player should be capable of exercising at high intensities at any time during a match. The ability to perform this type of exercise can be improved through aerobic high-intensity training. It is also important that a player is able to maintain a high physical and technical standard throughout a match. Therefore, a part of the training should aim at improving the capacity to exercise with varying running speeds for long periods of time (endurance). By performing aerobic low-intensity training the endurance capacity of a player can be increased. On the day following a match, or after several days of intensive training, a player may need to recover, which can be done by performing light physical activities – recovery training.

Anaerobic training

Anaerobic training can be divided into *speed training* and *speed endurance training* (see Fig. FT 1 – page 105).

An average sprint during a match lasts less than three seconds. However, as a sprint may be important for the final outcome of a match, it is advantageous for a player to perform speed training. In football, speed is not merely dependent on the physical capacity; it also involves fast decision making which must be translated into quick movements. The aim of speed training is to improve a player's ability to perceive, evaluate, and act quickly in situations where speed is essential.

107

During a short sprint (1-5 seconds), energy is produced primarily through breakdown of phosphates, but the lactate producing anaerobic system is also utilized (see page 27). During longer periods of high-intensity exercise energy is produced mainly via the latter system. High blood lactate concen- trations measured from top-class players during match-play indicate that the lactate producing energy system is important in football and should therefore be specifically trained. This can be achieved through speed endurance training, which improves the capacity to repeatedly perform high-intensity exercise.

Specific muscle training

Specific muscle training involves training of muscles with isolated move- ments. The aim of this training is to increase performance of a muscle to a higher level than can be attained solely by playing football. Specific muscle training can be divided into *muscle strength, muscle speed endurance*, and *flexibility* training (see Fig. FT 1 – page 105).

Training biceps using some form of external resistance, e.g. dumb-bells, is an example of a form of muscle strength training. Training the abdominal mus- cles using several repetitions of an appropriate exercise is an example of muscle endurance training. Stretching the hamstring muscles is an example of flexibility training.

Training methods

A major part of fitness training in football should be performed with a ball, since such training has several advantages. Firstly, the specific muscle groups used in football are trained. Secondly, the players develop technical and tactical skills under conditions similar to those encountered during a match. Thirdly, this form of training usually provides greater motivation for the players compared to training without the ball. When training with a ball, however, the players may not work hard enough, as many factors, such as tactical limitations, can lower the exercise intensity. To increase the demands of a training game new rules may be introduced (see page 139).

When a football field is unavailable the coach should be as creative as possible when organizing a training session. An example of a good alternative is a heading game, where the players alternately pass the ball with hands and head. In this way the fitness training is performed with movements which are similar to the ones used during a match. In addition, such games will involve tactical and technical elements which are relevant to football. In that respect much can be gained compared to running without a ball. Under some circum- stances it may be necessary to train without a ball. If this is the case the training should mainly be on grass, with the players wearing football shoes and performing movements that resemble those during match-play.

Players, especially the goalkeeper, can benefit from individual fitness training to cover the specific demands of the position in a team.

Individual training

In football, the physical demands of a player during a match are influenced by several factors, such as the player's tactical role and technical standard. Therefore, players in a team have different training needs. A part of the fitness training may therefore be performed on an individual basis, where the training can be focused on improving a player's strong and weak abilities. It is important to be aware of the fact that, due to hereditary differences, there will always be differences in the physical capacity of players, irrespective of training programmes. This fact is illustrated by results from tests made with players in the Danish World Cup team of 1986. Although all of the players in the team were close to their peak fitness level, the maximum oxygen uptake of the players ranged from 57 to 69 ml/min/kg body weight (the highest value found for a Danish football player is 76 ml/min/kg). Players who are physically weaker may be able to compensate through superior qualities in other aspects of the game. This type of player is also needed on a team, and it is important for the coach to chose a playing system and style which fits the strength of the available players. The strategy of a football team is often selected in such a way that players with high physical capacities perform the most work. For instance, midfield players usually possess a high endurance level and run a substantially longer distance than other players during a match. Individual physical demands must be considered when planning fitness training, but the extent of individual training is dependent upon several factors, such as the total training time available. Individual training can be performed in small groups because several players may have the same needs.

Training of young players

There is evidence to suggest that training of youth players does not need to be focused on improving physical performance. Often young players get sufficient physical training by regular drills and games. In a Danish study, 132 young players from football clubs, in which fitness training was not performed with players under 15 years of age, were tested using a football-specific endurance test (see page 88). The results from the different age groups are shown in Fig. FT 4 and can be compared to results for 82 senior players playing in the Danish league. For the boys younger than 15 years there was a pronounced increase in performance with age despite the fact that they did not perform any specific fitness training. Furthermore, the results of

Figure FT 4
Running distance during an intermittent field test (performance) for youth players (filled squares) and adult elite players (open square).

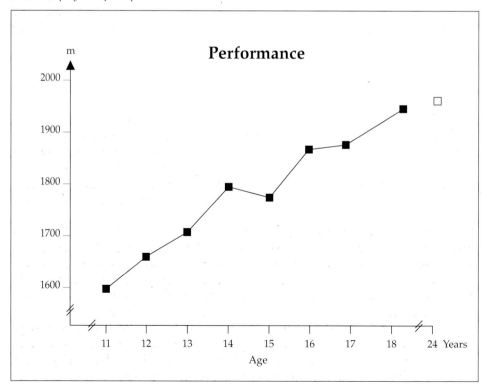

Young players improve their fitness level by training and by playing games. Therefore, they do not need to perform fitness training.

the 18 year old players were as high as those of the senior league players. It appears that a player can reach a top-class level as senior player without performing fitness training during the younger years. The time saved by excluding fitness training should be spent on training to improve technical skills, as the players will greatly benefit from this type of training when they become seniors.

When training young players one should be aware that there is a large difference in individual maturation within a given age group. The adolescent growth spurt may start as early as the age of ten or may not start until the age of sixteen. On average, girls mature about two years earlier than boys. As maturation status can have a profound effect on physical performance, care should be taken not to underestimate genuine football talents due to physical immaturity in comparison with the other players in the same age group. Another important aspect of youth training is the amount and intensity of training. The coach should carefully observe how the individual players respond to the training, as young players can easily be »overtrained«.

Fitness training for female players

The overall exercise intensity in female football is not as high as in the male game due to the lower physical capacity of female players. Nevertheless, as a result of the increasing popularity and rapid development of female football, greater physical demands are being placed upon female players. The activity profile of female football is very similar to that of male football (see Fig. FT 5), and there is little difference in the training potential of men and women, i.e. the response to training from a baseline level is similar. Therefore, male and female players should basically train in the same way and the training advice given in this book is applicable to both gender.

It is important to emphasize training at a high intensity for top-class female players. However, as alterations in the menstrual cycle may occur if the training suddenly becomes very demanding, it is advisable to increase the amount and intensity of exercise gradually. If any menstrual changes do occur, the player should either take a period of rest or follow a less demanding training program.

Figure FT 5

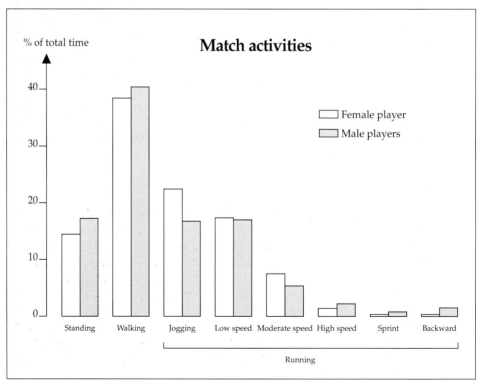

The activity profile of an elite female player during a match is the same as that of a male top-class player.

Summary

The performance potential of a player can be improved by fitness training, which can be divided into *aerobic training, anaerobic training,* and *specific muscle training*. Common to all types of fitness training is the fact that the exercise performed during the training should be as similar as possible to playing football. This is one of the main reasons as to why the majority of fitness training should be performed with a ball. As a supplement to the general fitness training, exercises may also be designed to accommodate the individual needs of the players. Training for young players, prior to and during early puberty, should not be focused on the physical aspect, but should mainly emphasize technical training. Fitness training for females and males should follow the same principles.

113

The Training
Session

The Training Session

This chapter outlines general principles of warm-up and recovery activities following a match and a training session. It also covers how to monitor a player's heart rate during training as well as how to use a training drill.

Warm-up

Warm-up allows a player to gradually adapt both physically and mentally to exercise.

Aims

1. To increase performance.

2. To decrease the risk of injury.

Effects

During exercise the active muscles produce heat. As the intensity of the exercise increases more heat is generated. Some of the heat is transferred from the muscles into the blood and is dispersed throughout the body. Thus, exercising with large muscle groups not only causes an increase in muscle temperature, but also results in a considerable rise in body temperature. During intense exercise the muscle temperature may rise to 43 °C while body temperature can reach 41 °C.

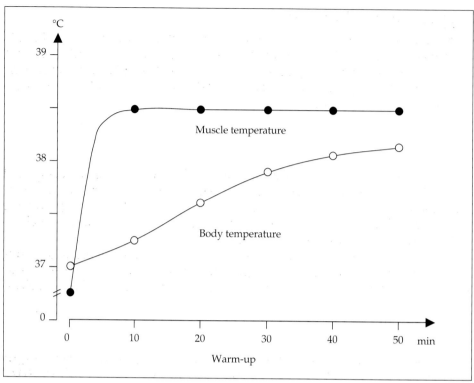

Figure TS 1
The figure illustrates the changes in body (open circle) and muscle (filled circle) temperature during 50 minutes of exercise. The body temperature increased gradually, whereas the muscle temperature only increased during the first 10 minutes, whereafter it remained constant.

Figure TS 1 illustrates what happens to the temperature of muscle and body during a warm-up. The muscle temperature reaches a stable level after about 10 minutes, whereas the body temperature is still rising after 50 minutes. A rise in muscle temperature increases the ability of the muscle to produce energy during exercise. This is one reason for the improvements in performance observed after a warm-up. Figure TS 2 shows the relationship between muscle temperature and performance during a brief sprint on a cycle ergometer. From the results in Fig. TS 1 and TS 2 it can be concluded that a warm-up should last for at least 10 minutes in order for the players to fully benefit from the increase in muscle temperature.

Many injuries occur due to an insufficient warm-up. A cold muscle is relatively rigid and resilient to sudden increases in tension caused by rapid movements. When the elastic components of the muscle are unable to accommodate the external tensions, the muscle will rupture. This is commonly referred to as a »pulled« muscle.

118

Application to football

Every training session or match should begin with a warm-up. In addition to the physical effects, the warm-up also has psychological benefits. Before a match it may help some players to control their nerves and concentrate on the match. For training, a warm-up can stimulate the players and prepare them mentally for the work ahead.

Organization

The exercise intensity should be low at the beginning of a warm-up and gradually increase. The tasks should be technically easy to perform; otherwise there is a risk that the overall activity level will be too low, and the warm-up will not have the desired effect. A warm-up should also include light stretching exercises (see page 126).

Both weather and temperature must be considered when planning a warm-up. When the air temperature is high, the temperature of the muscles and body increases rapidly and less time for warm-up is needed. Nevertheless,

Figure TS 2
The figure illustrates the relationship between muscle temperature and sprint performance. The higher the muscle temperature, the better the performance, e.g. at a muscle temperature of 41 °C performance was 15% greater than at 37 °C.

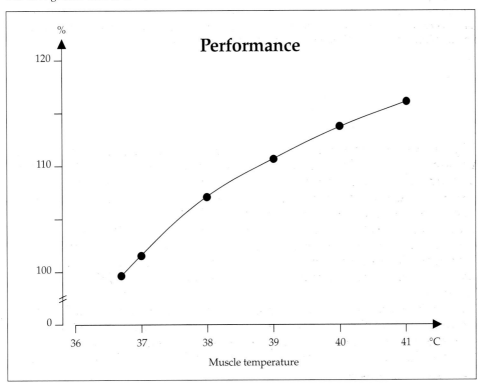

some warm-up exercises need to be performed to obtain a sufficiently high muscle temperature. In cold weather it is advisable that the players wear extra training clothes to decrease the loss of heat from the body, and to enable the muscle and body temperature to increase more rapidly.

Towards the end of a warm-up performed before a match the exercise intensity should be high (see Fig. TS 3). This is not necessary for a warm-up during training since the coach and the players can control the exercise intensity of the subsequent training drills. Other differences between warm-up for match and training are discussed below.

Pre-match warm-up

After cessation of exercise, the temperature of the previously activated muscles decreases quickly and is back to a pre-exercise level after approximately 15 minutes. A warm-up before a match should therefore continue until the start of the match. In top-class football the players often return to the changing room after the warm-up and stay there for more than 15 minutes. During this time many of the benefits gained during the warm-up are lost. If

Figure TS 3
The figure shows changes in heart rate for a player during a warm-up before training (solid-line) and prior to a match (dotted-line). Heart rate varied by approximately 25 beats/min within each of the three five-minute periods, and on average heart rate increased from one period to the next. Towards the end of the warm-up prior to the match, heart rates reached almost maximal value, whereas the values at the end of the warm-up before training were considerably below maximum level.

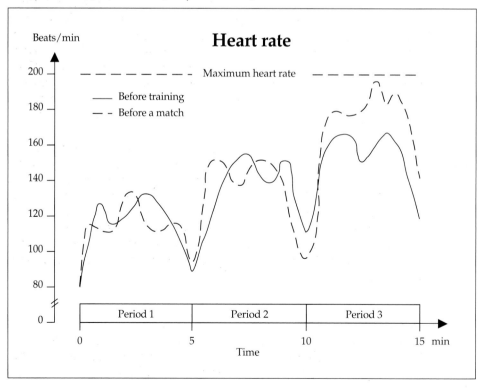

Warm-up before a match can be performed both individually and in groups.

the break is short (e.g. five minutes), however, the loss in muscle temperature can be regained by performing some activities immediately before kick-off.

A considerable decrease in muscle temperature may also occur at half-time. It has been observed that the running distance in the beginning of the second half is markedly shorter than that of the same period in the first half. One possible explanation for this difference is a decrease in muscle temperature during the break. Therefore, it is advisable that the players perform some kind of light activity at half-time, especially when the break lasts more than 10 minutes.

It is important to be aware of the psychological value of warming up prior to a match. The players should be allowed to do part of the warm-up on their own. For example, directly after changing, before a more structured team warm-up, and then again just before the start of a match. An important element of the pre-match warm-up is that the players work with a ball, so that they will have a feel for the ball prior to the game. In a warm-up before a match, 15 minutes could be spent to accommodate individual needs, followed by a warm-up for the team lasting 10 minutes and ending with five minutes for the players to exercise on their own.

Pre-training warm-up
When planning a warm-up programme for training the coach should try to be creative. To achieve an effective and motivating warm-up programme, the major part of the exercises should be performed with a ball.

To decrease the risk of injury, the warm-up should be initiated with some exercises that activate large muscle groups, for example jogging with or without a ball, before playing against opponents. After approximately five minutes of whole body exercises, light stretching exercises can be performed. The warm-up should then be continued with exercises for the main muscle groups used during football, which can be achieved by playing a »passive« small-sided game. After another series of stretching exercises the intensity of the warm-up activities can be increased. An example of the fluctuation in heart rate of a player during a pre-training warm-up programme is shown in Fig. TS 3 – see page 120.

A warm-up programme with the ball for 24 players is described below. The programme consists of three phases during which the exercise intensity is gradually increased. It lasts approximately 30 minutes, but can be shortened by excluding parts from each of the three phases.

Phase 1 (6 minutes)

a. All players start in one of the penalty areas passing balls randomly to each other (one ball for every two players). On a signal from the coach the players run to another area of the field and continue to pass the ball within this area. For example, on the first signal they run into the centre circle, on the next signal to the other penalty area, and then back to the centre circle, and so on. Passing can be replaced by alternatives such as dribbling with cross-overs. The total duration of this phase could be around five minutes.

b. The players are given one minute to gently stretch, maintaining each stretched position for only a few seconds.

Phase 2 (12 minutes)

A football field is divided into eight zones of equal size (see Fig. TS 4). The players are together in groups of six, with two zones for every six players.

a. Four players play against two players (4v2), with the two players trying to touch the ball. If one of the two players successfully touches the ball, this player then changes places with the player who made the mistake. A ball kicked out of the playing area is also regarded as a mistake. The players may only play in one of the two zones at a time. If the ball is played into the other zone, all the players should go to this zone before the ball can be passed back into the original zone. Total duration of the game is approximately five minutes.

b. A three-a-side game (3v3). Each team is trying to keep possession of the ball. One point is scored if a team can make 10 consecutive passes without the other team touching the ball. As in a. the players are only allowed to play in one zone at a time. Total duration of the game is approximately five minutes.

c. The players perform light stretching exercises for approximately two minutes.

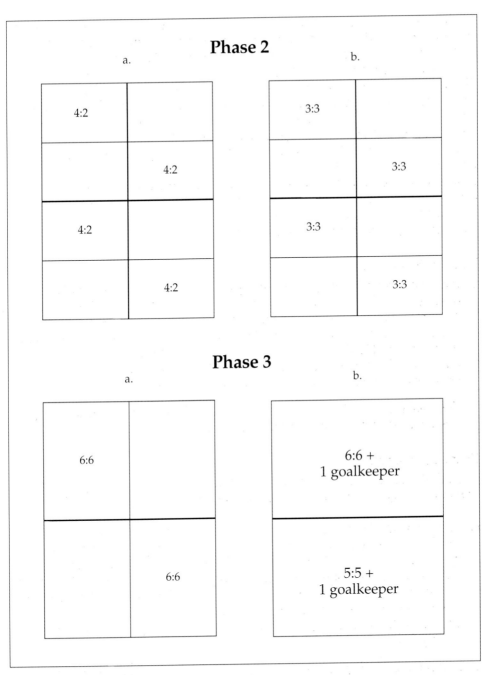

Figure TS 4
The figure shows the organisation of phases 2 and 3 of the warm-up programme described in the text.
There are 24 players including two goalkeepers. In phase 2 the field is divided into eight zones of equal
size. In the first part (a) four players play against two (4v2), and in the second part (b) three players play
against three (3v3). In phase 3 the field is divided into four zones of equal size. In the first part (a) six
players play against six (6v6) on each half of the field, and in the second part (b) six players play against
six (6v6) with one goalkeeper on one half of the field, and five play against five (5v5) with one goalkeeper
on the other half of the field.

Phase 3 (12 minutes)

a. The field is divided into four zones of equal size (see Fig. TS 4). The players are together in groups of 12, with two zones (half the field) per 12 players. A six-a-side game (6v6) is played with each team trying to keep possession of the ball. A point is scored if 10 successive passes can be made without the other team touching the ball. As before, the players must only play in one zone at a time. Total duration of the game is approximately five minutes.

b. A six-a-side game (6v6) in one half of the field and a five-a-side game (5v5) in the other. There is a goalkeeper in each half. A point is scored for passing the ball to the goalkeeper who must catch it and then throw it to a player in the same team. Total duration of the game is approximately five minutes.

c. The players stretch for around two minutes, holding each stretched position for 10-15 seconds.

Different drills with a ball can be used for warm-up. Here four players are playing against two players (see Phase 2a)

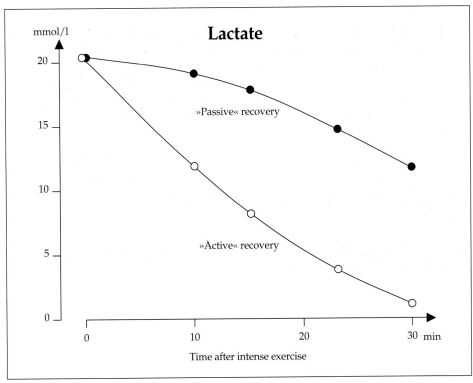

Figure TS 5
*The figure shows the blood lactate concentration after intense exercise followed by either »active«
(jogging – open circles) or »passive« (filled circles) recovery. The lactate concentration decreased at a
faster rate with »active« recovery. Thirty minutes after the cessation of exercise the resting blood lactate
level was reached during »active« recovery, whereas the level was more than 10 times higher than at rest
after 30 minutes of »passive« recovery.*

Recovery activities

A training session or match should end with a period of recovery activities
consisting of jogging and stretching exercises.

Jogging

During a match or an intense training session lactate accumulates in the active
muscles. Light recovery exercise will help to remove the lactate more quickly.
This is illustrated in Fig. TS 5, which shows that during low intensity running
blood lactate decreases at least three times more rapidly than at rest. The
faster removal is one of the reasons as to why a training session or a match
should end with low intensity activities such as jogging or a »passive« small-
sided game for at least five minutes.

Stretching

Stretching is defined as an exercise where a muscle is fully extended and held in that position for at least 15 seconds. It is important for a football player to be flexible, as poor range of movement can hinder performance and cause the muscle to rupture in situations during a match where the muscle is forced into an extreme position.

It has been demonstrated that the length of certain muscles in the legs are considerably shortened following a football match, and it can take more than two days before the normal length is restored. Playing matches and training frequently without performing regular stretching can result in a permanent shortening of the muscles. Thus ending a match or training session by stretching the main muscle groups used in football will help to restore the length of the muscles.

How to stretch

During a stretch, the two ends of a muscle are drawn away from each other. For example, a quadriceps muscle can be stretched by bending the leg and pressing the heel towards the buttocks while the hip is pressed forward.

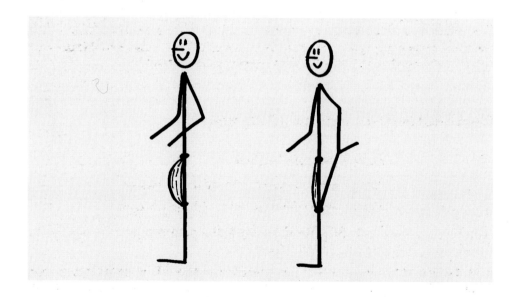

There are several ways to perform stretching exercises. A simple and efficient method is described below.

Slowly bring the muscle to a fully stretched position and hold this position for 10 seconds, then *carefully* stretch the muscle some more and hold this position for another 10 seconds.

Players can benefit by having a high flexibility. Here illustrated by the Danish central defender, Kent Nielsen, in the final of the 1992 European Championship against Germany.

When stretching there are certain rules to observe:

> *The muscles must be warm*
>
> *Always use slow movements and do not bounce*
>
> *Never stretch with a bent back and straight legs*
>
> *Be careful when stretching with a partner*

Both before and after a muscle is stretched it should be activated. If, for instance, the quadriceps muscles are to be stretched, the player can perform light kicking exercises or jumping before and after the stretching. Such activities also ensure that the muscles stay warm during the entire stretching programme.

A player should not start to stretch immediately after leaving the changing room as the muscles are cold and the risk of injury is high. For the same reason, a player should only perform light stretching exercises during a warm-up. A full stretching programme can be carried out after warm-up and after training.

127

A stretching programme

The six stretching exercises described below make up a short, but effective stretching programme for a football player. Each stretched position should be held for approximately 20 seconds, and activities performed between the stretching exercises should be of equal duration. The whole programme lasts approximately four minutes. If further stretching is desired, alternative exercises can be added or the programme can be repeated.

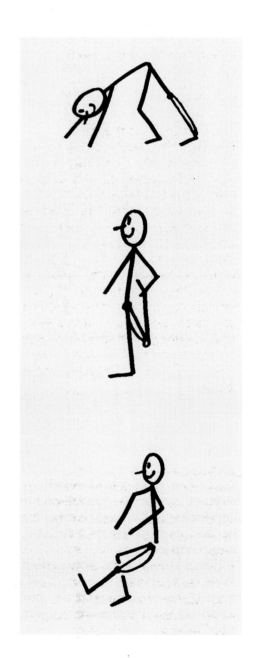

Calf muscles
Press the heel of the stretched leg towards the ground and keep the hip high.

Quadriceps muscle
Lift the knee, hold the foot with a hand, and press the heel towards the buttocks while pressing the hip forward.

Hamstring muscles
Stretch one leg forward with the toes pointing up. Bend the other leg. The body is held in an almost upright position and the buttock is pressed down. If the opposite arm is stretched forward the buttocks will be pressed further down.

Leg adductor muscles

With one leg bent and pointed forward, stretch the other leg to the side. Both feet are pointing forward and are kept on the ground. Slowly press the buttocks down. The upper body should be almost upright (slightly bent forward). Do not press with the hands on the stretched leg. The knee of the bent leg must be held directly above the foot (no twisting of the knee joint).

Deep abdominal muscles

One leg is bent and placed forward (the knee must not be in front of the ankle). The opposite leg is held back with the leg half bent and with the knee on the ground. The hip of this leg is pushed forward. The hamstring muscles of the leg held in front are partly stretched, while the deep abdominal muscles connected to the leg held in back are fully stretched. By regularly stretching the deep abdominal muscles the risk of getting a groin injury can be reduced; yet this type of exercise is often neglected among football players.

Buttock muscles

Cross one leg over the other and press carefully on the knee and thigh of the leg with the opposite arm. The other arm can either rest on the ground or be held behind the back which makes the exercise more difficult. Keep the upper body erect. To make the exercise easier, the lower leg can be stretched or the other arm can press on the knee.

Muscles should be stretched at the end of a warm-up.

Adaptation to recovery activities

Often players are heading straight for the changing room after a training session and a match. It may take some time before the players become accustomed to recovery activities and accept a change to this routine. The initial programme should therefore be simple and it should be led by the coach, who should frequently reinforce the value of recovery activities. As the players become aware of the positive effects of recovery activities they may perform the exercises on their own.

Monitoring heart rate during training

Monitoring a player's heart rate can be useful in order to make fitness training effective. However, there are certain points that should be considered before using heart rate determinations for training.

Reasons for monitoring heart rate

Heart rate determinations can give an indication of how hard a player is working and can be used to evaluate if the aim of a training is fulfilled. These measurements are especially useful when a player is expected to exercise at a high intensity. Regular monitoring of heart rate during training can also provide a good stimulus for the players to work harder.

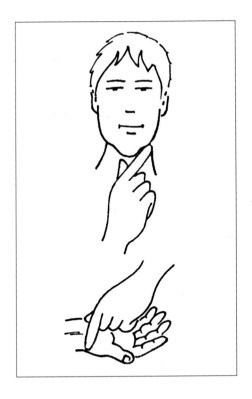

Figure TS 6
The figure shows two locations to measure heart
rate. One should never press on both sides of the
neck at the same time.

How to measure heart rate

Heart rate can be measured by the pulse from the large artery of a hand or the neck (see Fig. TS 6). The heart rate is expressed as the number of heart beats per minute. The number of beats can be counted for 10, 15, or 30 seconds. To obtain the number of beats per minute these values should be multiplied by 6, 4, or 2, respectively (see example in Scheme TS 1). The longer the counting time used, the smaller the measurement error will be. On the other hand, heart rate decreases fairly quickly upon cessation of exercise. To obtain information about heart rate during an exercise period, it is therefore best to use a counting time of 15 seconds immediately after the exercise.

Scheme TS 1

Counting time	Multiplication factor	Counted number x Factor	= Heart rate
6 sec	10	14 x 10	= 140 beats/min
10 sec	6	24 x 6	= 144 beats/min
15 sec	4	36 x 4	= 144 beats/min
20 sec	3	48 x 3	= 144 beats/min

It is important that players can measure their own heart rate as well as that of others. Once the players have learned the technique, heart rate measurements can be performed in a very short time. In order to maintain a high training efficiency, it may be advantageous to determine heart rate at the beginning of recovery periods.

The 15-second time period needed to measure heart rate can be controlled by the coach who shouts »3-2-1« and »GO«. A stop-watch is started on the command »GO« and the players start counting heart beats. The first beat is counted as zero. After exactly 15 seconds the coach gives a signal for the players to stop counting and the numbers obtained by the players are multiplied by four to give the number of heart beats per minute. The coach may then inform the players of the range in which the heart rate should be. In this way the players will receive feedback as to whether they have exercised at the desired intensity.

Modern telemetric equipment makes it possible to monitor heart rate during training and matches without any inconvenience for the players.

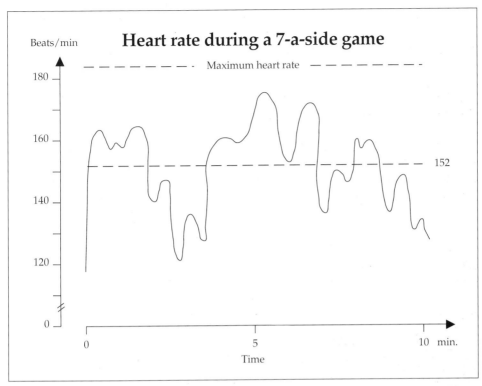

Figure TS 7
The figure shows changes in heart rate of a player during a seven-a-side game on half a field. Note the large variations in heart rate. The average heart rate was 152 beats/min.

Exercise intensity and heart rate

The exercise intensity of a player will vary frequently during a game. This is in part dependent on the position of the player in relation to the ball. To a certain degree the heart rate will reflect the variations in exercise intensity. Figure TS 7 shows an example of the fluctuations in heart rate for a player during a seven-a-side game using three-quarters of the field. This demonstrates that the time when heart rate is measured is crucial. The heart rate after three and five minutes was 122 and 176 beats/min, respectively. One might speculate that the exercise intensity of the player was too low when the heart rate was 122 beats/min, and too high when the heart rate was 176 beats/min. Neither assumption, however, would be correct as the player's average heart rate was 152 beats/min which was within the desired range for the game. Thus, to evaluate a player's average exercise intensity during a training game, heart rate measurements should be made on different occasions during the game.

In order to become familiar with heart rate measurements, a player's heart rate can be measured after different activities during a training game, and the values can be compared with those shown in Fig. TS 7.

Maximum heart rate

It is important to know the maximum heart rate of the individual players in order to interpret heart rate measurements (see page 19). A player's maximum heart rate can be determined in a simple way, as described below (see Fig. TS 8).

The player runs four laps around a football field at a moderate speed corresponding to a pace of about two minutes per lap (or another type of warm-up). This is followed by running one lap at a higher speed (in about 90 seconds), then half a lap in about 40 seconds, and finally half a lap at maximal speed which may take about 30 seconds. Immediately after finishing the test, the player's heart beats are counted for 15 seconds and this number is multiplied by four to give the number of beats per minute. The test lasts around 11 minutes for each player. The duration of the test can be as short as three minutes if another type of warm-up is used. If a whole team is to be tested, the players can start at intervals of 30 seconds, thus, 16 players can be tested (including warm-up) in 20 minutes. Another way to determine a player's maximum heart rate is to measure it immediately after a bout of presumed

Figure TS 8
The figure illustrates a method to determine a player's maximum heart rate.

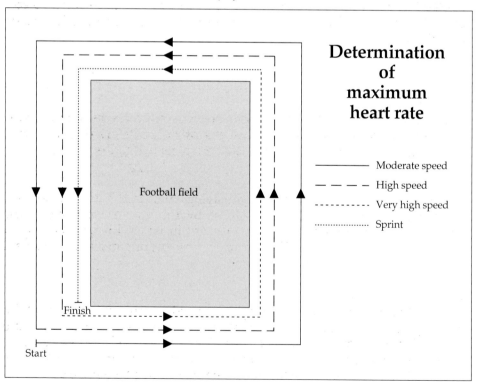

maximal intensity exercise during training. However, such measurements should be repeated several times to ensure that the true maximum heart rate has been obtained.

A player's maximum heart rate will not vary with changes in training status throughout the season, but it will decrease as a player gets older. It is therefore only necessary to determine a player's maximum heart rate once a year.

When to monitor heart rate

The coach has many things to do during a training session, such as organizing, instructing, and observing, so the additional responsibility of performing heart rate measurements may appear to be an unnecessary burden. However, such measurements can be made infrequently until the players and the coach are well acquainted with the procedures. Initially, the coach may only do heart rate measurements during selected training drills. When the expected range of heart rates for a given drill is known, random checks can be made.

Occasionally, heart rates should also be monitored during games which are designed to focus on aspects other than fitness. In this way the coach can obtain valuable information about how these games complement the fitness training.

One should be aware that the actual intensity of a game or exercise is influenced by many factors, such as motivation, technical standard of the players, and the condition of the ground. Another aspect is that players often keep a higher activity level than usual if they know that attention is being focused on their efforts.

Training drills

In the following chapters several training exercises and games (referred to as drills) will be presented. The descriptions of the drills are divided into a number of sub-sections, which are described in general terms below.

Area

The approximate dimensions of the playing area used for each drill are described. The actual size is determined by the number of players. The playing area is also illustrated by a diagram in which the area is marked inside a regular football field. Whenever possible the original lines of the field are used in order to facilitate preparation.

Number of players

A suggestion for the number of players needed to fulfil the purpose of the drill is given. Variations in the number of players that can be used are indicated in brackets, but this is only a guideline and does not mean that the drill cannot function with more or fewer players. If the number of players is changed, it may be necessary to change the size of the playing area.

Below the different codes for number of players are explained (five is used as an example):

5v5 (ten players in total – two teams of five players) means that five players from one team play against five from another team.

5v5+2 goalkeepers (twelve players in total – two teams of six players) means that five players from one team play against five from another team, each team has a goalkeeper.

5+5v5 (fifteen players in total – three teams of five players) means that ten players from two teams play against five players from a third team.

5+5v5+5 (twenty players in total – two teams of ten players) means that each team consists of two sets of five players that take turns to play. Five players from each team start the game while the other players rest. After a certain time substitutions are made for both teams.

2x5v5 (twenty players in total – two teams of ten players) means that five players from one team play against five players from another team, while at the same time the remaining five players from each team play against each other in another area.

Organization
The positions of the players at the start of the drill are described. Suggestions are made as to how to progress from one phase of the drill to the next.

Description
The drill is first described in general terms and then in more detail.

Rules
The rules for the drill are described. If nothing else is mentioned the drill is played with normal football rules.
Special terms are used for the number of ball touches allowed. A *minimum of two touches* means that a player has to touch the ball at least twice every time the player gets the ball; a *maximum of two touches* means that the ball must not be touched more than twice when a player has the ball. If the imposed conditions are broken during a drill, possession is given to the other team. A team gains *possession of the ball* when the ball is captured and two players from the team then touch it consecutively.

Scoring
A scoring system that can be used for each drill is described. Scoring can be achieved either by scoring a goal as in a normal game or through scoring points. A way in which a final result can be reached is also suggested.
Some form of scoring will often motivate the players. In order to ensure that this effect is sustained throughout the game it is important to keep to the rules of the drill and to count the scores correctly. It is advisable to let the players apply the rules and keep score themselves.

By altering the rules of a game, the intensity of a drill can be varied.

Type of exercise

Exercise can be classified as being either continuous or intermittent. Continuous exercise is performed at a fairly constant intensity for a prolonged period of time. During intermittent exercise the level of intensity changes markedly and can include rest periods. When intermittent exercise is described, suggestions are made for the duration of the exercise and rest periods. These can be varied in several ways within the given limits.

Variations

Variations to the drill are presented. Variations can be introduced simply for a change, or to alter the intensity of the exercise.

Hints for the coach

Suggestions are made as to how to introduce the drill to the players, especially if the drill includes specific conditions. An indication of the expected exercise intensity is also given. The coach should observe whether the actual intensity is as expected.

If the exercise intensity does not correspond to that desired, the players may not have fully understood the purpose of the drill. The coach should then explain the principles of the game again and elaborate on the possibilities that exist within the drill. Perhaps more time is needed for the players to become accustomed to the game. It may be that the drill does not function well with the particular group of players. In this case the drill should be adjusted, for

Figure TS 9
The figure illustrates the adjustment circle, which describes various areas in which a drill can be altered in order to change the exercise intensity.

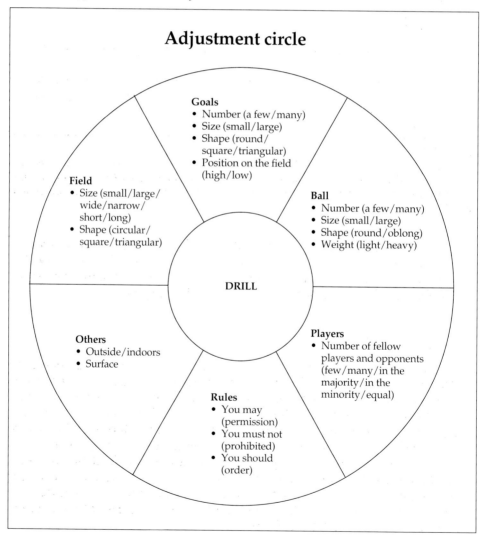

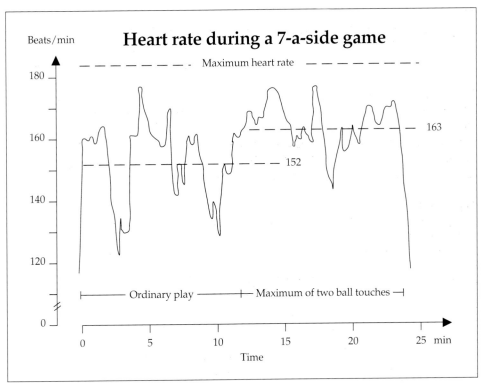

Figure TS 10
The figure shows heart rate of a player during a seven-a-side game played on half a field. After limiting the number of ball touches to a maximum of two, the average heart rate increased by 11 beats/min. Thus, by implementing a change in the rules of the game, the overall work rate of the player increased (see also Fig. TS 9).

example, by changing the number of players, the size of the playing area, or the number of ball touches (see below). Another possibility is to use the suggestions described within the drill under the section »change of intensity«. The probable effect of the described variations is also given.

Varying a drill

If the purpose of a training drill is not being fulfilled, changes should be made. In fitness training it is mainly the exercise intensity that needs to be controlled. There are many ways in which a drill can be adjusted, and some examples are outlined within the description of the drill. One possibility is to change the rules, e.g. all the players of a team must be in the attacking half of the field before a goal can be scored. The »adjustment circle« (see Fig. TS 9) shows various areas where changes can be made and Fig. TS 10 illustrates an example of the effect of implementing a suggestion given in the adjustment circle. The condition of a maximum of two ball touches was included in a seven-a-side game on half a field and resulted in an increase of the average heart rate from 152 to 163 beats/min.

Summary

Before a match or a training session a player should warm-up in order to improve performance and to reduce the risk of becoming injured. The exercises in a warm-up programme should be technically simple and begin at a low intensity and then gradually increase. After a match and a training session a player should perform recovery activities in order to recover as efficiently as possible.

Monitoring heart rate can be used to evaluate training effectiveness, but considerations should be made with regards to fluctuations in heart rate within a given drill and to a player's maximum heart rate.

Aerobic Training

142

Aerobic Training

Aims

1. To increase the capacity of the oxygen transporting system.

2. To increase the capacity of muscles to utilize oxygen during prolonged periods of exercise.

3. To increase the ability to recover rapidly after a period of high-intensity exercise.

Effects

The main physiological adaptations to aerobic training are:

- The blood volume increases and the heart becomes larger and stronger so it can pump more blood per unit of time. More oxygen can then be transported, thus increasing the aerobic energy production during high-intensity exercise.

- The capacity to utilize oxygen and to oxidize fat in the muscle increases. This means that less carbohydrate (glycogen) is used at a given exercise intensity and the limited stores of this fuel are spared.

The benefits for football are:

- A larger percentage of the energy required for exercise can be supplied aerobically, which means that a player can work at a higher exercise intensity for prolonged periods of time during a match.

- An improved endurance which allows a player to exercise at a higher intensity throughout a game.

- Less time is required to recover after a period of high-intensity exercise before being able to perform maximally in a subsequent match activity.

Aerobic training can also help to minimize deterioration of technical performance and lapses in concentration induced by fatigue, which may occur towards the end of a game.

Types of aerobic training

Aerobic training can be divided into three overlapping areas: *recovery training*, *aerobic low-intensity training* (Aerobic$_{LI}$), and *aerobic high-intensity training* (Aerobic$_{HI}$) (see Fig. FT 1 – page 105).

As aerobic training should mainly be performed with a ball, the definition of the three categories of aerobic training takes into account that the heart rate of a player will alternate continuously during training. Scheme AE1 illustrates the principles behind the various categories of aerobic training.

It is misleading to quantify training by the total exercise time. Any activity, whether it lasts for 15 or 90 minutes, can have a favourable effect on a player's aerobic work capacity.

Scheme AE 1 *Principles of aerobic training*

	Heart rate			
	% of HR$_{max}$		Beats/min	
	Mean	Range	Mean*	Range*
Recovery training	65%	40-80%	130	80-160
Lov-intensity training	80%	65-90%	160	130-180
High-intensity training	90%	80-100%	180	160-200

* If HR$_{max}$ is 200 beats/min

Recovery training

Aim

To achieve faster recovery after a match or an intensive training session.

Application to football

During a match or intensive training small ruptures may occur in the connective tissue and fibres of the muscle. This damage, which is often still present several days after it has been induced, causes the muscle to become stiff and

144

On the day after a match players can benefit from recovery training, which may be in the form of a game, e.g. tennis played with the feet.

hard. Performance is reduced and the ability to replenish glycogen stores is inhibited. The typical symptom that the player experiences is local muscle soreness.

During recovery training the players perform light physical activities, such as jogging and low intensity games. This type of training can help the muscle recover more efficiently and can reduce muscle soreness. Recovery training can also be used to avoid a condition known as »overtraining«. Throughout the season, when players are training frequently and playing many competitive matches, there may be times when the body is not able to recover completely. In such cases recovery training should replace more physically demanding forms of training.

Recovery training also has psychological benefits. The need to recover physically is often accompanied by a need to relax mentally. This may be obtained by performing exercises of low intensity and activities that differ from those normally used.

Principle

During recovery training the exercise intensity should be such that a player's heart rate is:

Average: Approx. 65% of maximal heart rate (HR_{max})

Range: 40%-80% of HR_{max}

For a player with a HR_{max} of 190 beats/min this corresponds to:

Average: Approx. 120 beats/min

Range: 70-150 beats/min

The heart rate should not exceed the recommended upper limit for more than a short period of time.

The training can take the form of either continuous or intermittent exercise. For the intermittent exercise the work periods should be longer than five minutes. Figure AE 1 shows an example of the fluctuations in heart rate for a player during recovery training.

Organization

The need for recovery training, after a match or intensive training session, will vary from player to player depending on fitness level and how hard the player worked. Some players can comfortably perform harder exercises than those of recovery training on the day after a match or intense training session. Therefore, the activities to be performed should be selected according to the individual need. In order to elevate the motivation of players who do not feel like training on the day following a match, it is advisable that the whole squad warms up together.

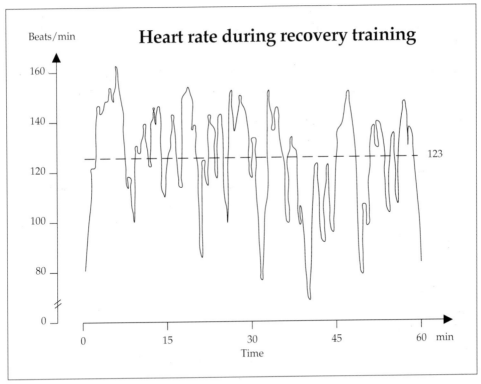

Figure AE 1
The figure shows heart rate of a player during a 60-minute period of recovery training. The training session consisted of a 10-minute warm-up period, followed by a game for about 25 minutes and another game (Drill 1 – see page 148) for approximately 25 minutes. The average heart rate was 123 beats/min with a range of 70 to 160 beats/min.

Recovery training drills

In recovery training it is good to use drills that do not heavily stress sore muscles and in which physical contact is avoided. Recovery training without a ball can consist of 20-40 minutes of jogging. Two drills for recovery training with a ball are described below.

147

Drill 1 – Football croquet (Fig. AE 2)

Area: Half a football field.

Number of players: 14 (2 to 24).

Organization: The players are divided into teams of two. Each team starts at any obstacle with a ball. All teams start at the same time.

Description: The players in each team work together and must alternate touching the ball. An obstacle is passed when the ball is played from one player to the other.

Rules: There are three different ways to pass an obstacle:

                        1. Two cones: the ball is played between the cones.

                        2. Four cones in the shape of a square: The ball is first played in one direction through the square and then diagonally through the other direction.

                        3. Four cones and a post: The ball is played between the cones and onto the post with one touch.

Scoring: The coach sets a lap time for the course. The players must then try to complete each lap in a time which is as close to the set time as possible. The players should not be given any information regarding their lap time during the activity. The winning team is the team that comes closest to keeping the correct tempo. For example, if the coach chooses a lap time of three minutes and stops the drill after nine minutes, the team which has come closest to completing three laps wins the game.

Variations: *a.* The ball must be kept moving at all times.

                        b. The players are allowed to touch the ball more than once (free touch) but the ball must be played between the cones with a first touch pass.

                        c. The number of times the ball can be touched is limited to a maximum of three per player.

                        d. No set time – the team that uses the least number of touches per lap wins.

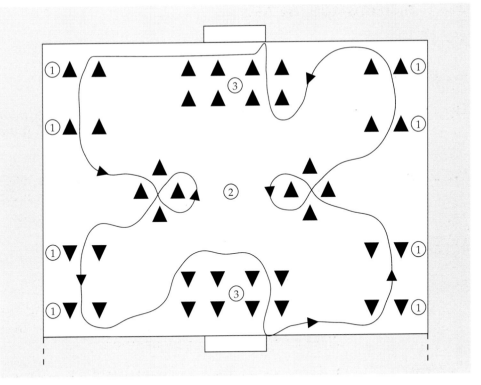

Figure AE 2

In the drills the following signs are used:

▲ Cone   ✕ Player

● Ball   ◯ Player

— Movement of a ball   ☐ Player

Hints for the coach:
The coach should demonstrate how to pass the different obstacles. It is important to explain clearly that the scoring system demands a controlled low tempo and that emphasis should not be placed on speed. The players should be allowed a practice lap, during which regular times are given. It is important that the lap time set by the coach necessitates a low tempo. The players should not be told the total duration of the drill or the total number of laps that have to be completed, as this defeats the competitive object of the game.

Change of intensity:
The exercise intensity of the drill should be very low. This is determined by both the lap time and how difficult it is to pass the obstacles. The latter can be varied in several ways, e.g. by changing the distance from the cones to the post.

Drill 2 – Football golf (Fig. AE 3)

Area: Unlimited area.

Number of players: 6v6 (1v1 – 13v13).

Organization: A number of cones are positioned within the playing area. Each player has a ball. A player from one team competes against a player from the opposing team.

Description: Players try to hit the cone with as few kicks as possible. After hitting the cone the players continue to the next cone, »teeing off« about five metres from the last cone.

Rules: None.

Scoring: The player that has used the fewest kicks to hit the cones wins the game and receives two team points. One point is awarded to each team if a game is tied. The game is won by the team which finishes with the most points.

Variations: *a.* Each team is divided into groups of three players. Each group has one ball. The players in the group have to play the ball every third time. The ball must not stop until it hits the cone.

                 b. Match-play golf. The player that needs the fewest kicks to hit a cone gets 1 point (tie = 0 points). If a cone is not hit within 10 kicks the player has to continue to the next cone. The game is won by the player that has scored the most points at the end, and this player's team receives two points.

Hints for the coach: The players should be carefully instructed about the rules and the placement of the cones (including the order of hitting them). The game can be made more entertaining by placing some of the cones in difficult positions, e.g. on a slope or behind a tree.

                 Change of intensity:
                 The game should be played with a low exercise intensity. However, the players should not stand still for long periods of time. Variation *b.* should reduce the duration of the waiting periods. In order to avoid a queue at the beginning of the game, pairs of players can start from different cones.

150

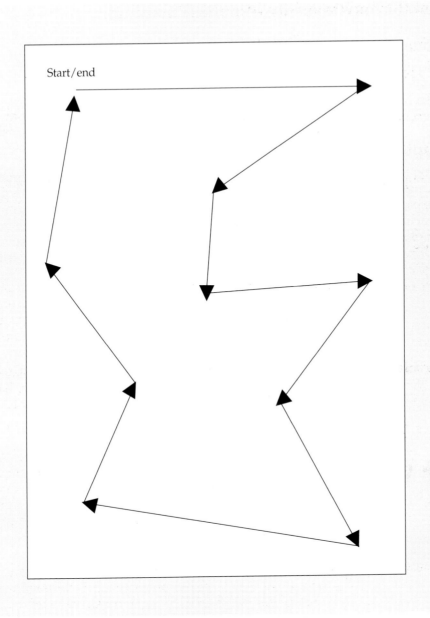

Start/end

Figure AE 3

Aerobic low-intensity (Aerobic$_{LI}$) training

Aims

1. To increase the capacity to exercise for prolonged periods of time.

2. To increase the ability to recover quickly after a period of high-intensity exercise.

Application to football

A top-class football player covers a distance of approximately 11 kilometres during a football match and also performs other energy demanding activities (see page 59). Therefore, it is important for players to have a high endurance capacity. This capacity can be improved through Aerobic$_{LI}$ training and complimented by Aerobic$_{HI}$ training (see page 160). The desired effect is to improve the ability to maintain a high work-rate and good technical performance throughout the game.

Figure AE 4
The figure shows heart rate of a player during an Aerobic$_{LI}$ game (Game 1 – see page 154).

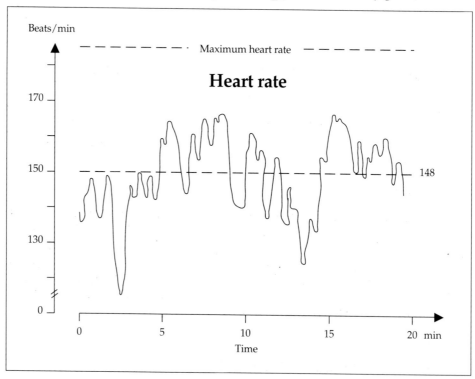

Players during an Aerobic$_{LI}$ game.

Principle

During Aerobic$_{LI}$ training the exercise intensity should be such that a player's heart rate is:

Average: Approx. 80% of HR$_{max}$

Range: 65%-90% of HR$_{max}$

For a player with a HR$_{max}$ of 190 beats/min this corresponds to:

Average: Approx. 150 beats/min

Range: 125-170 beats/min

The heart rate should not be below or above the recommended limits for more than a short period of time.

Organization

Aerobic$_{LI}$ training can take the form of either continuous or intermittent exercise. For the intermittent exercise the work periods should be longer than five minutes. Figure AE 4 shows an example of the fluctuations in heart rate for a player during an Aerobic$_{LI}$ training game. If the training is performed without a ball, it is recommended that exercise with varying intensities is used, e.g. alternating between exercise intensities corresponding to 70%, 80%, and 90% of HR$_{max}$ each second minute.

Aerobic$_{LI}$ training drills

Several games for Aerobic$_{LI}$ training are described below.

Game 1 (Fig. AE 5)

Area: Half a football field.

Number of players: 5v5 (3v3 – 8v8).

Organization: Each team defends a row of cones (five or more). The cones are positioned at least one metre apart in a straight line, in each team's own half of the field.

Description: With the ball, each team tries to knock over the cones of the opposing team. When a team succeeds, they place the cone back on the opponents line and, in addition, fetch one of their own cones and place it on the same line. This task must be done by the player who knocks down the original cone, the other players continue the game.
Note: Play is allowed both in front of and behind the line of cones.

Rules: None.

Scoring: The game is won by the team which has the fewest cones left after a set time.

Variations: *a.* When a player knocks down an opponent's cone it should be brought back to the own line of cones. The winning team is then the team which has the most cones at the end of the game.

b. The distance between the cones can vary or the cones can stand in small groups.

c. A cone can only be knocked down by a first time shot.

d. If a player who is transporting a cone between the two lines is hit by the ball, the cone must be returned.

e. The cones do not have to be placed on a line. They just have to be positioned somewhere in a team's own half of the field.

f. The game can be played with two balls.

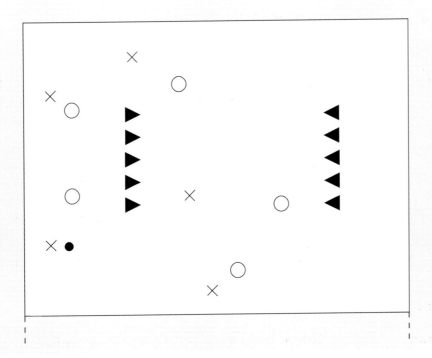

Figure AE 5

Hints for the coach: To prevent the players from working together in small groups, more cones can be added or the distance between the cones can be increased (see variations *b.* and *e.*). Once the players are familiar with the game they can be allowed to position the cones they are attacking or defending. The teams should be encouraged to discuss tactics, e.g. is it best to place the cones in small groups or to spread them out as much as possible? Variation *a.* can be used to make the game more difficult for the team that is ahead.

Change of intensity:
If the level of intensity is too low, a rule may be introduced so that a cone can only be knocked down when all the players from the attacking team are in the opponent's half of the field. The variations *b.* to *f.* should also increase the exercise intensity.

Game 2 (Fig. AE 6)

Area: Half a football field.

Number of players: 7v7 (4v4 – 11v11).

Organization: Each team has one ball.

Description: The teams must keep possession of their own ball and at the same time try to capture the ball from the other team.

Rules: If a team kicks one of the balls out of the playing area, possession is given to the other team (one point is scored – see Scoring).

Scoring: A team gets one point when it has possession of both balls. One ball is then returned to the other team and the play is resumed. The game is won by the team which has scored the most points after a given time period.

Variations: *a.* The number of consecutive ball touches allowed by each player is limited, e.g. a maximum of three.

b. The number of balls is 3 (or 4 – two per team). A point is scored when three balls are captured.

Hints for the coach: The teams should not divide up into two separate groups with one group of players always trying to capture a ball. This may be avoided by decreasing the size of the playing area or by variation *b.*

Change of intensity:
The exercise intensity may be increased with variations *a.* and *b.*

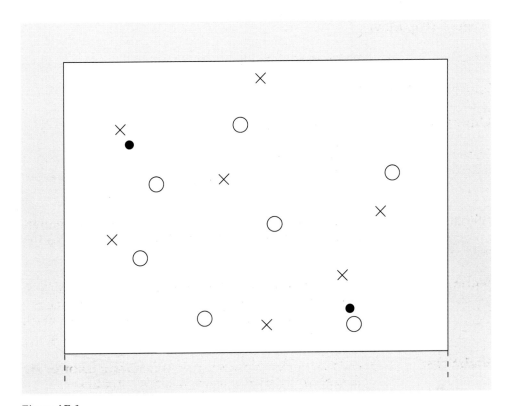

Figure AE 6

Game 3 (Fig. AE 7)

Area: Three-quarter of a football field divided into four zones with two full-size goals.

Number of players: 7v7 (3v3 – 11v11) + 2 goalkeepers.

Description: Ordinary football play.

Rules: All the players from one team, except the goalkeeper, must be in two adjoining zones.

Variations: *a.* The number of passes within a team are limited inside a zone, e.g. a maximum of five passes before the ball has to be played into a new zone.

                              b. Each team is allowed to be in three zones instead of two.

                              c. The players are no longer required to be in adjoining zones, instead the players from the attacking team (except the goalkeeper) must be inside the opponents' half of the field before a goal can be scored. All the defending players must also be in this zone. If they are not and a goal is scored, the score is doubled.

Hints for the coach: Start by explaining the rules of the two adjoining zones. In the transition from one zone to another, all the players from a team must be inside one zone. If this is too difficult fewer players can be used or variation *b.* can be applied.

                              Change of intensity:
                              Increasing the number of zones will often result in a decrease in the exercise intensity. Variation *a.* should increase the intensity, while *c.* may lower it.

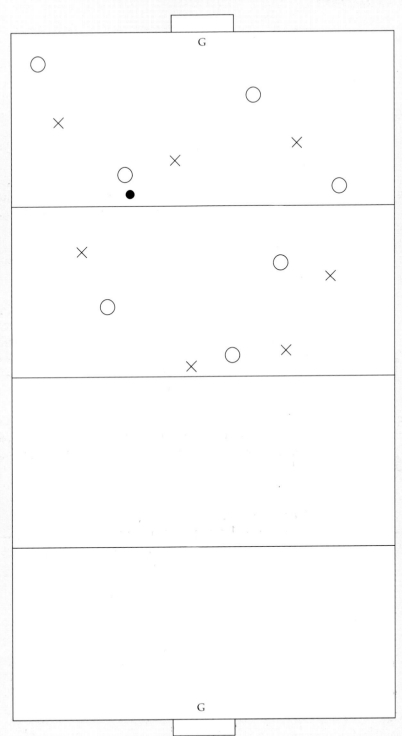

Figure AE 7

Aerobic high-intensity (Aerobic$_{HI}$) training

Aims

1. To increase the ability to exercise at a high intensity for long periods of time.

2. To increase the ability to recover quickly from high-intensity exercise.

Application to football

It has been demonstrated that the total distance covered by high-intensity exercise during a match is related to the standard of football, i.e. top-class players cover the most distance (see page 65). Therefore, it is important that players are capable of exercising at high intensities for prolonged periods of time. The basis for this ability is a well-developed capacity to perform aerobic exercise (high maximum oxygen uptake), which can be attained by Aerobic$_{HI}$ training.

Principle

During Aerobic$_{HI}$ training the exercise intensity should be such that a player's heart rate is:

Average:　Approx. 90% of HR$_{max}$

Range:　　80%-100% of HR$_{max}$

For a player with a HR$_{max}$ of 190 beats/min this corresponds to:

Average:　Approx. 170 beats/min

Range:　　150-190 beats/min

The heart rate should not be below the recommended lower limit for more than a short period of time.

Overlap with anaerobic speed endurance training

During Aerobic$_{HI}$ training the lactate producing energy system may also be highly stimulated for short periods of time (see Fig. FT 3 – page 106) which means that the training overlaps anaerobic speed endurance training. The coach should ensure that the exercise intensity during Aerobic$_{HI}$ training does not become so high that the training becomes exclusively speed endurance training. If the intensity is too high, the players will not be able to keep a high enough work rate during subsequent work periods and the desired effect of the Aerobic$_{HI}$ training will be lost.

Players during an Aerobic$_{HI}$ game (Game 3 – see page 176)

Organization

When using games for Aerobic$_{HI}$ training the exercise intensity for a player varies continuously, but a decrease in intensity for a short period of time will only cause a minor decrease in heart rate. Therefore, it is possible for a player to maintain a heart rate above 80% of maximum heart rate for the majority of the training. In addition to the intermittent exercise inherent to football, different intermittent training forms can be used in Aerobic$_{HI}$ training. Three of these forms (which to some extent overlap) are described below.

I. Fixed time intervals

The principle of the fixed time intervals is that the duration of the exercise and rest periods is set. If the exercise periods are longer than one minute, the rest periods should be shorter than the exercise periods, otherwise the overall exercise intensity will be too low. Some examples of paired work and rest periods are given in Scheme AE 2.

Scheme AE 2

	Exercise	Rest	Heart rate
a.	30 sec	30 sec	90-100%
b.	2 min	1 min	85- 95%
c.	4 min	1 min	80- 90%

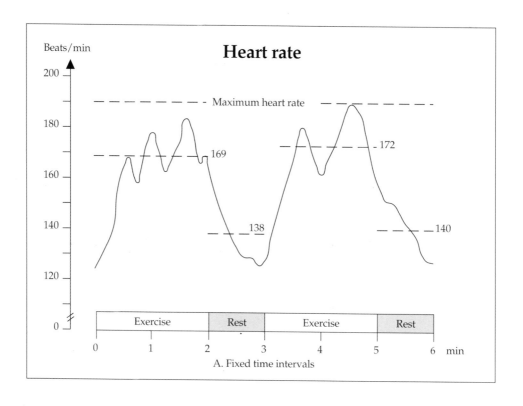

A. Fixed time intervals

The shorter the exercise periods, the higher the exercise intensity should be (according to the principles given for Aerobic$_{HI}$ training). Rest periods should include some form of recovery exercises, e.g. jogging.

The interval form Ia (see above) should not be confused with the similar interval form in anaerobic speed endurance training, as described on page 201, which has the same exercise and rest periods. There is a notable difference in the exercise intensity. During speed endurance training the intensity should be almost maximal for the entire exercise period, while it should be considerably lower during Aerobic$_{HI}$ training.

Figure AE 8a shows the fluctuations in heart rate of a player during an Aerobic$_{HI}$ training game with exercise periods of two minutes and rest periods of one minute.

The 15/15-principle

In a study, the effect of training by repeatedly alternating 15 seconds of running on a treadmill and 15 seconds of rest was investigated. This form of training is referred to as the 15/15-principle. During the training the aerobic energy system was taxed almost maximally, and the training was shown to improve the subjects' maximum oxygen uptake. Based on these findings the 15/15-principle is now commonly used in football training. However, such

162

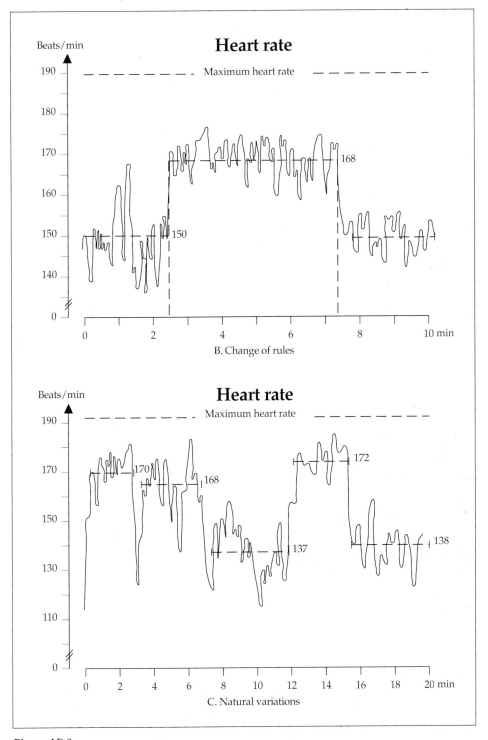

Figure AE 8
The figure shows heart rate of a player during Aerobic_{HI} games based upon three different principles:
(A) Fixed time intervals, (B) Alteration of the rules, and (C) Natural variations.

163

short exercise and rest periods are not effective in football training drills in which tactical aspects prevent a player from constantly performing high-intensity exercise, e.g. sometimes it can be tactically more correct for a player to jog than to perform high-intensity exercise. For example, during a three-a-side game on a third of the field, with full-size goals and two goalkeepers, there will always be short periods of exercise at a low intensity such as when a goal is scored or when the ball is kicked out of play. These pauses will greatly influence the average exercise intensity if the players are substituted every 15 seconds. Furthermore, a game of this kind can be frustrating as some players rarely get to touch the ball during an exercise period. When using games for Aerobic$_{HI}$ training the duration of the exercise periods should be at least 30 seconds. The use of the 15/15-principle in football illustrates that information from scientific research studies should be carefully evaluated before it is applied to football training.

II. Alteration of the rules

By changing the rules during a training game the exercise intensity may be varied. Set times can be implemented where the rules are changed to either increase or decrease the intensity. Figure AE 8b shows an example of fluctuations in the heart rate of a player during an Aerobic$_{HI}$ training game where the rules have been altered.

III. Natural variations

Training games can be structured so that the exercise intensity changes in a natural way. Figure AE 8c shows an example of the fluctuations of a player's heart rate during an Aerobic$_{HI}$ training game where the changes in intensity occurred due to natural variations.

Aerobic$_{HI}$ training drills

Games for the three intermittent training principles within Aerobic$_{HI}$ are described below. Some examples of training without the ball are also given.

Intermittent principle I – Fixed time intervals

Game 1 (Fig. AE 9)

Area: Approximately one third of a football field. The playing area is divided into three zones – two outer-zones (①+③) and a middle-zone (②). The two outer-zones have the same dimensions as the penalty area.

Number of players: 5v5 (3v3 – 10v10).

Organization: All players start in the same zone (one of the outer-zones).

Description: The players can pass the ball within the outer-zones and across the middle-zone, but the ball must not be touched in the middle-zone.

Rules: Only one player, from the team in possession of the ball, can be inside the outer-zone opposite to where the ball is. When the ball is played from one outer-zone to the other the players have to change zones before they are allowed to touch the ball.

Scoring: A team scores a point every second time the ball is played across from one outer-zone to the other and possession is maintained.

Type of exercise: Intermittent. Fixed time intervals, e.g. exercise periods of five minutes and rest periods of one minute.

Variations: *a.* A point is scored if a team can make ten successive passes. The rule of changing zones still applies.

b. A certain number of passes must be made, e.g. five, within an outer-zone before the ball can be played from one outer-zone to the other.

c. The number of ball touches per player is limited, e.g. a maximum of three.

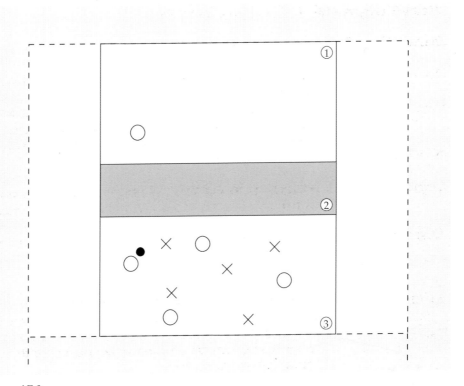

Figure AE 9

Hints for the coach: An important component of the game is the shift between zones. As soon as the ball has been played across the middle-zone the players should quickly change zones (high-speed running). During the play in the outer-zones the exercise intensity should also be fairly high, particularly for the defending team.

If variation *a.* is introduced the coach should emphasize the value of using both outer-zones, as the average exercise intensity of the game may be too low if the players have a tendency to stay inside one zone.

Change of intensity:
By varying the width of the middle-zone, the duration of the high-speed running between the outer-zones can be changed. Variation *b.* may lower the average exercise intensity while *c.* should increase it.

167

Game 2 (Fig. AE 10)

Area: Half a football field with four separate zones (①-④).

Number of players: 5v5 (3v3 – 8v8).

Organization: At least eight balls should be used, equally distributed in the four zones. Each team defends and attacks two zones (①+③ and ②+④). All players start outside the zones.

Description: The players must take balls from their own zones and try to dribble them into the zones of their opponents. If a ball is touched by an opponent, the player has to dribble it back to the zone it came from before another attack can be made.

Rules: No player can be attacked while inside a zone. Each team can only have two balls in play at a time.

Scoring: The team which has the most balls in the opponents' zones after a set game-time wins the game.

Type of exercise: Intermittent. Fixed time intervals, e.g. exercise periods of four minutes and rest periods of one minute.

Variations: *a.* A team gains possession of a ball when capturing it.

                      b. There is no limit to the number of balls in play at a time.

                      c. The players are allowed to pass the ball to each other, so that the player starting with the ball does not necessarily have to dribble it to one of the opponents' zones.

                      d. The two zones which a team is attacking and defending are placed diagonally (①+④ and ②+③).

                      e. The number of zones can be increased.

168

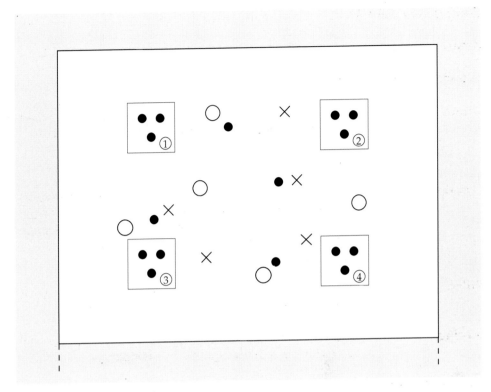

Figure AE 10

Hints for the coach: The exercise intensity will be the highest for a player who is dribbling the ball towards the opponents' zone, and for a defending player who is applying pressure to a player with a ball. Variation *b.* and *c.* may increase the overall intensity and should be introduced once the players understand the idea of the game.

Change of intensity:
An increase in the number (variation *e.*) and size of the zones makes it easier to score and should increase the overall exercise intensity. Variation *a.* may also increase the intensity.

Intermittent principle II – Altering the rules

Game 1 (Fig. AE 11)

Area:	Half a football field with two outer-zones (① +③) and a large middle-zone (②).
Number of players:	6v6 (4v4 – 10v10).
Organization:	One player (»outer-player«) is positioned in each of the outer-zones whereas the other players are in the middle-zone.
Description:	The teams must transfer the ball from one »outer-player« to the other.
Rules:	An »outer-player« has a maximum of two touches to pass the ball to a player from the team that it was received from. If the »outer-player« touches the ball more than twice or if the ball is played out of the playing area, the other team gets possession of the ball.
Scoring:	A point is scored if a team can transfer the ball from one »outer-player« to the other and then back to the first »outer-player« without the ball being captured by the opposing team. After scoring a point the team can continue and immediately score another point by transferring the ball to the opposite »outer-player«.
Type of exercise:	Intermittent. By alternating (e.g. each five minutes) between the ordinary game and variation *d.* or *e.* (see below) the overall exercise intensity can be varied.
Variations:	*a.* The number of times a player can consecutively touch the ball is limited, e.g. a maximum of three.
	b. The »outer-players« are only allowed one touch to play the ball, or the ball must not stop in the outer-zones.
	c. The teams have one »outer-player« in each outer-zone. The players have to pass the ball to an »outer-player« from their own team. The »outer-players« are allowed an unlimited number of ball touches.
	d. Man-to-man marking.
	e. All the players on the team in possession of the ball must be on the attacking half of the playing area when the ball is played to the »outer-player«.

170

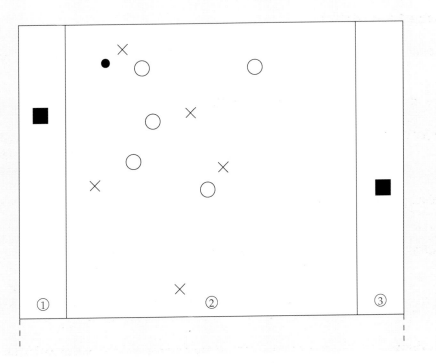

Figure AE 11

f. There are no »outer-players« and the size of the outer-zones is extended. A point is scored if a team brings the ball from one outer-zone to the other and returns it to the first zone without the ball being captured by the opposing team. All the players from the team must have been in all »three« outer-zones. The players on the team that is in possession of the ball are not allowed to touch the ball before they have been in the same outer-zone as the ball.

g. Goalkeepers are used as »outer-players« and they may use their hands, but may only take a maximum of four steps with the ball and hold the ball for 10 seconds.

Hints for the coach:
The players should be encouraged to pass to an »outer-player« as soon as they have captured the ball, and it should be emphasized that it is important to offer support to the »outer-players« after they have received the ball.

Change of intensity:
The exercise intensity can be controlled by varying the number of players and the size of the middle-zone. Variations *a.*, *b.* and *d.* to *f.* may increase the overall intensity. Variations *d.* and *e.* can be useful if some players always stay close to one of the outer-zones.

Intermittent principle III – Natural variations

Game 1 (Fig. AE 12)

Area: Half a football field, divided into three adjoining zones with two full-size goals at each end.

Number of players: 6v6 (4v4 – 9v9) + two goalkeepers.

Organization: Two players from each team are positioned in the three zones. After a set time the players change zones by rotating (see Fig. AE 12): The players from the defending zone move into the middle zone; the players from this zone move into the attacking zone; and the players from the attacking zone move into the defending zone.

Description: Ordinary football play.

Rules: The players have to stay within their own zones.

Scoring: Ordinary scoring.

Type of exercise: Intermittent. For example, exercise periods of four minutes, separated by 30 seconds of rest during which the players change zones.

Variations: *a.* Man-to-man marking.

b. A conditioned number of ball touches, e.g. a minimum of three.

c. Both players inside a zone must touch the ball before it can be passed into another zone.

d. The ball must be touched in the middle zone before it can be played into the attacking zone.

e. The players assigned to the middle zone are allowed to move into the two other zones.

f. When a goal is scored, the direction of the attack is changed.

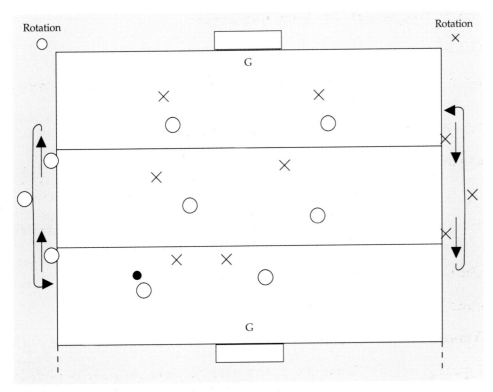

Figure AE 12

Hints for the coach: The players should work intensely when the ball is in their zone. When the ball is in the other zones, they should either defend against an opponent or create space for themselves in order to receive a pass. The game may be most intensive for the players in the middle zone. The changing of zones by rotation should ensure an equal overall exercise intensity for all players.

Change of intensity:
By changing the length and width of the zones the exercise intensity can be altered. Variation *a.* may be used to increase the work-rate but the intensity should not become so high that the training becomes anaerobic speed endurance training. Variations *b.* and *c.* should increase the duration of both the high-intensity exercise periods and the »rest periods«. Variation *d.* will ensure that the players in the middle zone are kept active, and variation *e.* may increase the physical demands placed on these players.

173

Game 2 (Fig. AE 13)

Area: A quarter of a football field.

Number of players: 5+5v5 (4+4v4 – 6+6v6).

Description: Two teams of five players play against one team of five players. The defending team must try to touch the ball. When the ball is touched the team that lost the ball becomes the defending team.

Rules: None.

Scoring: No points or goals are awarded in this game but if the defending team fails to touch the ball after a set number of passes, e.g. 10, this team has to touch the ball twice before it becomes an attacking team.

Type of exercise: Intermittent. Natural variations.

Variations: *a.* The defending team must gain possession of the ball in order to change with one of the other teams (to become one of the attacking teams).

                              b. The ball may not be passed to a player from the same team, i.e. the ball has to alternate between the two attacking teams.

                              c. Each player has a conditioned number of ball touches, e.g. a maximum of two.

Hints for the coach: It is important that the defending team maintains a high exercise intensity. Players of the two teams in possession of the ball should be encouraged to create space and to concentrate on good passing in order to keep the defending team working. The game should be re-started immediately after the defending team has touched the ball so that pauses are minimized.

                              Change of intensity:
                              Variation *a.* will increase the demands of the defending team while *b.* should increase the exercise intensity of the players that are trying to keep possession of the ball. Variation *c.* can be used to help the defending team to touch the ball, which may increase the overall exercise intensity.

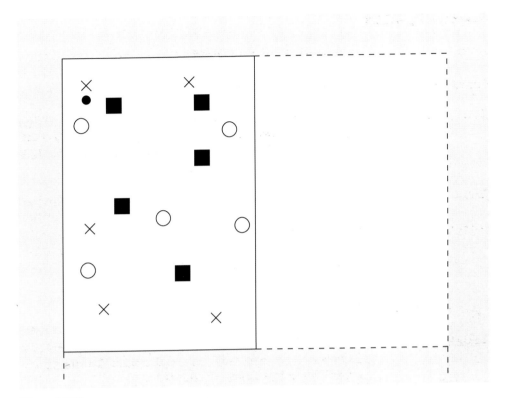

Figure AE 13

Game 3 (Fig. AE 14)

Area:	A football field divided into three zones – two outer-zones (①+③) and one middle-zone (②). One goal is placed in the middle of each half. The goals are placed back-to-back.

Number of players: 7v7 (5v5 – 9v9) + 2 goalkeepers.

Description: Ordinary football play.

Rules: In the middle-zone the number of ball touches is limited to a maximum of two. The goalkeepers may use their hands inside a certain area.

Scoring: Ordinary scoring.

Type of exercise: Intermittent. Natural variations.

Variations: *a.* Within the middle-zone the number of ball touches per team is limited to a maximum of six.

b. In the outer-zones the number of ball touches per player is conditioned, e.g. a maximum of two, but free play is allowed in the middle-zone.

c. All players from the attacking team must be in the same outer-zone before a goal can be scored. If not all of the defending players are within the outer-zone when a goal is scored then the score is doubled.

Hints for the coach: The exercise intensity should be the greatest when the teams play in the middle-zone.

Change of intensity:
By increasing the length of the middle-zone the physical demands can be elevated. Variations *a.* and *c.* should increase the average exercise intensity.

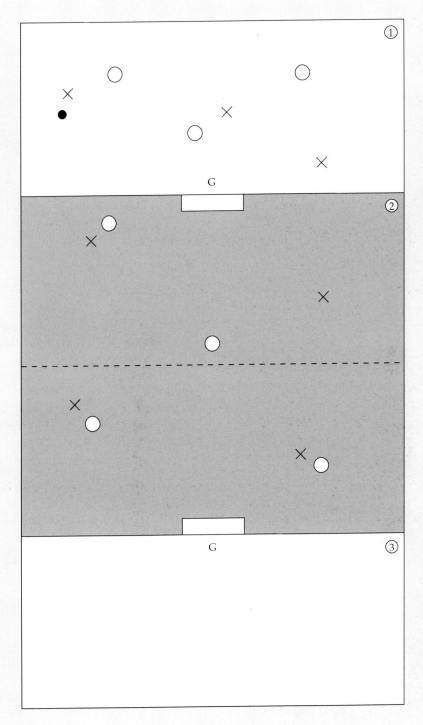

Figure AE 14

Aerobic$_{HI}$ training without a ball

Exercise 1 (Fig. AE 15)

Area:
A football field or a similar area.

Number of players: The whole squad.

Organization:
Two lines are marked approximately five meters away from each side of one of the goal-lines. The players are divided into three groups based on their running ability. The players in the group with the best runners (▢) have to run the longest distance (about 110 meters), while the group with the poorest runners (X) covers a shorter distance (about 100 meters), and the remaining players (O) start on the goal-line and cover an intermediate distance (about 105 meters).

Description:
All players start at the end with the three lines and run at a given speed to the opposite goal-line. After a set rest period they run back to the starting position. A signal is used (e.g. a whistle) to indicate when the players have to reach the opposite line.

Type of exercise:
Intermittent. Fixed time intervals. Exercise periods of 15-25 seconds with 15-25-second rest periods. Total duration could, for example, be 20 minutes (approximately 30 runs).

Variation:
Two of the three teams are positioned at one goal-line and the third team at the other. On a signal one of the two teams starts running to the opposite goal-line. When all players in the team have passed the goal-line in the other end, the team waiting at the line starts running to the opposite goal-line, and so on. The running time should be different for the three groups.

Hints for the coach: The selected running time should be such that the players keep a high speed but are able to maintain the speed for several exercise periods. Separating the group into three teams should ensure that the relative exercise intensity for each player does not vary too much. If there is an extreme difference in fitness level between players, the distances between the goal-line and the two lines can be extended (e.g. 10 meters), or the players can be divided into more groups (in which case more lines should be added).

Figure AE 15

Exercise 2 – Star run (Fig. AE 16)

Area: A football field or a similar area.

Number of players: 6v6 (2v2 – 12v12).

Organization: Cones are placed in the two outer corners of each penalty area, and at the points where the half-way line crosses the side-lines.

Description: Each player runs with a dispatch, e.g. a vest. On a given signal three players from each team start running from the edge of the centre-circle to different cones and back to the centre-circle. Thereafter, they run clockwise to the next cone and continue until all six cones have been visited. The dispatch is then given to a team-mate who performs the same course. This continues until a set number of rounds have been completed, e.g. five rounds per player.

Type of exercise: Intermittent. Exercise periods (one round) of approximately two minutes with two minute rest periods. Total duration could be 20 minutes (five rounds) for example.

Rules: The player has to turn around the cones but it is enough just to touch the perimeter of the centre-circle before continuing to the next cone.

Scoring: The team that first completes the set number of rounds wins.

Variation: After running to a cone and back to the centre-circle the dispatch is given to a team-mate who runs to the next cone and back to the centre-circle. The dispatch is then given back to the first player who continues to the next cone, and so on.

Hints for the coach: The players should maintain a high speed around the whole course and they should not sprint at the end of each run, as sprinting may lower the exercise intensity in the subsequent exercise periods.

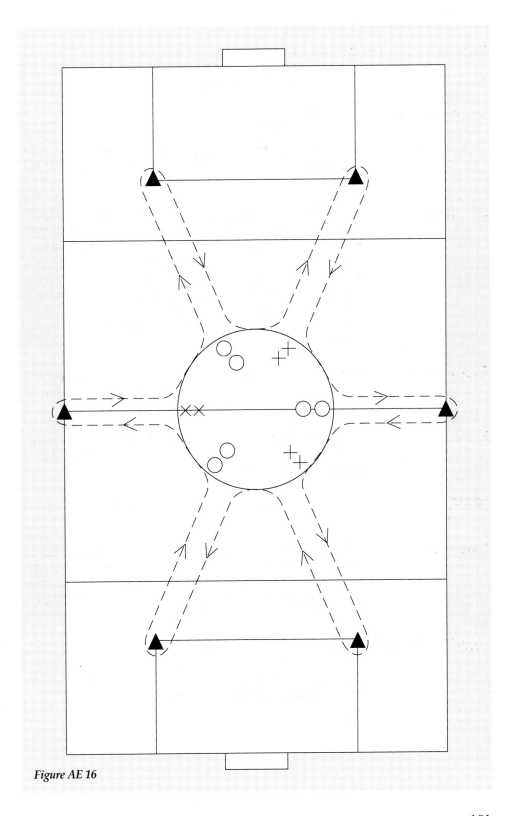

Figure AE 16

Exercise 3 – Pair running (Fig. AE 17)

Area: An area of about 5 x 50 meters.

Number of players: Unlimited number of pairs.

Organization: The players are divided into pairs consisting of one good and one not so good runner.

Description: On a signal a player from each pair starts running clockwise around the area with a dispatch, e.g. a vest. The other player from each pair walks or jogs around the running area. The players change roles by exchanging the dispatch.

Scoring: The pair completing the most rounds in a set time wins. Only the distance covered by the player with the dispatch counts.

Type of exercise: Intermittent. Exercise periods of 20-120 seconds with 20-120 second rest periods. The total duration could, for example, be 35 minutes, consisting of six periods of five minutes duration separated by one-minute breaks.

Variations: *a.* The players have to run a minimum of two and a maximum of four rounds during each work bout.

                              b. Each player has to cover five rounds at the first run, then 4, 3, 2, 1, 2, 3, 4, and finish with five rounds.

Hints for the coach: It should be emphasized that the players must not sprint. To obtain a high degree of competition, it is important that the pairs are equally matched. The players who are not running should walk or jog on the outer part of the test area so that they do not obstruct the »high-speed runners«. It might be necessary to introduce variation *a.* or *b.* if the »good« runner covers too many rounds in a row, and the team-mate consequently runs much less.

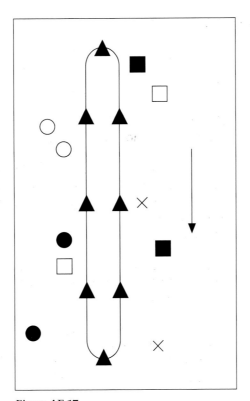

Figure AE 17

Summary

Aerobic work capacity is a fundamental component of fitness for a football player and can be improved by aerobic training. Aerobic training can be divided into three main areas. *Recovery training*, which aims at helping a player return to pre-exercise status as quickly as possible after a match or a hard training session. *Aerobic$_{LI}$*, which enables the player to work with a relatively high exercise intensity throughout a match, and *Aerobic$_{HI}$*, which enhances the ability to repeatedly exercise at a high-intensity during a match. In order to obtain the appropriate training effects, the guidelines within the different types of training should be followed (see Scheme AE 1 – page 144). Although the training drills described are classified as either Aerobic$_{LI}$ or Aerobic$_{HI}$, many of them can be adapted and used for both types of training simply by changing the size of the playing area and/or the number of players.

Anaerobic Training

Anaerobic Training

Aims

1. To increase the ability to act quickly and to rapidly produce power during high-intensity exercise.

2. To increase the capacity to continuously produce power and energy through the anaerobic systems.

3. To increase the ability to recover rapidly after a period of high-intensity exercise.

Effects

The main physiological adaptations to anaerobic training are:

- The synchronization between the nervous system and the muscles becomes more efficient.

- The amount of muscle enzymes involved in anaerobic energy production increases.

- The capacity to produce and remove lactate is elevated.

The benefits for football are:

- An improved performance of intense match activities, such as accelerating, sprinting, tackling, and shooting.

- An elevated ability to perform prolonged high-intensity exercise during a game.

- High-intensity exercise can be performed more frequently during a game.

Types of anaerobic training

Anaerobic training can be divided into *speed training* and *speed endurance training (see Fig. FT 1 – page 105).*

It is important to be fast in order to utilize an opening in the opponents defence.

Speed training

Aims

1. To increase the ability to perceive match situations that require immediate action (perceiving).

2. To increase the ability to take immediate action when needed (evaluating and deciding).

3. To increase the ability to rapidly produce force during high-intensity exercise (taking action).

Application to football

During a match a player performs many activities that require rapid development of force, such as sprinting or making quick changes in direction. As these activities may influence the outcome of a game, speed training is very important.

Principle

During speed training the players should perform maximally for a short period of time (less than 10 seconds – see Scheme AN1). The periods between the exercise bouts should be long enough for the muscles to recover to near resting conditions to enable a player to perform maximally in a subsequent exercise bout. For example, tests on professional Danish players showed that 25 seconds was not sufficient for them to recover fully after a seven-second sprint.

188

Scheme AN 1 Principles of speed training

Speed training			
Exercise (s)	Rest	Intensity	No. of repetitions
2-10	> 5 times exercise duration	Maximal	2-10

Speed training should be performed at an early stage in a training session when the players are not tired. However, it is important that the players have warmed up thoroughly. When a speed training exercise is performed for 5-10 seconds it also improves speed endurance, since considerable amounts of lactate are produced. The greatest effect of speed training is, however, on the high energy phosphate system. Figure AN 1 illustrates the relationship between the duration of exercise and the anaerobic energy production with and without lactate production.

Figure AN 1
The figure illustrates the relative contribution of anaerobic energy from breakdown of phosphates (shaded area) and from a process producing lactate (white area) during short-term intense exercise. The energy production from the use of phosphates accounts for a considerable part of the anaerobic energy production during bouts of exercise lasting less than 10 seconds.

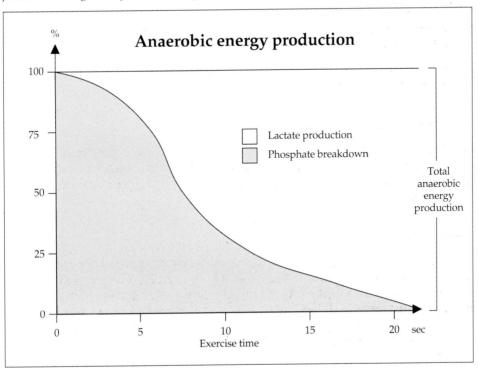

Organization

Speed training should mainly take the form of game-like situations – so-called *functional* speed training, since part of the desired training effect is to improve the players' ability to anticipate and react in different situations in football. Sprinting a set distance on a given command is an example of *formal* speed training. While this improves the ability to produce energy by the anaerobic systems, it has little effect on the ability to react in football-specific situations. This is due to the fact that the players respond to signals, e.g. a whistle, that do not resemble the stimuli for action which occur during a match. In addition, during this type of speed training the muscles involved in other rapid movements in football are not trained sufficiently.

Formal speed training has traditionally been the predominant form of speed training in football. Thus players often associate speed training with sprinting without a ball. For psychological reasons it might therefore be necessary to include this form of training once in a while, although the overall effect for football is not optimal. The benefits may be improved with certain adaptations; for example, the start signal could be the bounce of a ball. One reason as to why formal speed training is popular, is that it is easy to organize and its objectives can be well defined, whereas the planning of functional speed training requires more imagination and the coach needs to continually assess whether the objectives of the training are being achieved. When selecting the form of speed training however, it should be recognized that the overall benefits from functional speed training are far greater than those that can be achieved by formal speed training.

Speed training drills

A number of drills suitable for functional speed training are described below.

Speed in a game is not only dependent on the ability of the muscles to produce energy rapidly but also related to the ability of a player to quickly perceive, evaluate, and decide.

Drill 1 (Fig. AN 2)

Area: Half a football field with one full-size goal.

Number of players: 16 (4 – 22) + 1 goalkeeper.

Organization: The players work in pairs. The drill may start from different positions on the field.

Description: Two players stand in front of a server. The server kicks the ball towards the goal. The players start to sprint immediately after the ball has been served. The player who reaches the ball first tries to score, i.e. becomes the attacker, while the other player becomes the defender.

Scoring: Ordinary scoring.

Variations: *a.* Both players start with their backs to the goal, i.e. they are facing the server.

b. One player starts in front of the other player (for example three metres apart) with the ball. The player with the ball is the attacker and must dribble with high speed towards the goal, the other player is a defender who must chase at maximal speed to try to prevent the attacker from scoring.

c. The same as variation *b.*, but the player must dribble the ball around a cone.

d. One player starts with the ball in front of the other player. The player makes a short wall pass to the server (who is nearer the goal) and then attacks the goal. The defending player chases as in *b.*

Hints for the coach: It is important that the players try hard to get to the ball first. The player who gains possession of the ball should be encouraged to make a direct run towards the goal and shoot. By varying the position of the serve, the players will need to concentrate throughout the exercise.

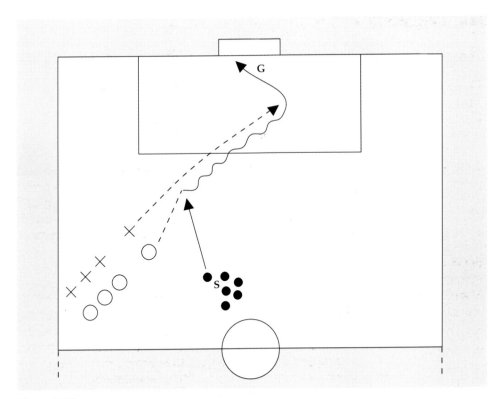

Figure AN 2

Drill 2 (Fig. AN 3)

Area:
A large circular area with a smaller inner circle, e.g. the centre-circle of a field.

Number of players: 10 (6 – 15).

Organization:
All players start with a ball inside the inner circle.

Description:
The players dribble their ball inside the inner circle and attempt to kick the other balls out of this area. When a ball is kicked out of the inner circle, the player that had this ball must sprint to try to reach it before it rolls out of the outer circle. The player then walks back to the inner circle dribbling the ball.

Rules:
None.

Scoring:
If the ball passes the outer circle the player that had the ball gets one negative point and the player that kicked it out gets one point. The player that has the most points after a certain time has won the game.

Variations:
a. The players are divided into two teams and should only try to kick out the opponents' balls. A point is scored for every ball kicked out of the outer circle. The player who has lost possession of the ball must sprint after it to try to stop it rolling out of the outer circle. The game is won by the team with the most points after a set game time.

b. The players are divided into two teams. Each player on one team (attacking) starts with a ball inside the inner circle. The players of the other team (defending) have to be in the area between the perimeter of the inner circle and the perimeter of the outer circle. On a command from the coach the attacking players have a limited time, e.g. 10 seconds, to dribble the ball to the edge of the outer circle. The players of the defending team should try to prevent this. The teams alternate between attacking and defending. A point is scored for every player on the attacking team who reaches the edge of the outer circle in possession of a ball within the allocated time. The points are added up after a certain number of rounds and the game is won by the team with the most points.

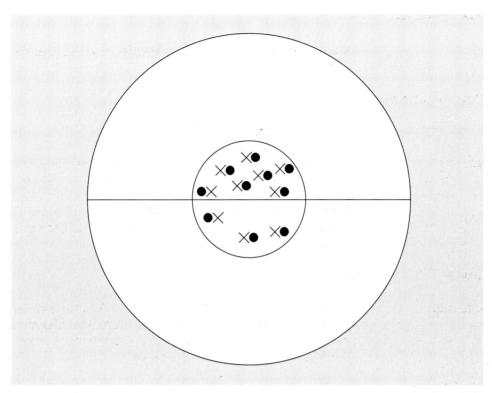

Figure AN 3

Hints for the coach: When a ball is kicked out of the inner circle, the player should be encouraged to *immediately* sprint after it to try to stop it rolling out of the outer circle. It is important that the players walk on their way back to the inner circle after a sprint so that they rest sufficiently. Using the variations *a.* and *b.* should help to make the game more competitive and thus increase the motivation of the players.

Game 1 (Fig. AN 4)

Area:	A football field with a middle-zone and two full-size goals.
Number of players:	3v3+6v6 (3v3+3v3 – 4v4+8v8) + 2 goalkeepers.
Organization:	Three players from each team are »middle«-players who must not leave the middle zone. The remaining six players are »sprint«-players. After a set time the three »middle«-players change with three of the »sprint«-players from the same team.
Description:	The game consists of two sub-games.

Sub-game 1
The »middle«-players play 3v3 with one ball in the middle-zone (the »sprint«-players do not participate), where they defend and attack a row of cones. When a team knocks over one of its opponents' cones then one of their own cones is transferred to the opponents' row of the cones (see Game 1, page 154).

Sub-game 2
A »middle«-player from sub-game 1 can at any time pass the ball out of the middle-zone towards one of the goals for one of the »sprint«-players (from the same team) to chase and try to score a goal. The »sprint«-player may only score if the ball is reached inside the shaded area (see Fig. AN 4). A player from the other team can also attempt to gain possession of the ball as soon as it leaves the middle-zone and, if successful, this player can score without any restrictions. Only one player from each team is allowed to compete for the balls passed from the middle-zone.

As soon as a ball is passed out of the middle-zone in sub-game 1, a »middle«-player from the opposing team runs to fetch a new ball which is positioned behind each team's row of cones (by the »sprint«-players), and the game is continued.

Rules:	The goalkeepers must stay inside the penalty area.
Scoring:	One point is given for knocking down a cone in sub-game 1 whereas three points are given for scoring a goal in sub-game 2. The game is won by the team with the most points after a set game time.
Variations:	*a.* Two players from each team may sprint after the ball. *b.* Sub-game 1 is played with two balls at the same time.

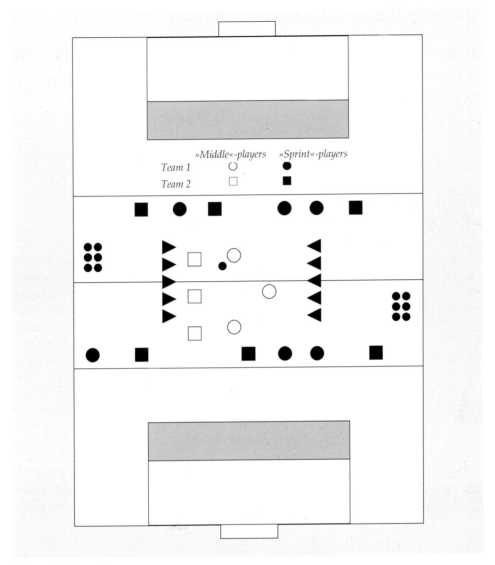

Figure AN 4

Hints for the coach:

The task of the »middle«-players is to either knock down the opponents' cones or to make an accurate pass so that one of their »sprint«-players can receive the ball inside the shaded area. The »sprint«-players must chase the ball or an opponent with maximum speed, but should walk back towards the middle zone after each sprint in order to recover. The inclusion of variation *a.* will increase the number of sprints. However, the quality of each sprint may decrease if the subsequent rest periods are too short. Variation *b.* should increase the number of sprints as it will give the players in sub-game 1 more time and space to make a pass out of the middlezone. It may be necessary to increase the number of players in sub-game 1 if this variation is used.

Speed endurance training

Aims

1. To increase the ability to *rapidly* produce power and energy via anaerobic energy-producing systems.

2. To increase the capacity to *continuously* produce power and energy through the anaerobic energy-producing systems.

3. To increase the ability to recover after a period of high-intensity exercise.

Application to football

Findings of high blood lactate concentrations in top-class players during match-play indicate that the lactate producing energy system is highly stimulated during periods of a game (see page 72). Furthermore, analysis of matches has shown that the higher the level of football, the more high-speed running is performed. The capacity to produce lactate and to repeatedly perform high-intensity exercise should therefore be specifically trained. This can be achieved through speed endurance training.

In order to examine the effect of speed endurance training on performance, a study was performed with players from a top-class Danish squad. Half of the players on the squad performed six weeks of functional speed endurance training, twice a week for 30 minutes per session, in addition to the normal training. The other half of the squad did not change their training. All players were tested before and after the six-week period using a football-specific field

Many activities in a game stimulate the lactate-producing energy system.

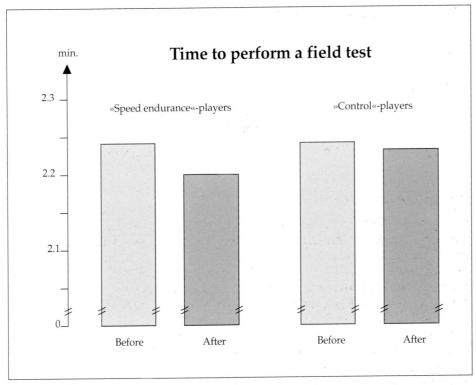

Figure AN 5
The figure shows field test performance of two groups of top-class players tested twice during the season. In the period between the two tests, one group of players performed the ordinary training (»control«-players – on the right), whereas the other group performed their ordinary training combined with additional speed endurance training (»speed endurance«-players – on the left). The »control«-players did not improve performance, whereas the »speed endurance«-players had a better test result after the period.

test. The testing showed that the players who performed speed endurance training had improved their test results after the training period, whereas the performance of the other players was unchanged (see Fig. AN 5).

Both the match analyses and the training study demonstrate that speed endurance training can be beneficial for football players. However, it is recommended that this type of training is only used with top-class players, as the training is very demanding both physically and mentally. When there is a limited amount of time available for training, time can be better utilized for other forms of training. To summarize:

1. Speed endurance training can be effectively used for top-class players.

2. Speed endurance training should have a low priority and may be completely omitted for non-elite players.

3. Speed endurance training should not be used with players under 16 years of age.

Man-to-man contact requires a high rate of energy production from the anaerobic systems.

Principle

Speed endurance training can be divided into *production* training and *maintenance* training. The purpose of production training is to improve the ability to perform maximally for a relatively short period of time, whereas the aim of maintenance training is to increase the ability to sustain exercise at a high intensity.

The exercise intensity during speed endurance training should be almost maximal, which means that the training must be performed according to an interval principle. During training games with exercise periods of 10-20 seconds it may be difficult to achieve the desired training effect, so exercise periods of more than 20 seconds are recommended. In the production training the duration of the exercise bouts should be relatively short (20-40 seconds), and the rest periods in between the exercise bouts should be comparatively long (2-4 minutes) in order to maintain a very high intensity throughout the production training. In the maintenance training the exercise periods should be 30-120 seconds and the duration of the rest periods should approximately equal the exercise periods, so that the players progressively become fatigued. Scheme AN 2 illustrates the principles of the two categories of anaerobic training.

If the exercise periods during speed endurance training last for one minute or more, heart rate measurements may be used to indicate whether or not the exercise intensity is high enough. Towards the end of such exercise periods heart rates should be close to maximum. Figure AN 6 shows heart rate and blood lactate values for a player during and after the exercise periods in a speed endurance maintenance training session. The training was performed on a third of a field and consisted of a two-a-side game with man-to-man marking. One minute of exercise was interspersed by one minute of rest.

Scheme AN 2 Principles of speed endurance training

I. Maintenance training				
	Exercise (s)	Rest	Intensity	No. of repetitions
I a	30-90	As exercise duration	Almost maximal	2-10
I b	30-90	Aerobic low-intensity game for a maximal duration of 3 times exercise duration	Almost maximal	2-10

II. Production training				
	Exercise (s)	Rest	Intensity	No. of repetitions
II a	20-40	> 5 times exercise duration	Almost maximal	2-10
II b	20-40	Aerobic low-intensity game for a minimum duration of 5 times exercise duration	Almost maximal	2-10

Organization

In reality, during speed endurance training games the players do not exercise at a maximum level of intensity throughout an exercise period. There are many factors that will affect the exercise intensity of a game, such as the tactical requirements. Figure FT 3 (see page 106) shows examples of how the exercise intensity can vary for a player during speed endurance games.

To ensure that the exercise intensity is high throughout an exercise period, it is often necessary to motivate the players verbally, especially towards the end of the period. It is also important that there are enough balls available during the drills to minimize interruptions which will interfere with the desired high tempo.

In speed endurance training the rest periods between the bouts of high-intensity exercise should include recovery activities, e.g. players can jog to fetch the balls.

Figure AN 6

The figure shows heart rate and blood lactate concentration of a player during a two-a-side training game with man-to-man marking on a third of the field. The player's heart rate approached maximum level towards the end of the one-minute work periods and decreased to about 120 beats/min during the rest periods. Blood lactate concentrations after the second and third exercise periods were 11 and 12 mmol/l, respectively, indicating a marked production of lactate. Thus, the drill served its purpose as a speed endurance maintenance training game.

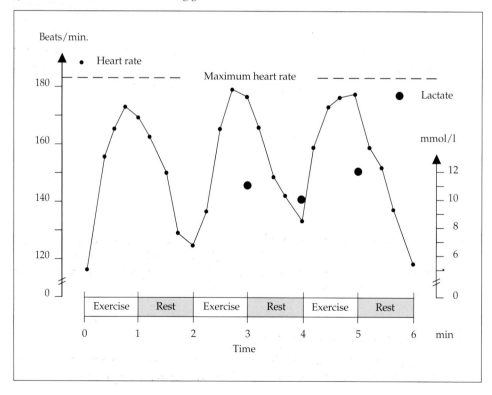

Players during a speed endurance two-a-side training game (see also Fig. AN 6).

Speed endurance maintenance training should be conducted at the end of a training session, as the players will be physically affected for some time after this training. It is, however, important that the players perform some type of light exercise after the training to allow for rapid recovery.

Speed endurance training drills

A number of training drills which can be used for speed endurance training are described below. Some exercises without a ball are also given.

Speed endurance maintenance training drills

Game 1 (Fig. AN 7)

Area:	A quarter of a football field with one full-size goal.
Number of players:	2+2v2+2 (1+1v1+1) + 1 goalkeeper.
Organization:	Each team consists of 2 x 2 players who take turns to play.
Description:	Ordinary football play with both teams attacking the same goal. The game is started by the server (S) passing a ball into the playing area. If a team loses possession of the ball by the goalkeeper catching it or if it is kicked out of the playing area, the next ball is served to the opposing team. After scoring a goal the same team gets the next ball from the server.
Rules:	None.
Scoring:	Ordinary scoring.
Type of exercise:	Fixed time intervals, e.g. an exercise period of 1-2 minutes with rest periods of the same duration.
Variations:	*a.* Use man-to-man marking.
	b. When a team gains possession of the ball, the ball must be taken into the shaded zone before attacking the goal.
	c. Only the players who are inside the shaded zone when the ball is received from the server are allowed to participate in the following attack.

Hints for the coach:
It is important to continuously motivate the players to exercise at a high intensity. In variation *a.* the demands of the drill are further increased and a reduction in the duration of the exercise period may be necessary in order to maintain the desired exercise intensity. If one player cannot cope with the marking of an opponent, the intensity of the other two players can be affected, hence, it is important to have players of equal ability marking each other. Variation *b.* should decrease the number of shots and ensure that all players are exercising at a high intensity. In variation *c.* the players must be aware that running back very fast prevents the opponents from interfering during the attack. This rule should ensure a higher overall exercise intensity, even though some players may be standing still for short periods. In variation *c.* the physical demands may be further increased by reducing the size of the shaded area.

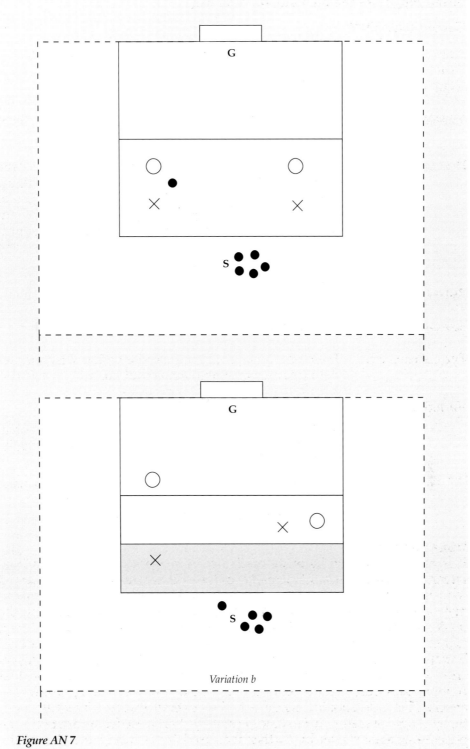

Variation b

Figure AN 7

Game 2 (Fig. AN 8)

Area: A third of a football field with five small goals.

Number of players: 3+3v3+3 (2+2v2+2 – 4+4v4+4).

Organization: Each team has 2 x 3 players who take turns playing. Each team attacks and defends two of their own goals and a common goal in the middle of the field.

Description: Ordinary football play. The team that gets the ball after a goal is scored continues the game, but the next scoring must be done in another goal.

Rules: None.

Scoring: Scoring can be done both ways through a goal.

Type of exercise: Fixed time intervals, e.g. exercise periods of one minute interspersed by one-minute rest periods.

Variations: *a.* Man-to-man marking.

                                       b. A goal is scored by playing the ball through a goal to a team-mate on the other side of the goal.

Hints for the coach: The players of the team that has possession of the ball should try to create space for themselves, while the opposing team should be encouraged to work hard to regain possession of the ball as quickly as possible. If the defending team adopts the tactic of having one player in each of the goals it may be necessary to increase the width of the goal or increase the number of goals. A larger distance between the goals should result in a higher overall exercise intensity. Variation *a.* should also increase the physical demands. However, the exercise intensity might be lower for some players if there is a large difference in the physical capacity of the two players who are marking each other. This problem can be partly solved by including variation *b.*

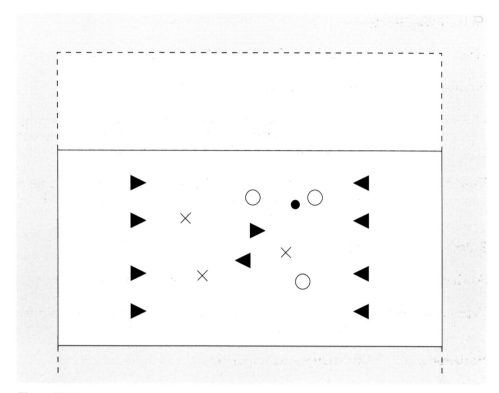

Figure AN 8

Game 3 (Fig. AN 9)

Area: A football field, divided into four zones – two middle-zones (②+④) and two outer zones (①+③).

Number of players: 2x4v4 (2x3v3 – 2x5v5).

Organization: Four players from each team are in each of the two middle-zones. The game consists of two sub-games and begins with sub-game 1. At a given signal from the coach the players alternate between the two sub-games as indicated by the arrows and signs on Fig. AN 9.

Description: The game consists of two sub-games.

Sub-game 1
Eight players play against eight with one ball in the two middle zones (4v4 in each zone). The players must try to keep possession of the ball within their team.

Sub-game 2
Four players play against four in the outer zones (①+③). The players must try to play the ball through the small goals (cones) to a team-mate.

Rules: The players must stay inside their appointed zone during each of the sub-games. During sub-game 2 the players are not allowed to run through the goals.

Scoring: In sub-game 1 a point is scored for making a set number of consecutive passes, e.g. 10, without the other team touching the ball. In sub-game 2, a point is scored for passing the ball through one of the goals to a team-mate.

Type of exercise: Fixed time intervals, e.g. in sub-game 2 the exercise period can be around two minutes, while in sub-game 1 it can be three minutes.

Variations: *a.* Use man-to-man marking in sub-game 2.

b. Scoring during sub-game 2 is only allowed if the receiving player makes a first time pass to a team-mate and the pass does not go through the goal.

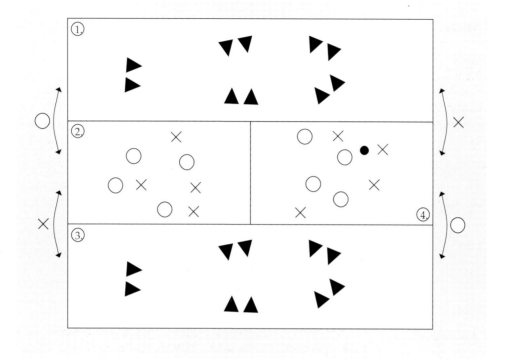

Figure AN 9

Hints for the coach: The actual speed endurance training occurs in sub-game 2 in which the players should be encouraged to exercise at close to maximal intensity.

Sub-game 1 allows the players to recover from sub-game 2. Therefore, the tempo in sub-game 1 should be relatively low, but the players should be encouraged to keep moving. The exercise demands in sub-game 2 can be controlled by changing both the number and width of the goals. Variation *a.* should increase the overall exercise intensity in sub-game 2. Variation *b.* can also increase the exercise intensity and is effective if one team has scored several more goals than the other team.

Exercises without a ball

Exercise 1 (Fig. AN 10)

Area: Half a football field.

Number of players: Unlimited. A team consists of three or four players.

Organization: Cones are positioned as shown in Fig. AN 10 and each team starts between two cones.

Description: Each player runs with a dispatch, e.g. a vest. At a given signal the first player follows the route illustrated in Fig AN 10 back to the start where the dispatch is passed to a team-mate, who repeats the run. This continues until each player has performed a set number of runs, e.g. three runs per player.

Scoring: The game is won by the team that finishes the set number of runs first.

Type of exercise: Intermittent, e.g. exercise periods of approximately one minute with two-minute rest periods. Total duration, e.g. 23 minutes (two rounds consisting of three runs with approximately five minutes between each round).

Variation: Players start at both ends of the row of cones and pass the dispatch accordingly.

Hints for the coach: The players should run almost maximally during each shuttle. To keep the players motivated it is important that the teams are as equal as possible in terms of fast and slow players. The variation will shorten both the exercise time and the duration of the rest periods.

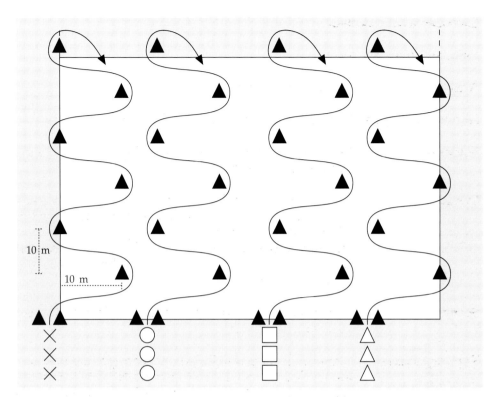

Figure AN 10

Speed endurance production training drills

Drill 1 (Fig. AN 11)

Area:

A small circular area (radius approximately three metres) inside a large circular area (radius approximately 20 metres).

Number of players: 5 (4-8).

Organization:

A server (S), a »speed endurance« player (SE), and a minimum of two balls. The players take turns exercising.

Description:

The server plays a ball towards the perimeter of the outer circle. SE must try to stop the ball rolling out of the outer circle. SE then dribbles the ball back into the inner circle at maximal speed. The server plays another ball as soon as SE is back inside the inner circle.

Rules:

None.

Scoring:

The number of balls that SE stops from rolling out of the outer circle.

Type of exercise:

Fixed time intervals, e.g. exercise periods of 20-30 seconds and rest periods of 2 minutes (4 x 30 seconds).

Variations:

a. Only one ball is used. SE chases the ball and passes it directly back to the server, who then serves it with a first-time pass.

b. Two players compete for the ball. The player that gets the ball should try to pass the ball back to the server whereby one point is received. The other player must try to prevent the pass. The server either serves with a first-time pass as in *a.* or serves a new ball.

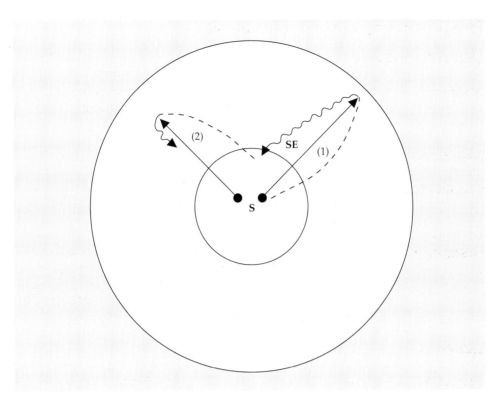

Figure AN 11

Hints for the coach: It is important that the exercise is performed at maximum intensity. The server can control the overall demands of the drill and should give SE a realistic chance of reaching the ball before it rolls out of the outer circle. In variation *a.* and *b.* the ball should be played back to the server as quickly as possible, otherwise the overall exercise intensity may be too low. An effective method of ensuring that the ball is played back quickly is to restrict the number of ball touches to a maximum of three. Extra balls should be kept ready in case the back pass is missed.

Drill 2 (Fig. AN 12)

Area: A third of a football field with one full-size goal.

Number of players: 6 (5-8) + 1 goalkeeper.

Organization: A server (S), a »speed endurance« player (SE), a cone, and several balls. The players take turns exercising.

Description: The server passes a ball to SE who shoots at the goal and then runs around the cone before the next shot.

Rules: None.

Scoring: The number of goals scored within a set time.

Type of exercise: Fixed time intervals, e.g. exercise periods of 20 seconds and rest periods of 2.5 minutes (i.e. 5 x 20 + 5 x 10 seconds).

Variations: *a.* SE receives the ball in the air and either shoots directly or after being in control of the ball.

b. SE may dribble around the goalkeeper.

c. SE takes free-kicks (i.e. the server positions the ball every time).

Hints for the coach: The players should be encouraged to sprint around the cone immediately after their attempt at the goal. In variation *b.* it may be necessary to restrict the number of ball touches, e.g. a maximum of four, in order to prevent the exercise intensity from becoming too low.

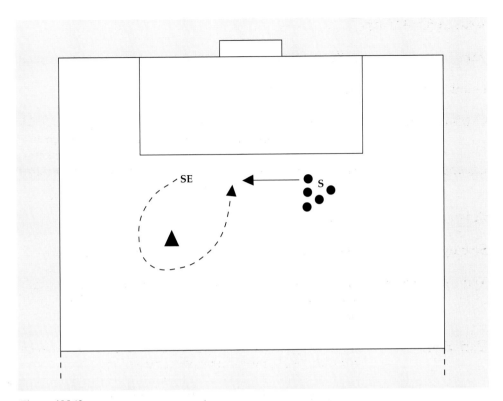

Figure AN 12

Game 4 (Fig. AN 13)

Area:	Half a football field with two full-size goals.
Number of players:	6v6 (5v5 – 9v9) + 2 goalkeepers.
Organization:	Several balls are scattered around the field. The game consists of two sub-games and starts with sub-game 1. At a given signal the players change between the two sub-games. After sub-game 2 the balls must be scattered around the playing area again.
Description:	The game consists of two sub-games.

Sub-game 1
Ordinary football with one ball and normal scoring.

Sub-game 2
All the balls may be used. The players should within a given time try to score as many goals (in the opponents' goal) as possible, using the balls that are scattered around the edge of the playing area (if a goal is scored the ball must stay inside the goal until the end of that period). Each team should also try to prevent the opposing team from scoring.

Rules:	None.
Scoring:	A goal is worth five points in sub-game 1 and one point in sub-game 2.
Type of exercise:	Intermittent. Sub-game 1 can be performed for a period of around five minutes while the duration of sub-game 2 may last up to 40 seconds.
Variations:	*a.* Both teams are divided into defenders and attackers in sub-game 2. The defenders should try to prevent the opposing attackers from scoring and vice-versa.

b. During sub-game 2 the players work in pairs and play against a pair of opponents, with one ball at a time.

c. During sub-game 2 a player from the attacking team can only score if inside the goal area.

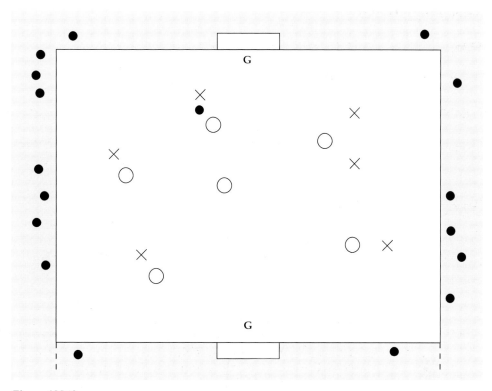

Figure AN 13

Hints for the coach: During sub-game 2 the exercise intensity must be almost maximal (speed endurance production training). The coach should emphasize that hard work can be rewarded by more goals. Initially sub-game 2 might appear rather disorganized, but, generally, the players quickly understand the idea of the game. During sub-game 1 the exercise intensity should be relatively low, which may be obtained by reducing the size of the playing area or by increasing the number of players.

Variations *a.* and *b.* should increase the overall demand. Variation *c.* may be used if the intensity during subgame 2 is too low because the players are trying to score with long shots.

Exercise without a ball

Exercise 2 (Fig. AN 14)

Area:	A football field or a similar area.
Number of players:	15 (three teams of five players).
Organization:	Two cones are positioned behind the goals and two cones are positioned at the points where the centre-line and the side-lines meet. One player from each team stands at each of the cones. The extra player in each team is positioned at the starting cone.
Description:	At a signal one of the players at the starting cone runs in a clock-wise direction. This player carries a dispatch, e.g. a vest, which is passed to the team-mate at the next cone.
Type of exercise:	Intermittent, e.g. exercise periods for each player of approximately 15 seconds with 60-second rest periods. Total duration, e.g. 3 x 5 minutes (three rounds per player).
Scoring:	The team that first completes the set number of rounds has won.
Hints for the coach:	The players should perform maximally in each run. To keep the players motivated it is important that the teams are as equal as possible in terms of fast and slow players.

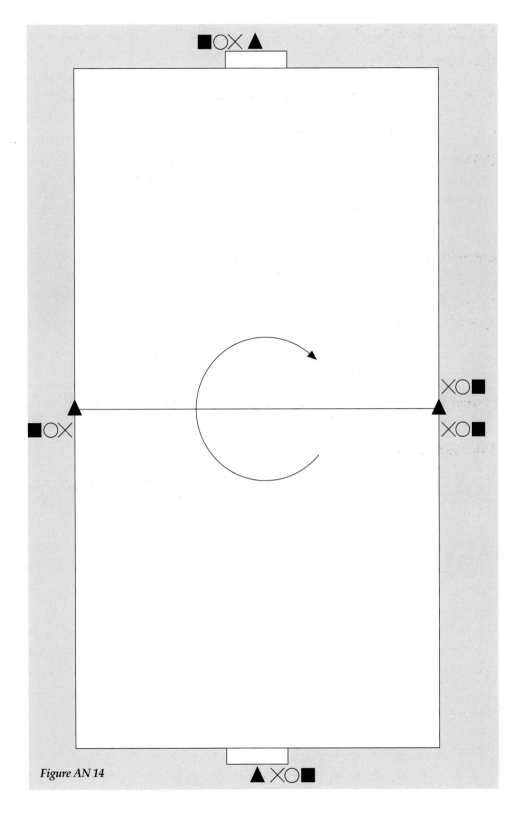

Figure AN 14

219

The anaerobic energy system is frequently activated during match-play. Therefore, it is important to perform anaerobic training.

Summary

Anaerobic training consists of *speed* training and *speed endurance* training, of which the latter can be divided into *production* training and *maintenance* training.

In football, speed is not merely dependent on physical capacity, but also involves rapid decision making which must then be translated into quick movements. Therefore, the aim of speed training is also to improve a player's ability to perceive, evaluate, and act quickly in match situations where speed is essential. In order to obtain this effect speed training should mainly be performed with a ball.

Speed endurance training increases the muscle's ability to rapidly produce force and improves the capacity of muscles to maintain a high power output. This type of training can enable a player to exercise at a high intensity more frequently and for longer periods of time. This ability is especially important for top-class players.

Specific Muscle
Training

Specific Muscle Training

Strength and endurance of the muscles used in football will improve over many seasons of play. In order to achieve further and quicker improvements however, the muscles need to be trained specifically. This type of training is called specific muscle training, and can be divided into muscle strength training, muscle endurance training, and flexibility training (see Fig. SM 1). Flexibility training consists of stretching exercises that are described in the chapter »The Training Session« (see page 117). In the present chapter muscle strength and muscle endurance training are discussed.

Application to football

Muscle strength and muscle endurance training are beneficial for a football player. In this type of training, however, only the muscles used in the exercise are trained and the adaptations are specific to the type of exercise performed. The latter aspect is illustrated in Scheme SM 1 (see page 226), which presents results from a study in which the effect of different types of muscle training

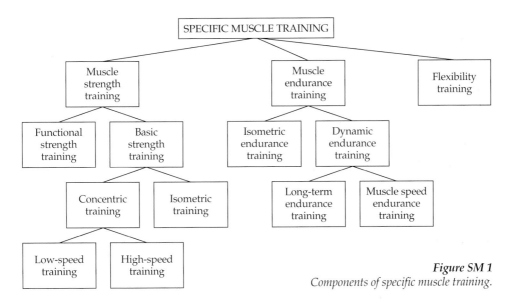

Figure SM 1
Components of specific muscle training.

Type of specific muscle training	Amount of training	Improvement			
		Strength		Endurance	
		Isometric	Concentric	Isometric	Concentric
I. Isometric endurance	60% of maximum strength held 5 sec 150/day, 5 weeks	4%	6%	*122%*	41%
II. Concentric endurance	60% of maximum strength, lifted 150/day, 5 weeks	0%	29%	0%	*5040%*
III. Concentric strength	Maximum strength, lifted 10/day, 5 weeks	19%	*41%*	27%	45%

Scheme SM 1

was studied. The subjects performed either isometric muscle endurance training (I), concentric muscle endurance training (II), or concentric muscle strength training (III – for definitions see page 48). The improvements in strength and endurance that occurred with training are shown as a percentage of the baseline value. For all training conditions the largest improvement was seen when the type of exercise used for testing was the same as that performed during training sessions. These values are highlighted in Scheme SM 1. For example, with concentric muscle endurance training (II) a large increase in concentric endurance was observed, but there was no increase in isometric endurance. It should also be noted that while it is possible to achieve a large increase in the endurance capacity of a muscle within a short period of time, a longer time is required for significant increases in muscle strength. The results of this study demonstrate that it is important to know how the muscles have to be trained when performing specific muscle training.

Kick performance is in part dependent on the strength of the leg muscles.

Muscle strength training

Aims

To increase muscle strength in order to:

1. Increase muscle power output during explosive activities in a football match such as tackling, jumping, and accelerating.

2. Prevent injuries.

3. Regain strength more quickly after an injury.

Application to football

Generally football players need to be relatively strong in most of the large muscle groups of the body, as muscle strength is an important component of many match activities such as tackling and sprinting. However, the muscle strength required is dependent on several factors, such as a player's style of

Figure SM 2
Football strength is defined as the force generated during a movement in match-play, e.g. a kick. Football strength is dependent on coordination strength, which is the force developed during an isolated football-specific movement, e.g. kicking a ball that is laying still (dead ball). Both football strength and coordination strength are dependent on the basic strength of the muscles involved in the movement. Basic strength can be tested with the use of strength testing equipment (see photo page 51).

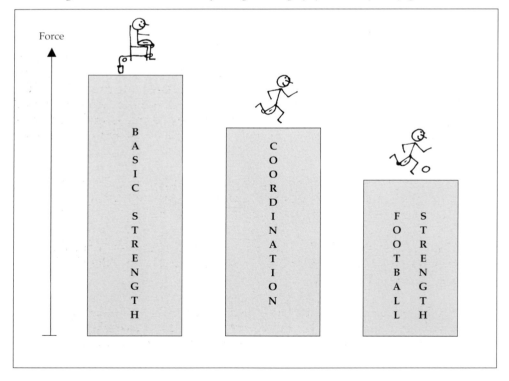

play and position in the team. For example, due to the explosive nature of the movements that a goalkeeper has to perform during a game, this player has a special need for a high level of muscle strength. Furthermore, some players may benefit by having particular strength in specific muscle groups. For example, a player who specializes in long throw-ins may improve this task by increasing the dynamic strength of the chest muscles. Youth players in the transitional stage before senior football will have a particular need as they will encounter players who, due to a longer training background, have greater strength.

One important function of the muscles is to protect and stabilize joints of the skeletal system. Hence, strength training is also of importance in preventing injuries as well as the re-occurrence of injuries. A prolonged period of inactivity, e.g. due to an injury, will considerably weaken the muscles. It has been demonstrated that five weeks after immobilization of a leg, the strength of the quadriceps muscle can be reduced by 50%. Thus, before a player returns to football training after an injury, a period of strength training is needed. Strength training should also be performed after the player has returned to football training and should be continued until pre-injury strength is regained. The length of time required to regain strength is dependent on the length of the inactivity period but generally several months are needed. For a group of players observed two years after a knee operation, it was found that the average strength of the quadriceps muscle of the injured leg was only 75% of the strength in the other leg. In spite of this, the players believed that they were as strong as they were before the injury.

Muscle strength in football

A player's ability to exert force during a football match is not solely dependent on the strength of the muscles involved in the movement. The power output is also influenced by the player's ability to coordinate the action of the muscles at the right time (timing). In order to understand the factors that limit power development in a movement in football, three classifications of strength are introduced: *basic strength, coordination strength, and football strength.*

> *Basic strength* refers to the strength of the muscle groups involved in a given movement when the muscles are contracting in a similar way as during the movement (see Fig. SM 2).

> *Coordination strength* refers to the player's ability to coordinate the different muscle groups in a given movement and to utilize basic strength (see Fig. SM 2).

> *Football strength* refers to how much force is produced during an action in football, for example a shot (see Fig. SM2). This is in part determined by the ability to utilize the coordination strength at the right time (timing).

229

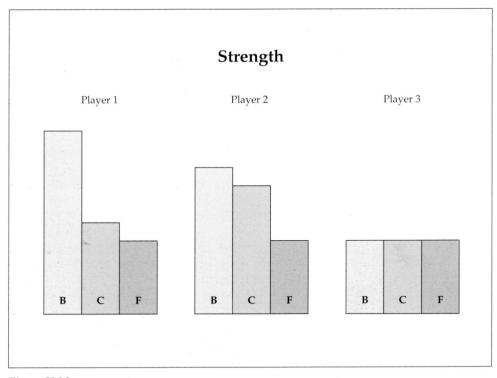

Figure SM 3

The figure gives a theoretical illustration of three players with the same football strength, e.g. they are able to kick the ball an equal distance during match-play, but with different levels of basic strength and coordination strength.

Player 1 is not able to utilize a high level of basic strength due to an inability to coordinate. Player 2 has difficulty in transferring high basic strength and good coordination strength to football strength. Player 3 is able to compensate for poor basic strength due to a good ability to coordinate and to time a movement.

B = basic strength, C = coordination strength, F = football strength.

A high level of basic strength cannot be effectively utilized during match-play if a player is not able to coordinate the activation of the different muscle groups during a movement (see Fig. SM 3 – player 1). In a similar way, the ability to coordinate the muscles involved is of limited use if a player does not have a good sense of timing in a game situation (see Fig. SM 3 – player 2). This is the reason why smaller players, who possess a well-developed ability to coordinate and time movements, are often able to compete, e.g. in a heading, with players who are taller and have higher basic strength levels, but who have a poor ability to coordinate and time their movements. For players who have a good sense of timing, basic strength and coordination strength will limit football strength (see Fig. SM 3 – player 3). When planning a muscle strength training programme, it is important to recognize that the ability to utilize strength during a game depends on several factors.

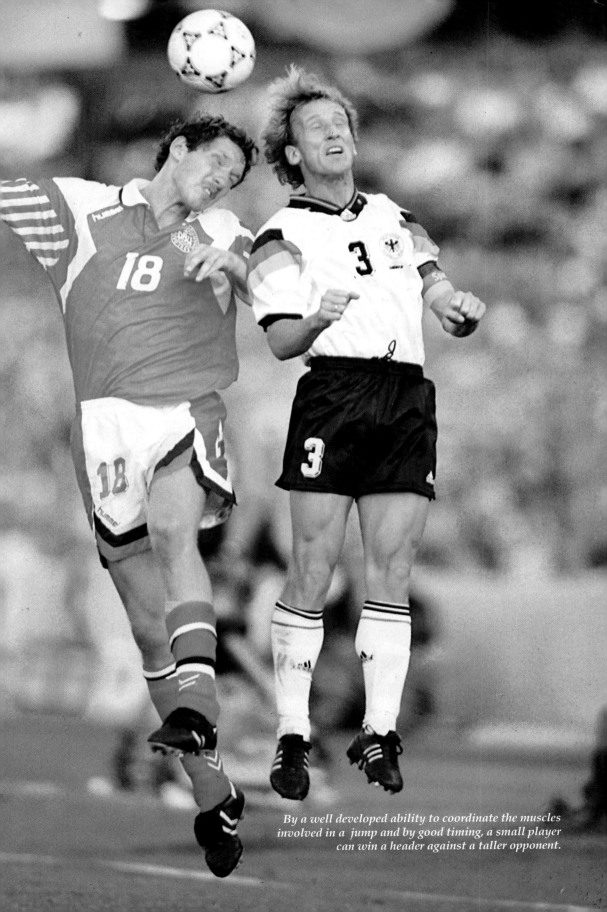

*By a well developed ability to coordinate the muscles
involved in a jump and by good timing, a small player
can win a header against a taller opponent.*

Types of strength training

Strength training for football players can be divided into *functional* strength training and *basic* strength training (see Fig. SM 1 – page 225).

Functional strength training
In functional strength training movements related to football are used. The training can consist of games where football movements are performed under conditions that are physically more stressful than normally, e.g. playing on an unusually soft surface, such as sand, or playing while wearing a weighted jacket (not more than 3-5% of body weight). Alternatively, functional strength training can take the form of maximal force development in isolated movements relevant for football. The advantage of functional strength training is that the improvements in muscle strength can be effectively utilized during match-play, whereas one disadvantage is the difficulty in controlling and adjusting the resistive load.

Figure SM 4
*The figure illustrates the effect of a period of **functional strength training** on the various aspects of strength. The strength levels before, after, and several months after the strength training period are shown on the left, in the middle (A), and on the right (B), respectively. The shaded areas indicate the improvement in strength immediately after and several months after the strength training period. By performing ordinary football training after the strength training period, the improvement in coordination strength could be better utilized during match-play (compare with Fig. SM 5 – page 234).*

B = basic strength, C = coordination strength, F = football strength.

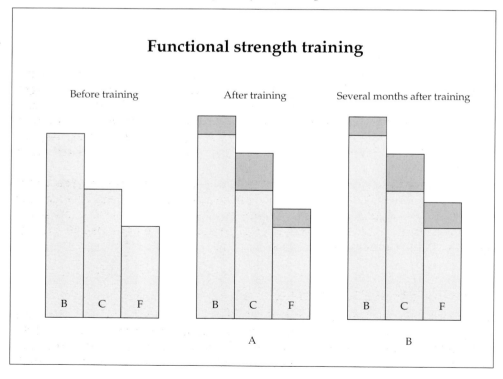

232

Strength training may reduce a player's risk of injury.

Basic strength training

During basic strength training muscle groups are trained in isolated movements. For this type of training different kinds of conventional strength training machines or free weights can be used, which allow for simple adjustment of the resistive load. This makes it easy for the players to train on their own once a training programme has been designed. One disadvantage of basic strength training is that the strength gains are specific to the particular movement.

Basic strength training does not necessarily require weight training machines or free weights, as the body weight can be used as the resistive load, for example when doing push-ups. Although this type of training makes it difficult to adjust the resistance, the work performed can be varied by changing the number of repetitions in a set.

Effects of strength training

Functional strength training improves both basic strength and coordination strength, which have a beneficial effect on football strength (see Fig. SM 4). Basic strength training will lead primarily to improvements in basic strength, with only a small immediate effect on coordination strength and football

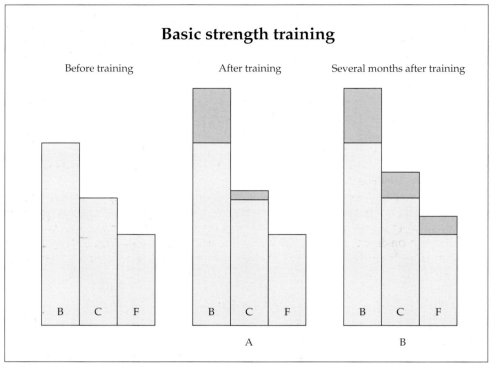

Figure SM 5
*The figure illustrates the effect of a period of **basic strength training** on the various aspects of strength. The strength levels before, immediately after, and several months after the strength training period are shown on the left, in the middle (A), and on the right (B), respectively. The shaded areas indicate the improvement in strength immediately after and several months after the strength training period. Immediately after the basic strength training period there was no increase in football strength, but the ordinary football training performed after the strength training resulted in a better coordination of the stronger muscles and improved utilization of the basic strength during match-play (compare with Fig SM 4 – page 232).*

B = basic strength, C = coordination strength, F = football strength.

strength (see Fig. SM 5). This is partly because the movements during such training differ from movements in football. For example, the quadriceps muscle is conventionally trained with an angle of 90° between the leg and the upper body, whereas the angle at which this muscle group works during football is mainly larger (see Fig. SM 6). In order to effectively utilize improvements in basic muscle strength during match-play, strength training should be combined with playing football (see Figs. SM 4b and SM 5b).

The results of a study with Danish top-class players demonstrate the effect of various types of strength training in a period without regular football training. Two groups of players performed basic strength training with the quadriceps muscles. One group trained with heavy resistant loads at low movement speeds (HR-slow), while the other group trained with lighter resistant loads at faster movement speeds (LR-fast). A third group performed functional strength training (FS – see kicking exercise page 241). The training period lasted three months (off-season) and the players trained three times per week. Kick performance was tested before and after the training period. Improvements in basic strength were found in the training groups, with the greatest increase observed for the HR-slow group. On the other hand, the FS-group achieved the largest improvement in kick performance, whereas only a modest increase was found for the LR-fast and HR-slow groups (see Figure SM 7). Apparently, the players performing the basic strength training could only to a very limited extent transfer the improvement in basic strength to football strength (see also Fig. SM 5).

In a study with players from the Belgian top-class team Anderlecht, basic strength training was performed twice a week throughout the season in parallel with the ordinary training. The strength training resulted in an increase in the basic strength of the quadriceps muscles (see Fig. SM 8). Before and after the strength training period, the players' ability to kick was tested to

Figure SM 6
The figure focuses on the angle between the thigh and the upper body during an exercise often used to train the quadriceps muscle (thigh muscles – on the left) and during a kick (on the right). The angle during the training is 90°, whereas the angle ranges between 130 and 240° during a kick.

assess the ability to exert force in a football-related movement. Due to the strength training, the distance the ball travelled in the air after a kick was increased from 48 to 51 metres (see Fig. SM 8). This shows that by combining strength training and football training, players can utilize an increase in basic muscle strength.

Strength training can be advantageous for football players. However, there can also be negative effects if the training is not well-structured. If too much muscle mass is gained the player may lose football-specific qualities such as technical skills. An imbalance in strength between muscle groups may also occur which can alter locomotive characteristics and increase the risk of injury. For example, it has been found that individuals with low strength in the hamstring muscles relative to the strength of the quadriceps muscle are susceptible to injuries in the hamstrings. Furthermore, strength training may also decrease flexibility if the trained muscles are not regularly stretched.

Figure SM 7
The figure shows kick performance (speed of the ball) of Danish elite players before and after a three-month period in which the players only performed a limited amount of football training (off-season). During this period three groups of players performed different types of strength training, whereas one group (control) did not conduct strength training. One group trained concentrically at slow speeds (low-speed), a second group trained concentrically at fast speeds (high-speed), while the third group trained functionally (functional). The groups that performed strength training increased their basic muscle strength, but they had only moderate increases in kick performance, with the greatest increase found for the functional group.

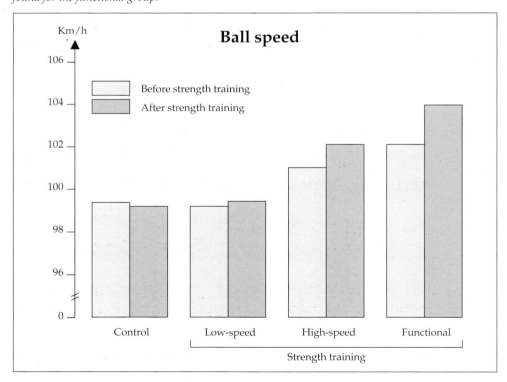

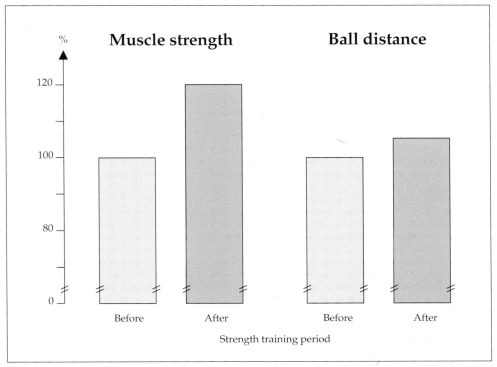

Figure SM 8
The figure shows basic strength of the quadriceps muscle (on the left) and the longest distance a ball could be kicked (on the right) by players from Anderlecht before and after a period of basic strength training. Muscle strength, and to a lesser extent, kick performance, were increased after the strength training period.

Designing a strength training programme

In planning a strength training programme several factors should be considered. The quantity and the structure of training as well as how the muscles should be trained need to be taken into account. Guidelines for these factors are given below.

Quantity of a strength training programme

The amount of time used for strength training is dependent upon several factors:

- The available training time. Strength training should not take up too much of the total time available for training, except for certain periods of the year (see page 294).

- The motivation and self-discipline of the players. These factors are important as strength training is of little use without a maximal voluntary effort.

237

- The baseline strength level of the individual player. The need for strength training is less for stronger players than it is for weaker players. However, the playing style of each player, as well as of the whole team, has to be taken into account.

- Facilities available.

Structure of a strength training programme

Strength of muscles increase faster than the strength of tendons, ligaments, and connective tissue. Therefore, if too much strength training is performed at an early stage, an imbalance between the strength of the muscle and the strength of the surrounding structures may develop. When maximal loads are applied this may lead to the rupture of tendons, ligaments, or connective tissue.

The risk of injury can be minimized by complying with the following suggestions at the beginning of a strength training period:

> *Start with relatively low weight loads and concentrate on good technique.*

> *Start with few repetitions of each exercise.*

> *Allow sufficient time for recovery between each training session.*

An example of the frequency and number of sets per training session during and after an intensive strength training period is given below.

Start (4 weeks):		
First week:	1-2 sessions	2 sets per session
Second week:	1-2 sessions	3 sets per session
Third week:	2-3 sessions	3-4 sets per session
Fourth week:	3 sessions	3-4 sets per session
Training phase:		
Per week:	3 (max 4) sessions	3-4 sets per session
Maintenance phase:		
Per week:	1-2 sessions	2-4 sets per session

How to train the muscles

Adaptation to strength training is localized to the muscle groups used during the training and specific to the type of movements performed, so it is important to know how the muscles work when playing football. Scheme SM 2 indicates the function of individual muscle groups in football.

238

The scheme shows that a football player should focus on training the leg muscles eccentrically and concentrically at slow and fast movement speeds, whereas the muscles of the upper body should primarily be trained concentrically at low speeds and isometrically. However, individual needs may require alternative modes of training.

Scheme SM 2

	Concentric speed low high		Isometric	Eccentric
Muscle of the leg				
Anterior lower leg muscles	●	●	⊕	⊕
Posterior lower leg muscles	●	●	⊕	●
Leg extensors (Quadriceps)	●	●	⊕	●
Leg flexors (Hamstrings)	●	●	⊕	●
Leg adductors	⊕	⊕	⊕	●
Buttock muscles	●	●	●	●
Muscles of upper body				
Abdominal muscles:				
Side	⊕	⊕	●	○
Front	⊕	⊕	●	○
Deep	●	⊕	●	⊕
Back:				
Upper	●	⊕	●	○
Lower	●	⊕	●	○
Chest muscles	⊕	⊕	○	○
Shoulder muscles	⊕	⊕	○	○
Neck muscles	⊕	○	⊕	○
Muscles of the arm				
Arm flexor (biceps)	⊕	○	⊕	○
Arm extensor (triceps)	○	○	○	○

Explanation of symbols: Use in football:

○ = minor
⊕ = moderate
● = major

239

A player's kick performance can be evaluated by measuring the ball velocity after a kick.

Organization

The following points are important when performing strength training:

> *Players should warm up before the training commences.*
>
> *Sufficient rest should be allowed between repeated exercise bouts for a given muscle group.*
>
> *Each repetition should be performed with a maximum effort.*
>
> *If feeling any kind of pain that is not solely related to fatigue, players should stop training.*
>
> *A strength training session should end up with stretching exercises.*

Strength training is most effective if the muscles have been thoroughly warmed up before the exercises begin. The warm-up should include whole body exercises that raise the overall body temperature (see page 118). In addition, the muscle groups that are to be used during the training should be specifically warmed up; this can be achieved by performing the exercises with light loads.

If a muscle group is repeatedly trained within a short period of time, the effect of the training will decrease as the muscles get tired. So alternating exercises, which use different muscle groups will increase the overall training effect. After intensive activity a muscle becomes considerably shorter. To prevent a permanent shortening after strength training, every training session should end up with stretching exercises (see page 126).

Functional strength training – practical application

When functional strength training is performed as isolated movements, each exercise should be performed with a maximum effort. After each repetition, a player should rest a few seconds to allow for a higher force production in the subsequent muscle contraction. The number of repetitions in a set should not exceed ten, and rest periods between sets should be longer than one minute.

Exercises for functional strength training

Kicking
The muscles that are active when kicking a ball can be trained by performing kicking movements with added resistance. The resistance should be relatively low in order for the speed of the kick to be high. As an alternative to using a weight training machine, a strong elastic band, fastened to a fixed object at one end and attached to the player's foot at the other end, may be used. One limitation with the elastic band however, is that the resistance becomes greater as the band is stretched, therefore decreasing the movement speed towards the end of the kick.

For the ankle

Jumping in a barrel.
Half a barrel is used. The player skips or jumps inside.

Balancing.
The player tries to keep balance on a balancing board while rocking from side to side.

Jump training

To improve jump performance plyometric training can be used. In this type of training the muscles are first stretched and then immediately shortened, e.g. jumping down from a box and then, instantaneously, jumping up on ground contact. On landing, the quadriceps muscles are stretched (eccentric work) as the downward movement is retarded, and then shortened (concentric work) to propel the body upwards. Plyometric training has been shown to be an effective way of improving the performance of explosive movements and has been used for several years in other sports such as volleyball.

Due to the explosive nature and large impact force associated with this form of training, the risk of injury can be high if proper safety precautions are not taken. The training should preferably be performed on grass or a hard rubber mat, and never on a concrete floor. If a wooden floor is used, the players should wear shoes with a thick and strong rubber sole to help absorb impact forces. It should be noted that some muscle soreness may occur in the days following the first sessions of plyometric training.

Some plyometric training exercises are described below.

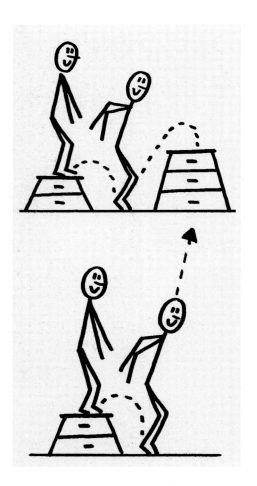

Exercise 1

a. Jumping down from a bench (or a gymnastic box) and up onto another bench using either both legs or one leg. Contact with the ground should be instantaneous.

b. Jumping down from a bench and immediately jumping vertically on landing. The vertical jump can take the form of an imaginary attempt to head the ball. A ball suspended from above may be used.

The height of the benches should be close to 30-40 centimetres (not higher than 60 centimetres). Contact time on the ground should be minimal. The jumps should not be performed while carrying or wearing an extra load, as the risk of injury is too great.

242

Progression

The height of the bench that the player jumps onto in *a*. can be gradually increased. The height should not be too high, however, as this will increase the risk of injury.

Variation

Start the vertical jump with bent legs.

Hints for the coach

The player should land on the front part of the feet, allowing the legs to bend, i.e. the quadriceps muscles are stretched. From a bent-legged position the player jumps explosively upwards. The whole movement should be performed smoothly and include a powerful arm swing during the jump upwards. The angle between the thigh and the vertical should not be more than 60° at the lowest point on landing (see Fig. SM 1), i.e. the thighs remain above the horizontal level. If the player is landing on the heels after jumping down from the box, the height of the box should be lowered. Note: Jumping over a hurdle with a non-fixed horizontal bar is safer than jumping onto a box.

In *b*. the player can practice heading technique while in the air by bending the upper body backwards and then pushing it explosively forwards for the imaginary contact of the forehead with the ball.

Exercise 2 – Hurdle jumping

A player jumps over hurdles (maximum of four) in a continuous motion. The exercise begins with the player standing with both feet together in front of the first hurdle. The player can jump with both legs together, with one leg, or change legs after each jump, e.g. take off with one leg, then land and take off with the other leg, etc. The hurdles should have non-fixed horizontal bars.

Progression

The height of the hurdles can gradually be raised.

Variation

Start by running to the hurdle.

Hints for the coach

The height of the hurdles should never prevent the player from performing the exercise rhythmically. The exercise will not have the desired effect if the player stops after landing.

Goalkeepers performing specific muscle training in order to improve their jumping ability.

Exercise 3

The player jumps up onto a box from a one-leg take off and then jumps off powerfully with the same leg. The other leg drives up while the arms swing forward and up.

Progression

The height of the box can be gradually raised.

Variations

a. Start by running to the box.

b. The non-jumping leg is used for the take-off from the box.

Hints for the coach

The transition from landing on the box to the take-off should be smooth. It should be emphasized that the non take-off leg and the arms should be pulled up powerfully during and after the take-off.

Exercise 4 – Gazelle jumping

Three running steps are followed by a jump with a one leg take-off. The three running steps are then repeated and followed by a take-off with the other leg. The whole cycle is then repeated.

Variations

a. After three running steps, take-off with one leg, then land and take-off with the other leg, then three more running steps. This cycle is repeated. Alternate between left leg and right leg for the first take-off.

b. After three running steps, take-off with one leg, land and take-off with the same leg, then take three more running steps. Repeat the cycle with the other leg.

Hints for the coach

The take-off must be powerful. This is helped by driving the arms and the non take-off leg explosively up to approximately a horizontal level. The jumps should be high and long. Lines can be drawn on the ground for the players to jump between.

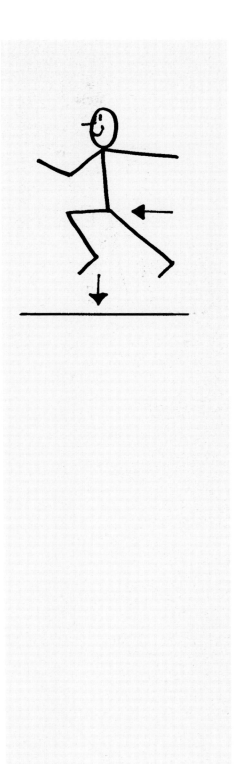

Exercise 5 – Jumping test

Jumping ability can be tested in a simple way. The player jumps up and tries to touch a bar that can be raised and lowered. The highest successful jump is used as the test result. If several players are to be tested at the same time, the test can take the form of a high-jump competition where the height of the bar is gradually increased and each player is given a maximum of three attempts.

Measuring jumping ability before and after a jump training period gives a good indication of how effective the training has been. Testing can also help to motivate the players to train harder (see page 81).

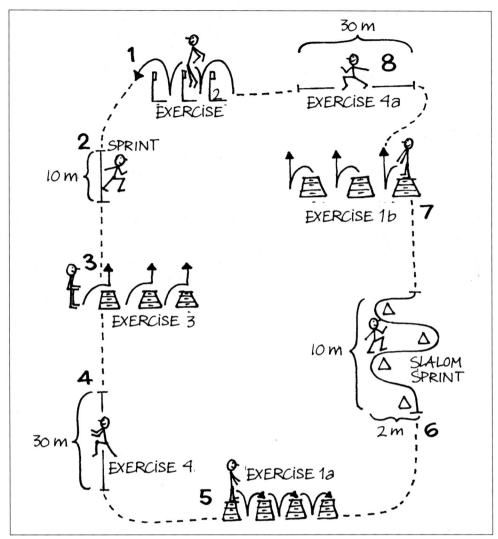

Figure SM 9

1. Exercise 2
2. 10 metre sprint
3. Exercise 3
4. Exercise 4
5. Exercise 1a
6. Slalom sprinting
7. Exercise 1b
8. Exercise 4a

Jumping and sprinting exercises

Figure SM 9 illustrates several examples of jump and sprint training exercises that can be performed in a gym or outside on the field. The exercises are performed at different stations, and together they represent a circuit training programme. Most of the exercises included in the circuit have been described previously. When using this programme it is important that the players do not run between the stations so that each exercise can be performed with a maximum effort.

249

Many activities in soccer demand high force development combined with good coordination of the muscles involved.

Basic strength training – practical applications

Basic strength training can be performed with weight training machines or with free weights. Strength training with free weights is described below, but the same principles apply when using weight machines. To account for the separate forms of contraction of a muscle, the basic strength training can be divided into *isometric*, *concentric*, and *eccentric* muscle strength training (see Fig. SM 1 – page 225).

Eccentric muscle strength training is difficult to perform with machines and free weights because eccentric muscle strength exceeds concentric muscle strength. Since large weight loads are needed, a player will have difficulties in returning the weights to the starting position after each repetition. Therefore, only concentric and isometric strength training is described below.

Concentric strength training

It has been observed that performing concentric strength training with high loads and low velocities can have a beneficial effect on maximal force development at slow contracting speeds, e.g. during a tackle in football. On the other hand, strength training at slow speeds improves strength during fast movements only to a minor extent. Similarly, training with light loads at moderate velocities will mainly increase force development at these speeds and only result in a small improvement in strength at low speeds. Therefore, it is advisable to divide the concentric strength training into *low-* and *high-speed training* (see Fig. SM 1 – page 225). In general for football, the leg muscles should be trained at both low and high speeds, while the muscles of the upper body should be trained mainly at low speeds (see Scheme SM 2 – page 239).

Maximum performance tests

Before starting a strength training programme a baseline measurement of muscle strength for each player should be obtained.

Maximum concentric strength refers to the largest load that can be lifted for a given movement. This is defined as 1RM (RM= repetition maximum). Another measure which is useful for concentric strength training is 5RM. This is the maximum load that can be lifted for five consecutive repetitions of a given movement. In general 1RM is about 1.2 x 5RM. This relationship may be used for estimating the value of 1RM if the value of 5RM is known, and vice-versa. Due to risk of injury the players should not perform the 1RM test until they have become well accustomed to the different exercises and the weight-lifting equipment. It is safer to conduct 5RM determinations, which can be made rather soon after the start of a training programme.

Principle

In concentric strength training different principles may be used. A new principle which allows for muscle groups to be trained at both low and high speeds is described below. It is referred to as the »5-15« principle, as a set consists of either five or 15 repetitions of a given exercise. With a set of five repetitions (low-speed), the load is the same as that for 5RM and with 15 repetitions (high-speed) it is 50% of 5RM (see Scheme SM 3). For example, if the 5RM value has been determined as 38 kg then the low-speed load will be 38 kg and the high-speed load 19 kg.

Scheme SM 3 Principles of basic concentric muscle strength training

	Work load	Number of repetitions	Rest between repetitions (s)	Number of sets
Low-speed	5RM*	5	2-5	2-4
High-speed	50% of 5RM	15	1-3	2-4

* RM: Repetition maximum

		Speed	
		Low	High
Repetitions		5	15
Muscle of the leg			
1. Anterior lower leg muscles	(ex. 1*)		
2. Leg extensors	(ex. 2)		
3. Leg flexors	(ex. 3)		
4. Leg adductors	(ex. 4)		
5. Buttock muscles	(ex. 5)		
Muscles of upper body			
6. Side abdominals	(ex. 6)		
7. Front abdominals	(ex. 7)		
8. Upper back muscles	(ex. 8)		
9. Lower back muscles	(ex. 9)		
10. Chest muscles	(ex. 10)		
11. Shoulder muscles	(ex. 11)		
Muscles of the arm			
12. Arm flexor	(ex. 12)		

* The numbers refer to exercises on pages 256-258.

Scheme SM 4

When 5RM is determined for the various muscle groups scheme SM 4 may be filled in and used during the training. Scheme SM 5 shows an example of how such a scheme may look in practice.

		Speed	
		Low	High
Repetitions		5	15
Muscle of the leg			
1. Anterior lower leg muscles (ex. 1)		100	50
2. Leg extensors (ex. 2)		30	15
3. Leg flexors (ex. 3)		20	10
4. Leg adductors (ex. 4)		–	–
5. Buttock muscles (ex. 5)		60	30
Muscles of upper body			
6. Side abdominals (ex. 6)		6	–
7. Front abdominals (ex. 7)		6	–
8. Upper back muscles (ex. 8)		30	–
9. Lower back muscles (ex. 9)		16	–
10. Chest muscles (ex. 10)		10	–
11. Shoulder muscles (ex. 11)		–	–
Muscles of the arm			
12. Arm flexor (ex. 12)		–	–

Scheme SM 5

Compared to scheme SM 2, scheme SM 5 does not include the anterior lower leg muscles and the deep abdominal muscles. Generally, these muscles are so strong that they do not need to be trained separately.

Organization

Each exercise should be performed with a maximum effort. After each repetition a player should rest a few seconds to allow for a higher force production in the subsequent muscle contraction. A heavier weight load should be followed by a longer rest period (see scheme SM 3).

Quantity

If both low- and high-speed training is needed for a muscle group, then two to four sets of both five and 15 repetitions should be performed. Two to six sets are performed if the muscle group is to be trained either at low- or high-speed (five or 15 repetitions, respectively). For any given muscle group there should be a rest period of at least two minutes between each set. During this time the players can perform exercises for other muscle groups.

Example

A training session based on the above training principle is presented in Scheme SM 5. The player should perform a total of three sets of five and 15 repetitions for the muscle groups 1, 2, 3, and 5 (the numbers refer to Scheme SM 5), and six sets of five repetitions for the muscle groups 6 to 10 (6 and 7 together in one exercise). The training is performed in three identical parts. The players continuously alternate between training the leg muscles and the muscles of the upper body. Scheme SM 6 illustrates part 1.

Scheme SM 6

Exercise	First round Repetition	Second round Repetition
1	15	5
6 + 7	5	5
2	5	15
8	5	5
3	15	5
10	5	5
5	5	15
9	5	5

Parts 2 and 3 are performed in the same way as part 1. If the duration of each set, with subsequent rest periods, is about one minute, each part will last approximately 20 minutes. The whole programme will then take about an hour to complete.

Goalkeepers can especially benefit from strength training. This is illustrated here by the action of the Danish National goalkeeper, Peter Schmeichel, in the final of the 1992 European Championship against Germany.

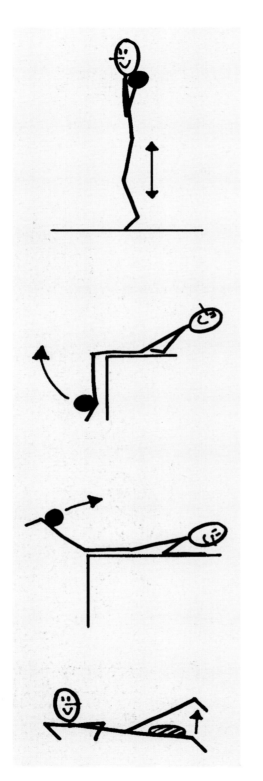

Exercises for basic strength training

Exercise 1 – calf muscles
Push up onto the toes while carrying a weight on the shoulders.

Exercise 2 – Quadriceps muscle
Kick forwards and upwards. Keep the upper-body still.

Exercise 3 – Hamstring muscles
Bend the legs backwards and upwards.

Exercise 4 – Leg adductor muscles
The load, e.g. a sandbag, is fixed on the lower leg and lifted up towards the other leg.

Exercise 5 – Buttock muscles

Lie on a bench with the feet tucked under a fixed object, e.g. a metal bar. The load (weights or a sandbag) is held behind the head. The exercise must be performed with a straight back which should only raise up to the horizontal level.

Exercise 6 – Front abdominal muscles

The legs are lifted off the ground with the knees bent. The load (weights or a sandbag) is held behind the head. The upper body is lifted upwards.

Exercise 7 – Side abdominal muscles

The legs are lifted off the ground with the knees bent (as in Exercise 6). The load (weights or a sandbag) is held behind the head. The upper body turns alternatively to the left and right.

Exercise 8 – Upper back muscles

Sit on a bench and pull the bar down to the neck. The back should be kept straight.

Exercise 9 – Lower back muscles

As in Exercise 5, but with a larger part of the body lying on the bench.

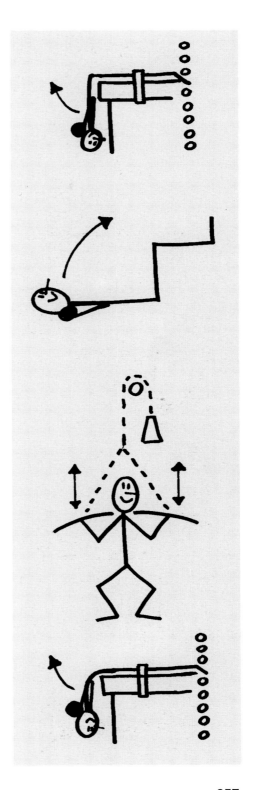

257

Exercise 10 – Chest muscles

With elbows slightly bent, the dumb-bells are moved diagonally backwards and then lifted so that they meet again in front of the body (corresponding to the movement for a throw-in).

Exercise 11 – Shoulder muscles

The arms lift the dumb-bells up to a horizontal level and then slowly lower them.

Exercise 12 – Biceps

Stand against a wall with a straight back. The palms of the hands should be turned up. The bar is lifted to the chest and slowly lowered.

A player's jumping skill is not only dependent on the basic strength of the involved muscles, but also on the player's ability to coordinate the muscles and to time the take-off.

Progression – concentric strength training

The first strength training sessions may be used to introduce the players to the equipment and to determine 5RM values.

During an intensive strength training period new 5RM determinations should be made about every third week so that training loads can be adjusted according to the acquired strength gains. This is necessary in order to achieve further improvements in strength. Figure SM 10 shows typical improvements in strength during a strength training period.

Example

After the initial introduction the 5RM load for a given muscle group, e.g. calf muscles, is determined to be 90 kg. In this case the training loads will be:

5RM	5RM-50%5RM
80	40

After three weeks the 5RM load is determined to be 105 kg, so the training loads will now be:

5RM	5RM-50%5RM
100	50

After another three weeks the 5RM load has increased to 115 kg, so the training loads will now be:

5RM	5RM-50%5RM
110	55

Isometric strength training

When performing isometric strength training it is important to train the muscles at joint angles that are relevant to football.

Determination of maximum isometric strength

Maximum isometric strength is defined as the largest load a player can hold in a specified position for five seconds. As with concentric strength training, the players will need time to become accustomed to the exercise before a maximum test is performed.

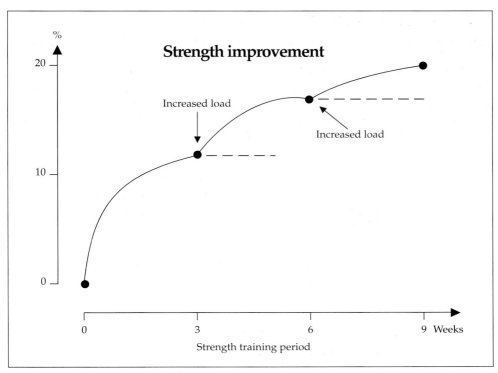

Figure SM 10
The figure illustrates increase in muscle strength during a nine-week strength training period in which the weight load was increased after three and six weeks. The dotted-line illustrates a hypothetical change in strength without an increase in the load during the period.

Principle
A large weight load (representing 85-100% of the maximum strength for a given joint angle) is held in a given position for five to 15 seconds (see Scheme SM 7). A set consists of about 10 repetitions separated by rest periods of approximately equal duration as the work time. There should be at least three minutes of rest between each set. During each training session, between two and four sets should be performed for each muscle group.

Scheme SM 7 *Principles of basic isometric muscle strength training*

Work load	Number of repetitions	Rest between repetitions (s)	Number of sets
85-100% of maximum held for 5-15 s	5-10	Same as exercise duration	2-4

For isometric strength training the exercises described on pages 256-258 may be performed holding the positions at joint angles which are specific to football. It should be noted that isometric strength of the leg adductor muscles is of importance for the prevention of injuries in the groin. The simple exercise described below may be used for improving the isometric strength of this muscle group.

Exercise 13 – Leg adductor muscles (isometric strength)
A ball is placed between the legs and both legs press inward to compress the ball.

Muscle endurance training

Training a group of muscles by repeating the same movement for more than 15 seconds is called muscle endurance training.

Aims

To increase endurance of a muscle in order to:

1. Improve the capacity of the muscle to sustain exercise.

2. Improve the ability of the muscle to recover after intense exercise. The muscle can thereby perform high-intensity contractions more frequently during a game.

Application to football

Most of a football player's muscles need to have a high concentric and a moderate isometric endurance capacity, whereas eccentric endurance is of less importance.

Any form of exercise helps to maintain or improve the endurance of the active muscles. This means that by regular training and matches, players can develop a high level of muscle endurance, especially for the leg muscles. For the muscles of the upper body however, it may be beneficial to develop a higher level of endurance. This can be obtained by muscle endurance training. Scheme SM 8 summarizes the recommended priority of endurance training for the muscles of the upper body.

Types of muscle endurance training

Muscle endurance training can be divided into *isometric* and *concentric* muscle endurance training, of which the latter can be divided into muscle speed and long-term endurance training (see Fig. SM 1 – page 225). In muscle speed endurance training, which is primarily a form of anaerobic training for the active muscle group, the exercises are performed at a high speed for a duration of between 15 and 60 seconds. A lower exercise speed is used for long-term endurance training and here the energy is primarily supplied aerobically. This section will focus on isometric and muscle speed endurance training as long-term muscle endurance is generally trained sufficiently during ordinary football training.

Scheme SM 8

	Concentric speed		Isometric
	low	high	
Muscles of upper body			
Abdominal muscles:			
Side	●	⊕	●
Front	●	⊕	●
Deep	⊕	○	●
Back:			
Upper	●	⊕	●
Lower	●	⊕	●
Chest muscles	○	○	○
Shoulder muscles	○	○	⊕
Neck muscles	○	○	○
Muscles of the arm			
Arm flexor (biceps)	⊕	○	⊕
Arm extensor (triceps)	○	○	○
Explanation of symbols:	Priority in muscle endurance training:		
	○ = low		
	⊕ = moderate		
	● = high		

During muscle endurance training, it is important that the muscles work in a similar way as when playing football since the improvements are specific to the type of exercise used during the training. For example, concentric muscle endurance training does not improve isometric muscle endurance and vice-versa (see scheme SM 1 – page 226). Scheme SM 8 can be used to ensure that the muscles are trained in an efficient way. Large improvements in concentric and isometric endurance can be achieved in a relatively short period of time (see scheme SM 1). These improvements are, however, lost very rapidly if the endurance training is not maintained. Coaches at all levels of the game have traditionally used circuit training programmes or similar forms of muscle endurance training during the pre-season period. Towards the start of the season, however, this type of training is often terminated and most of the increases in endurance are lost.

Figure SM 11
In the figure the solid-line represents endurance capacity of a muscle group during a four-week period of intensive muscle endurance training and during the following four weeks without muscle endurance training. The dotted-line shows the endurance level during an eight-week period of regular muscle endurance training with short sessions.
When the intensive programme was performed a considerable increase in muscle endurance was obtained, but the endurance was rapidly lost after the training had stopped. After six weeks, the endurance was poorer compared to that obtained by the regular programme with short training sessions in spite of less total time having been spent on the latter training.

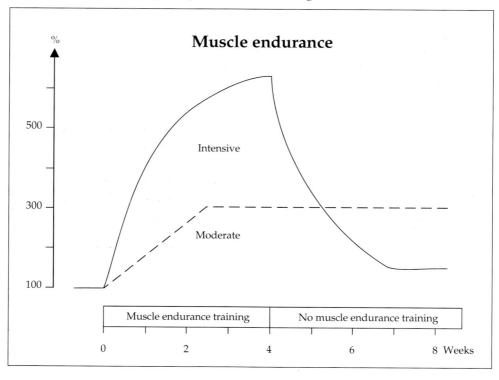

Figure SM 11 gives an example of muscle endurance for a player before, during, and after an intensive circuit training period. The player showed major improvements in muscle endurance as a result of a four-week circuit training period, but most of the endurance gained was lost three weeks after the cessation of this form of training. Thus, the overall effect of the circuit training was poor. It has also been demonstrated that this type of training only has a very small effect on the maximum oxygen uptake.

Instead of using time-consuming circuit programmes during the pre-season period, it is more suitable to introduce and have the players regularly perform a football-related muscle endurance programme lasting less than 10 minutes. It should consist of exercises that can be performed both outdoors and indoors as the programme should be performed throughout the year. The effect of such a programme is illustrated in Fig. SM 11.

It is most efficient to perform muscle endurance training at the end of a training session just prior to the stretching exercises.

Organization

The exercises are performed for 15 to 60 seconds, either at a fixed joint angle (isometric) or as a concentric movement at a constant frequency (see Scheme SM 9). The exercise should be repeated two to four times for each muscle group separated by rest periods of equal duration as the exercise periods.

Scheme SM 9 Principles of muscle endurance training

Training form	Work	Duration		Number of sets
		exercise (s)	rest (s)	
Muscle speed endurance	Constant frequency (20-60 per min)	15-60	as exercise duration	2-4
Isometric endurance	50-80% of maximal force	15-60	as exercise duration	2-4

Exercises

The exercises below make up a muscle endurance programme, including both isometric and concentric exercises, which is suitable for football players.

Exercise 1 – Front abdominal muscles (concentric)
While laying on the back the legs are lifted off the ground with the knees bent. The upper body is lifted up.

Exercise 2 – Back muscles (isometric)
While laying on the stomach the upper body is lifted and the arms are stretched forward. This position is held and the player looks down at the floor.

Exercise 3 – Side abdominal muscles (concentric)
While laying on the back the legs are lifted off the ground with the knees bent. The upper body turns alternatively to the left and right.

Exercise 4 – Lower back muscles (isometric)
While laying on the stomach the legs are kept straight and lifted so that the thighs do not touch the floor. The arms are stretched forward and rest on the floor. This position is maintained and the player looks down at the floor.

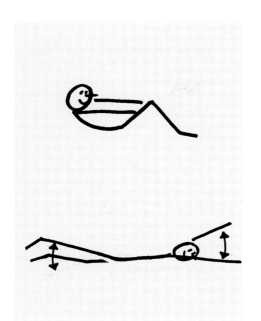

Exercise 5 – Front abdominal muscles (isometric)

While laying on the back the legs are bent with the feet on the ground. The upper body is lifted so that the hands are beside the knees. The lower back is pressed onto the ground and this position is held.

Exercise 6 – Back muscles (concentric)

While laying on the stomach one leg and the arm opposite the leg are moved up and down. The player looks down at the floor.

Players performing a muscle endurance training exercise (Exercise 6).

Sub-study

To experience the effect of muscle endurance training the following simple experiment can be carried out. To test the endurance of the abdominal muscles, determine how many sit-ups a player can perform at a given frequency (e.g. 30 per minute) from the starting position illustrated on Fig. SM 12. The test should be performed both before and at the end of a period of endurance training for the abdominal muscles, as well as one month after the training. The test should be supervised to ensure that the exercise is performed correctly and to record the time to fatigue.

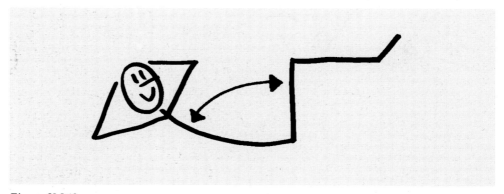

Figure SM 12
The figure illustrates an exercise for the abdominal muscles which may be used in the experiment on muscle endurance training.

Scheme to use for the study

	Before	After	One month after
Number of abdominal exercises			

Compare the results obtained with the numbers shown in Figure SM 11 – (see page 264).

During match-play the muscles develop high forces in various actions. In a tackle the leg muscles work isometrically.

Summary

By training muscle strength and muscle endurance, performance of a muscle can increase to a higher level than can be attained by just playing football. In order to set up an efficient programme for specific muscle training, several factors need to be considered. Of major importance are the type and speed of the movements used during training. The muscles should be trained in a manner that resembles actions in football.

269

Planning the Season

Planning the Season

Football players need a high level of fitness to cope with the physical demands of a game and to allow for their technical skills to be utilized throughout a match. Therefore, fitness training is an important part of the overall training programme. However, the amount of emphasis placed on fitness training depends on several factors, such as the players' competency in other areas of the game (see Fig. PL 1 – page 274), and the exercise intensity during training sessions which are not specifically designed to develop fitness.

When planning fitness training the phases of a football year should be taken into account. A year can be divided into a pre-season, a season, and a mid-season break. This chapter will focus on how to prioritize the various areas of fitness training throughout the year. The description will be divided into general fitness training and specific muscle training. It should be emphasized that due to specific demands of a team there may be major deviations in the priority of the aspects of fitness training. Furthermore, a coach should be prepared to change or adjust a planned training session at any time, e.g. it may sometimes be appropriate to avoid intensive training in order to allow the players to rest mentally and physically.

General fitness training

Pre-season

The term »pre-season« covers the period between the last match of one season and the first match of the next. The pre-season can be sub-divided into a *maintenance period* and a *re-building period*. The maintenance period is from the last match of the previous season to the resumption of team training, and the re-building period is from the resumption of team training until the first match of the next season. The duration of these periods varies from country to country. In some countries the maintenance period is about eight weeks and the re-building period five to eight weeks. In other countries the total pre-season period is four to six months with a maintenance period of two to three months.

Traditionally, the maintenance period has been used for mental recovery with very little physical training, and the first month of the re-building period has focused mainly on fitness training with an emphasis on long distance

Figure PL 1
The figure shows a hypothetical example of how two teams differ in quality within the four main areas of football, i.e. social/psychological, tactical, technical, and physical. The two teams are of the same fitness level but team 1 is superior in the other areas. Therefore, team 1 should spend more time on fitness training than team 2, which should focus on improving its tactical and technical abilities.

running and muscle endurance training. The training at the beginning of the re-building period has often been very intensive as coaches want to ensure that players reach »top form« for the start of the competitive season. This can partly explain why a high frequency of injuries occur during this period. A more efficient way of planning the pre-season training is described below.

The maintenance period

(from the end of one season to approximately eight weeks before the start of the next season)

By maintaining a certain amount of endurance training after the end of the season, the decrease in fitness, which always occurs after cessation of normal training and competition, will be minimized. This means that the players will have a good basic fitness level for the start of the re-building period. In order to help the players to relax mentally, parts of the training in the maintenance period can consist of other ball games, e.g. field hockey or basketball. The number of training sessions per week is dependent on many factors, but between one and four times per week, with additional individual training, may be suitable. During the last month before the re-building period the training frequency should be increased to at least two sessions per week.

Detailed planning
An example of the training frequency and exercise intensity for non-professional players during a week in the maintenance period is illustrated in Scheme PL 1. The intensity of the training is represented by a number (scale: 1-5). A higher number indicates a higher intensity. Training with intensity 3 or 4 in the maintenance period should be regarded as training with the main aim of improving or maintaining the level of fitness.

Scheme PL 1

Time period	0 - 15	15 - 30	30 - 45	45 - 60	60 - 75	75 - 90	minutes
Day:							
Monday	Warm-up	3	3	4	3	3	Recovery
Thursday	Warm-up	3	3	3	4	3	Recovery

Recovery = Recovery activities

The re-building period
(approximately eight weeks before the start of the season)

During the re-building period fitness training should mainly consist of games and exercises with a ball. This ensures that the relevant muscles are being trained, and allows for technical and tactical aspects to be practiced under physically taxing conditions. As the start of the season approaches, the number of training sessions should be gradually increased. In some countries the playing surface is changed (e.g. sand/gravel to grass) during the re-building period which can cause problems for the players as their muscles are stressed in a different way. In order to decrease the risk of injury the transition between playing surfaces should be gradual.

During the re-building period training matches are a good and appropriate form of fitness training, but they should not be played before the players are prepared physically for the demands of a full match.

Training camps
Clubs often organize a training camp or tour during the re-building period. This may be for a week or just a couple of days. Unfortunately, many coaches consider training camps to be a good opportunity to develop high levels of fitness, and therefore include up to three intensive training sessions per day. This is a mistake which invariably results in many injuries. Many teams,

including top-class teams, return from training camps with several injured players and a group of players who are both physically and mentally exhausted.

Training camps should be renamed »recovery« camps, and fitness training should not be the most important aspect of such a camp. Having the team assembled for an extended period of time can have many benefits. Since the players are together under less stressful circumstances than normally, it can enhance team spirit, and more time can be spent on developing technical skills and tactical strategies, both in theory and practice.

Detailed planning

An example of the training frequency and exercise intensity for a typical week for a non-professional team during the re-building period is illustrated in Scheme PL 2 (the total duration of a training session is 90 minutes).

Week schedule

Time period	0 - 15	15 - 30	30 - 45	45 - 60	60 - 75	75 - 90	minutes
Day							
Monday	Warm-up	3	3	4	3	3	Recovery
Tuesday	Warm-up	3	5	3	4	3	Recovery
Thursday	Warm-up	3	5	2	4	3	Recovery
Saturday	Warm-up		Training match				

Scheme PL 2

Explanation of codes:

1 = Very low intensity.   *4 = High intensity.*
2 = Low intensity.   *5 = Very high intensity.*
3 = Moderate intensity.

The intensity of the training is represented by a number (1-5). A higher number indicates a higher intensity. Only periods with an intensity of 4 or 5 should be considered as fitness training, i.e. training which is performed with the main purpose of improving the physical capacity of the players. During periods with an intensity of 2 or 3, priority is placed on other areas of the game, such as tactical strategy.

It may be advantageous for players to work in smaller groups during the re-building period. A training model which is easy to organize and which can also have a motivating effect on the players is »station«-training. Figure PL 2 shows three examples of how »station«-training may be organized. There are 3 or 4 stations where either an $Aerobic_{LI}$ or an $Aerobic_{HI}$ game is played.

276

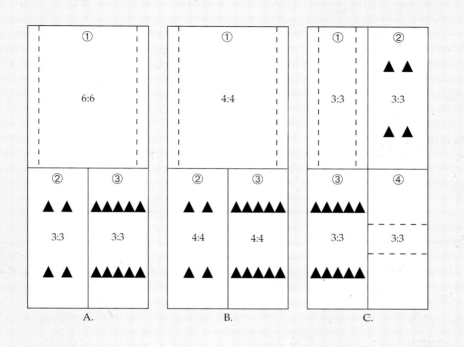

Figure PL 2
The figure gives three examples of how »station training« can be organized. There are three stations in A and B, and four in C. Twenty-four players are divided into two teams.

In A there are 12 players (six from each team) at station ①, and six players (three from each team) at station ② and ③. After a given time-period the players change stations. The players from stations ② and ③ rotate to station ①, while the players from station ① advance to station ② and ③. After one more period, the players from stations ② and ③ return to station ①, while the players from station ① go to the station where they have not yet been. With this kind of organization the players will have the same six opponents.

In B there are eight players (four from each team) at each station, and in C there are six players (three from each team) at each of the four stations. When changing stations in B and C, the two teams at a station move in opposite directions so that the opponents change (the players will meet again).

The players may alternate between performing an Aerobic$_{LI}$ and an Aerobic$_{HI}$ game. This can be achieved by performing Aerobic$_{LI}$ games at stations ② and ③, and Aerobic$_{HI}$ games at stations ① and ④. Examples of games:

Station 1: Game 1, page 170
Station 2: Ordinary football play but with scoring both from in front of and from behind a goal.
Station 3: Game 1, page 154
Station 4: Game 1, page 166

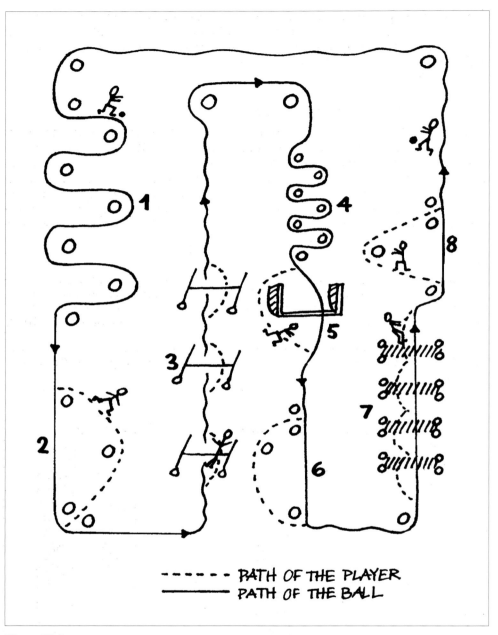

Figure PL 3

The figure shows an example of an obstacle course that can be performed with a ball. The solid-line shows the path of the ball and the dotted-line illustrates the course of the player.

Explanation of codes:
(1): slalom dribbling; (2): passing the ball forward and meeting it again after running around the cones; (3): passing the ball forward and then jumping over hurdles; (4): same as (1); (5): passing the ball over a big goal and retrieving it on the other side; (6): same as (2); (7): passing the ball forward and meeting it after jumping across the marked areas; (8): same as (2).

If bad weather prevents access to a good playing surface, the players can run with the ball around an obstacle course. Players are easily motivated by this type of training, and at the same time they exercise using movements specific to football. An example of an obstacle course is shown in Fig. PL 3.

Effect of pre-season training

A top-class Danish team followed a pre-season training schedule similar to the one described above. Six weeks before the start of the re-building period the players trained twice a week. The training frequency during the re-building period was gradually increased to five times per week. The fitness level of the players was evaluated with a number of tests before and after the re-building period. The results of these tests are shown in Fig. PL 4 and are compared to results obtained during the season. Although the increase in

Figure PL 4
The figure shows the maximum oxygen uptake and the endurance capacity of players on a Danish elite team on three occasions during the year: towards the end of February – just before the players started the re-building period; in the beginning of April – just after the start of the season; and in the middle of June – during the first half of the season. The values are expressed in relation to those obtained in February (100%).
During the re-building period the maximum oxygen uptake and endurance capacity were only slightly lower than during the season. Thus, the short re-building period was sufficiently long for the players to reach a high fitness level.

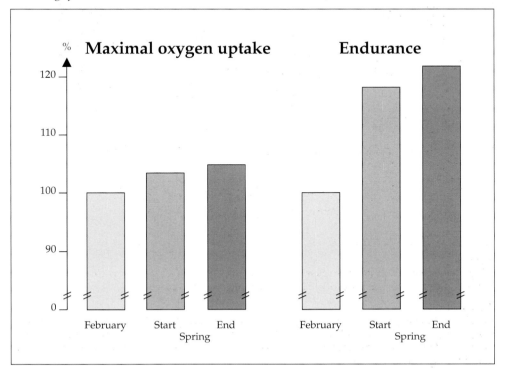

maximum oxygen uptake was rather small during the re-building period, the level obtained was almost as high as that during the season. More impressive was the large increase in endurance capacity during the re-building period. The ability of the players to exercise for prolonged periods of time was almost as good at the start of the season as it was during the season. This demonstrates that it is possible for the players to have a high level of fitness before the start of the season by means of this structuring of the pre-season period. When the season started the team had no injured players and went on to win the first three matches.

Tests results from players in the Danish club Brøndby, who were competing in the 1987 European Cup, also demonstrate that it is possible to reach a high level of fitness in a relatively short period of time, provided that the initial fitness level is already fairly high. These players were tested three times during the year: in early January before an intensive preparation period for a European Cup quarter-final match, in early March, a few days before this match, and in October during the season. The results showed that the players' physical capacity at the time before the match was just as high as during the season (see Fig. PL 5).

These studies demonstrate that football players can reach peak physical performance at the beginning of the season, even with a short re-building period (5-8 weeks) in the club. However, this is assuming that there has not been a marked decrease in the physical capacity during the maintenance period.

To prepare for a European Cup quarter final match against O'Porto, the players on the Danish team Brøndby had to reach peak fitness level during an eight-week re-building period.

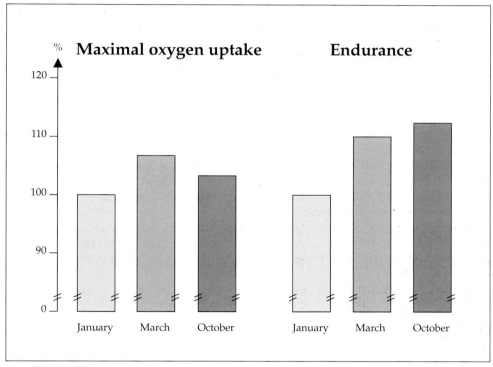

Figure PL 5
The figure shows the maximum oxygen uptake and the endurance capacity of players from the Danish team Brøndby on three occasions during 1987: in the beginning of January – just prior to the start of the re-building period; in the middle of March – just before a European Cup match; and in October – during the second half of the season. The values are expressed in relation to those obtained in January (100%). During the re-building period the maximum oxygen uptake reached a level which was slightly higher than during the season, whereas the endurance capacity after the re-building period was slightly lower than during the season. Thus, the relatively short re-building period was long enough to enable the players to reach an adequate fitness level.

Beginning the re-building period with a relatively high fitness level will allow for a slow development of the players' physical capacity when club training starts again, and time can be spent on improving other performance characteristics in football, e.g. technical skills. By a gradual transition between individual training out of the club and the training at the club, the muscles are well prepared for high-intensity exercise. In this way muscle soreness, which is especially common after the first training sessions during the start of the re-building period, can be avoided. The risk of getting injured is reduced and the players are often well-motivated when training eventually becomes more intensive. In addition, there is a lower risk of both mental and physical »overtraining«. In northern countries where pre-season training occurs in the winter, postponing the re-building period means that fewer training sessions will be performed under difficult weather conditions.

Figure PL 6 shows changes in physical performance during the pre-season with three different forms of planning. A comparison is made between the changes in physical performance achieved by pre-season training according to the above suggested planning, and programmes with no training during the maintenance period and with either a shorter or longer re-building period.

Summary – Pre-season

The pre-season period can be divided into a maintenance period and a re-building period. During the maintenance period mainly Aerobic$_{LI}$ training should be performed to ensure a good physical foundation before the start of the re-building period. During the re-building period it is important to play matches regularly at a high competitive level. Such matches should be supplemented by frequent sessions of Aerobic$_{HI}$ training, speed training, and for elite players, speed endurance training. Training camps are recommended but should not be used primarily to increase the physical capacity of the players. Scheme PL 3 indicates how much priority should be given to the individual forms of training during the maintenance and re-building periods. The higher the number (1-5), the more important the training form.

Scheme PL 3

| | Pre-season | | | |
	Maintenance period		Re-building period	
Aerobic				
Low-intensity training	3344*	4444	4455	5555
High-intensity training	2223	3234	4445	4555
Anaerobic				
** Speed endurance training	1111	1111	2234	4555
Speed training	1111	1111	2234	4555

  * Each value represents one week.
 ** The extent of speed endurance training is dependent on the performance level of the team.

Explanation of codes:

1 = *Very low priority (need not be trained).*
2 = *Low priority (may be trained).*
3 = *Moderate priority (should preferably be trained).*
4 = *High priority (should be trained).*
5 = *Very high priority (must be trained).*

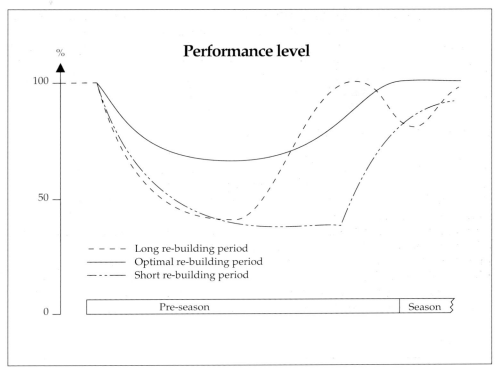

Figure PL 6
The figure provides a theoretical illustration of the changes in a player's fitness level as a result of structuring the pre-season in the way recommended in the text (solid-line). Also included are the changes in fitness level with two other programmes in which no training was performed during the maintenance period, and the re-building period was either long (dotted-line) or short (double dotted-line).

By maintaining a certain level of activity during the maintenance period, the decrease in fitness level after the season is reduced and the players can reach peak performance with a relatively short re-building period. With a long re-building period the players may peak before the season, whereas with a short re-building period the players may not have a sufficient fitness level at the start of the season, if they do not train during the maintenance period.

Season

During the season the level of fitness achieved during the re-building period should be maintained and perhaps even improved.

Studies have shown that there is a relationship between the standard of play and the amount of high-speed running during a match, so players should have a high ability to repeatedly perform intense exercise. This capacity can be improved by Aerobic$_{HI}$ training and anaerobic training. Coaches do not always put sufficient emphasis on these types of training during the season. In a study with Danish top-class players, the effect of a seven-week mid-season break consisting of three weeks of holiday followed by a four-week re-building period was evaluated. After the re-building period, the players were better at performing high-intensity exercise compared to before the mid-season break (see Fig. PL 7). Apparently the intensity of the training during the first half of the season had not been high enough. In another study with Danish top-class players, heart rate was measured during several matches and during the type of training which the coach considered to be the most physically demanding. During the matches the heart rate was on average higher than 170 beats/min for about 25% of the game, while the

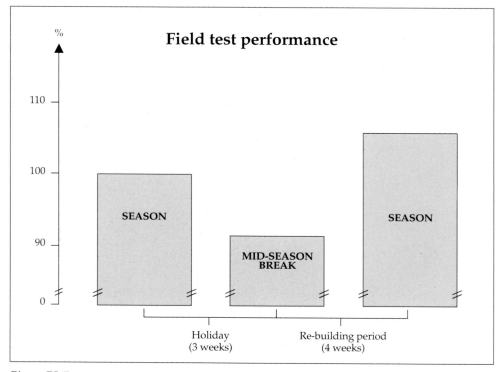

Figure PL 7

The figure shows performance in a field test performed during the season, after three weeks of holiday, and after a four-week re-building period (start of the second half of the season). The values are expressed in relation to the level during the season (100%)

The players showed a better performance after the re-building period compared to during the season, suggesting that the players' ability to perform intense exercise was not high enough during the season. For further results from this study see Fig. PL 10 (page 290).

corresponding period during training was 4% (see Fig. PL 8). Thus, the exercise intensity during the fitness training was considerably lower than the intensity during the matches.

The endurance capacity of players may be maintained by regularly supplementing the match programme with prolonged training sessions (once or twice per week) that include $Aerobic_{LI}$ games. It is essential that the exercise intensity is fairly high and that there are only short interruptions during the sessions.

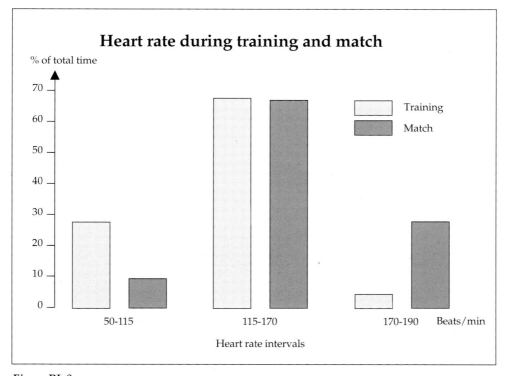

Figure PL 8
The figure compares heart rate of Danish top-class players during fitness training and during a match. The values are expressed in percent of training time and match time, respectively. The time periods when heart rate was between 50-115 (to the left), 115-170 (in the middle), and 170-190 beats/min (to the right) are shown. It is clear that the players' heart rates were consistently higher during the matches compared to the training, indicating that the exercise intensity during the training was considerably lower than during the matches.

Detailed planning

An example of the training frequency and intensity for a typical week during the season is illustrated in Scheme PL 4.

Week schedule *Scheme PL 4*

Time period	0 - 15	15 - 30	30 - 45	45 - 60	60 - 75	75 - 90	minutes
Day:							
Monday	Warm-up	3	3	3	Recovery		
Tuesday	Warm-up	3	5	3	4	3	Recovery
Thursday	Warm-up	5	2	4	4	3	Recovery
Saturday	Warm-up	2	3	2	Recovery		
Sunday				Match			

Explanation of codes:

1 = Very low intensity. *4 = High intensity.*
2 = Low intensity. *5 = Very high intensity.*
3 = Moderate intensity.

The intensity of the training is represented by a number (1-5). A higher number indicates a higher intensity (for further explanation see page 276).

The schedule presented is representative of a training pattern for a non-professional team with four training sessions per week. A team that trains twice a week can follow the training intensities for Tuesday and Thursday. Naturally, the absolute training intensity will be lower than that expected of an elite team, but the general outline can still be followed.

For a top-class club with part-time or full-time professionals, it is reasonable to include Wednesday as an extra training day. Training twice per day may be performed on certain days, e.g. Tuesday and/or Thursday. For the top-class players it is important to get adequate rest, and to eat and drink properly between training sessions (see pages 299 and 319). Some of the training sessions should be less demanding, e.g. practise of free-kicks and corners.

During the season or a tournament the players may perform alternative activities in order to relax both physically and mentally.

Summary – season

Aerobic$_{HI}$ training should be given a high priority during a season. Speed training, and for top-class players, speed endurance training, should also be performed regularly. Endurance capacity may be maintained by frequently including prolonged training sessions with only short rest periods. Scheme PL 5 indicates how much priority should be given to each form of training during the season. The higher the number (1-5), the more important the type of training.

Scheme PL 5

| | Season | | | | | | |
	First half			Second half			
Aerobic							
Low-intensity training	4343*	4343	433	343	4343	4343	4343
High-intensity training	5555	5555	555	555	5555	5555	5444
Anaerobic							
**Speed endurance training	3453	4534	543	453	4534	5345	3453
Speed training	5555	5555	555	555	5555	5555	5544

* Each value represents one week.
** The extent of speed endurance training is dependent on the performance level of the team.

Explanation of codes:

1 = Very low intensity.
2 = Low intensity.
3 = Moderate intensity.
4 = High intensity.
5 = Very high intensity.

Mid-season break

In some countries the season is divided into two halves separated by a mid-season break, which can be from four to 18 weeks. Like the pre-season, the mid-season break can be divided into a maintenance period and a re-building period.

A study was conducted with a top-class Danish club in an attempt to clarify how much and what type of training should be performed during these periods. The players were monitored before, during, and after a seven-week mid-season break. The players did not train during the first three weeks, and during the following four weeks they trained with a main focus on improving physical capacity (see Fig. PL 9).

The results from the study are illustrated in Figs. PL 8 (see page 284) and PL 10 (see page 290). As expected, the three-week holiday caused a considerable decrease in performance capacity, but after the four-week re-building period the players performed better in a high-intensity exercise test compared to before the holiday period. However, after the re-building period the endurance capacity had not returned to the level before the break.

Figure PL 9
The figure shows the training activities of a group of Danish elite players before, during, and after a three-week holiday. The values are expressed in relation to the activity level before the holiday (100%). The level of physical activity decreased markedly during the holidays, whereas the activity level was slightly higher during the re-building period compared to before the holiday period.

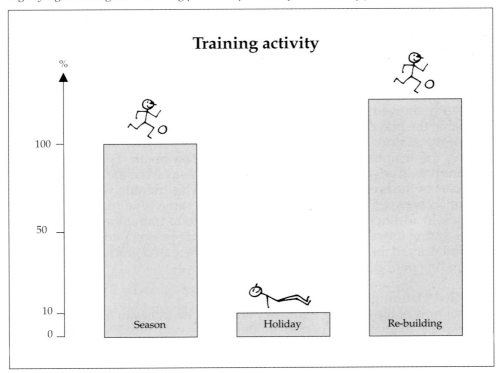

Summary – mid-season break

The mid-season break can be divided into a maintenance period and a re-building period. It is important that the players are active during the maintenance period to ensure a gradual transition between the two periods. Towards the start of the second half of the season high-intensity training should be emphasized. Scheme PL 8 shows an example of how much priority should be given to each form of training during a seven-week mid-season break. The higher the number (1-5), the more important the type of training.

Scheme PL 8

| | Mid-season break | |
	Maintenance period	Re-building period
Aerobic		
Low-intensity training	444*	454
High-intensity training	333	455
Anaerobic		
**Speed endurance training	111	354
Speed training	222	455

* Each value represents one week.
** The extent of speed endurance training is dependent on the performance level of the team.

Explanation of codes:

1 = Very low priority (need not be trained).
2 = Low priority (may be trained).
3 = Moderate priority (should preferably be trained).
4 = High priority (should be trained).
5 = Very high priority (must be trained).

During a mid-season break it is important to perform aerobic low-intensity training.

Specific muscle training

The extent of specific muscle training should be determined by the training time available and should only take up a minor part of the total training over the year.

Muscle strength

A long-term training programme, with two or more training sessions per week, is necessary to achieve significant improvements in muscle strength. Strength can, however, be maintained by training only once a week (see Fig. PL 11). Therefore, it is recommended to give strength training a high priority during the pre-season period when more time is available, particularly during the maintenance period when playing football is given a low priority. During the re-building period it is appropriate to reduce the amount of basic strength training and instead emphasize functional muscle strength training.

Figure PL 11
The figure shows muscle strength before and after a 10-week period of strength training performed three times a week, as well as after a period when the strength training was reduced to once a week. The values are expressed in relation to the level before the strength training period (100%).
During the period of frequent strength training the subjects had a marked increase in muscle strength, and they were able to maintain their improvement in the following weeks despite a reduction in the training frequency to once a week. Thus, muscle strength can be maintained with limited training.

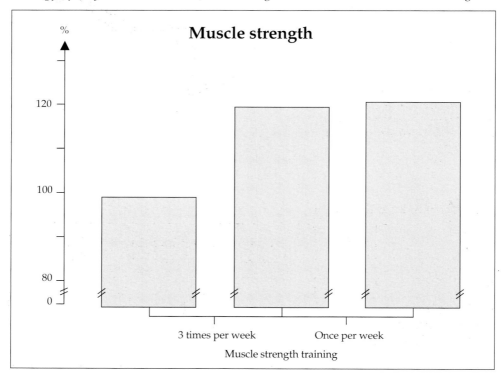

During the season, the amount of basic strength training should be reduced to a level where muscle strength can be maintained. In this way the strength training will not have a negative effect on other areas of performance, such as coordination, once the season has started.

Sub-study

To examine changes in muscle strength a simple experiment can be carried out.

The 5RM value for the quadriceps muscle of one leg is determined as the heaviest weight that the player can raise from an angle of 90º between the lower leg and the thigh to full extension (horizontal) five consecutive times (see Fig. PL 12). The test should be performed before and immediately after a strength training period of approximately 10 weeks, in which the quadriceps muscle has been trained concentrically. The test should be repeated about a month after the end of the strength training period.

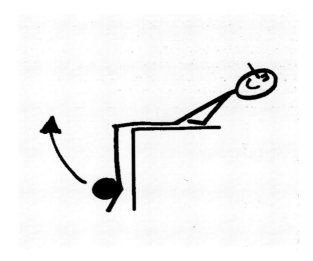

Figure PL 12
The figure illustrates an exercise for the quadriceps muscle which may be used in the experiment on muscle strength training.

Scheme to use for the study

	Before	After 4 weeks	Immediately after	A month after
Strength of the quadriceps muscle (5RM)				

Muscle endurance

It is possible to greatly improve muscle endurance in a short time (see Scheme SM 1 – page 226). However, muscle endurance is lost very rapidly if it is not maintained through training (see Fig. SM 11 – page 264). Therefore, periodical training of muscle endurance does not serve any purpose. It is more appropriate to use a short muscle endurance programme (see page 266) that is performed throughout the entire year, with the possible exception of the maintenance period in the pre-season, when it can be reduced.

Summary – Specific muscle training

In the first part of the pre-season it is feasible to emphasize basic strength training. As the start of the season approaches, the amount of basic strength training should be reduced, and more time should be allocated to functional strength training and playing football. The amount of muscle endurance training should be fairly consistent throughout the year. The time which traditionally has been spent on muscle endurance training during the re-building period may instead be used for strength training.

Scheme PL 9 illustrates how much priority should be given to each form of specific muscle training. The higher the number (1-5), the more important the type of training.

	Maintenance period		Re-building period		Season
Muscle strength training					
Basic	3334	5555	5543	2222	2222
Functional	2222	3333	3344	4343	4343
Muscle endurance	1111	1112	3333	3333	3333

Scheme PL 9

Explanation of codes:

1 = *Very low priority (need not be trained).*
2 = *Low priority (may be trained).*
3 = *Moderate priority (should preferably be trained).*
4 = *High priority (should be trained).*
5 = *Very high priority (must be trained).*

	Pre-season				Season			Break	Season			
Aerobic training												
Low-intensity	3344	4444	4455	5555	4343	4343	4334	4445	4343	4343	4343	4343
High-intensity	2223	3234	4445	4555	5555	5555	5553	3345	5555	5555	5555	5444
Anaerobic training												
*Speed endurance	1111	1111	2234	4555	3453	4534	5431	1135	4453	4534	5345	3453
Speed	1111	1111	2234	4555	5555	5555	5552	2245	5555	5555	5555	5544
Muscle strength training												
Basic	3334	5555	5543	2222	2222	2222	2222	2222	2222	2222	2222	2222
Functional	2222	3333	3344	4343	4343	4343	4343	4343	4343	4343	4343	4322
Muscle endurance training	1111	1112	3333	3333	3333	3333	3333	3333	3333	3333	3333	3322
Flexibility training	3232	3434	4444	4444	4444	4444	4444	4444	4444	4444	4444	4444

* The extent of speed endurance training is dependent on the performance level of the team.

Explanation of codes: See page 296.

Summary

Scheme PL 10 evaluates the priority of the different types of fitness training during various periods of the year. The higher the number (1-5), the more important the form of training. The scheme is based on an eight-month season with a six-week mid-season break (for practical reasons each month is assumed to have four weeks).
The planning of training is contingent upon the level of competition. Fitness training for recreational players that train a couple of times per week should mainly focus on aerobic training and anaerobic speed training. Players that are training more often should emphasize Aerobic$_{HI}$ training and anaerobic speed endurance training. For elite players, fitness training should also include specific muscle training, particularly muscle strength training.

Nutrition

Nutrition

In this chapter the importance of nutrition in football is discussed and dietary recommendations to accommodate nutritional requirements for training and matches are provided.

Muscle glycogen utilization during football

During a football match carbohydrate is used for the production of energy (see page 32). Figure NU 1 (see page 302) shows the relative amount of carbohydrate, which is stored as glycogen, in the quadriceps muscle of a group of Swedish players before a match, at half-time, and after the match. The low level of muscle glycogen at half-time and after the match illustrates that a large amount of carbohydrate was used.

For four of the players the muscle glycogen stores were almost depleted after the first half. From video-film analysis it was found that these four players covered considerably less distance than the other players during the second half, thus indicating that their level of physical performance was reduced by the low muscle glycogen levels. It can be assumed that the players would have been better prepared for the second half if the muscle glycogen stores had been higher prior to the match.

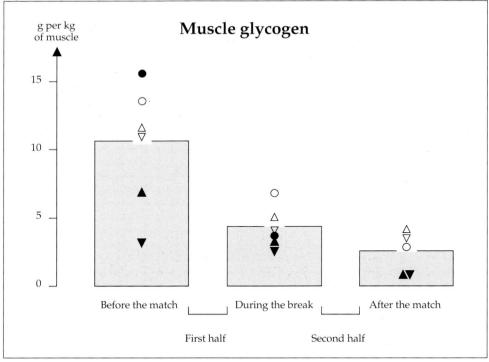

Figure NU 1
The figure shows the average and individual values of glycogen in a quadriceps muscle of six players before, during half-time, and after a match. Before the match two of the players had low muscle glycogen stores and at half-time most of the players had almost depleted their stores. Consequently, during the second half the players used less carbohydrate than during the first half. One player (●) stopped at half-time after a high use of glycogen in the first half.

Diet and intermittent exercise performance

It is well established that performance during long-term continuous exercise is improved by intake of a carbohydrate rich diet in the days before the exercise. In order to evaluate whether a high-carbohydrate diet also affects performance during prolonged intermittent exercise, which is inherent to football, a study on eight professional Danish players was performed.

A football-specific intermittent exercise test was used to evaluate performance. The test consisted of two parts. In the first part the players performed 45 minutes of walking and running at different speeds with and without a ball on a grass field according to a standardized protocol. The players covered a distance of 6856 metres. After a 15-minute break, the players then carried out the second part, which consisted of intermittent running on a motor-driven treadmill (see Fig. NU 2). The players first ran in seven 5-minute periods at varying speeds (see Fig. NU 2A), during which they covered a total distance

302

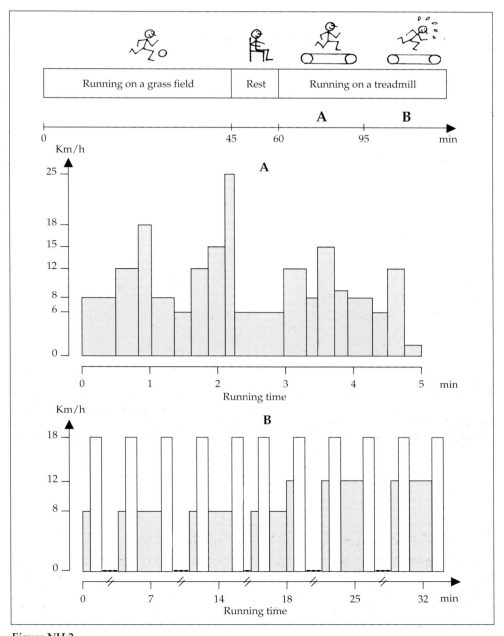

Figure NU 2

The figure shows a protocol of the football-specific intermittent exercise test used to evaluate performance in a dietary study with Danish professional players.

First the players performed controlled movements specific for football with and without a ball for 45 minutes. The players then rested for 15 minutes followed by intermittent running on a motor driven treadmill. In the first 35 minutes the players performed seven 5-minute intermittent exercise bouts as shown in A. The players then alternated between low-intensity running (8 km/h) for 10 seconds and high-speed running (18 km/h) for 15 seconds, and after 18 minutes the lower speed was increased to 12 km/h (B). The players continued in this manner until they were exhausted.

303

of 5677 metres. Then, they performed intermittent running, alternating between high-speed running for 15 seconds and low-speed running for 10 seconds (see Fig. NU 2B). The players continued until they were exhausted and the test result was the total distance covered. The average exercise intensity during the tests was 70-80% of the maximum oxygen uptake, which resembles the average intensity during a match (see page 71).

The players performed the test on two occasions separated by 14 days. On one of the occasions the test was carried out with the players having consumed their normal diet during the days before the test, and on the other occasion the players performed the test having consumed a high-carbohydrate diet prior to the test. Both tests were carried out three days after a competitive match with the diets maintained during the two days following the match. In order to control the food intake, each player was given a selection of foods and a list of instructions explaining which type of food to consume. The players recorded what kind and how much food they had eaten. From this information the nutritional and energy content of the diets was ascertained. Fig. NU 3 shows the relative carbohydrate intake with the two diets.

Figure NU 3
The figure shows the carbohydrate content (expressed as a percentage of the total energy intake) of food ingested during the »normal« and high-carbohydrate diet before the tests (to the left), and the average running distance covered in the tests (to the right). After ingesting the high-carbohydrate diet the players ran, on average, about one km longer than after consuming the »normal« diet.

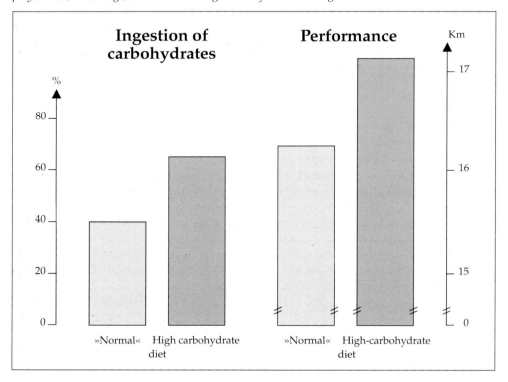

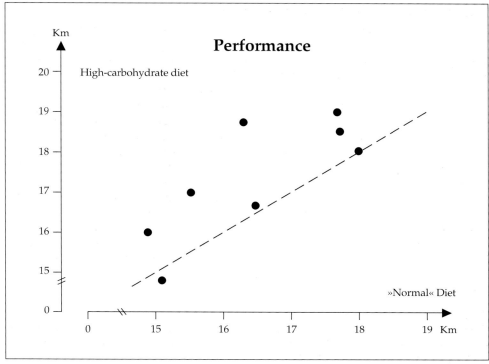

Figure NU 4

The figure compares the individual distances covered during the tests after the »normal« and high-carbohydrate diet in the dietary study with Danish professional players. Values placed above the oblique line indicate that a player covered a longer distance after the high-carbohydrate diet. Five players ran a considerably greater distance after the high-carbohydrate diet, whereas three of the players covered almost the same distance in the two tests.

The test leaders were not aware of which diet the players had been given until the entire study was completed. Neither were the players told of the purpose of the study until after the second test. In order to minimize any other sources of experimental error, the players were randomly assigned the two diets so that during each test occasion some of the players had consumed the high-carbohydrate diet while others had consumed the normal diet.

The results of the study showed that after following the high-carbohydrate diet, the players ran, on average, 1 kilometre more compared to after the normal diet (see Fig. NU 3). Individual values are illustrated in Fig. NU 4. Three of the eight players ran approximately the same distance in both tests, whereas five obtained a considerably better result after consuming a high-carbohydrate diet. Thus, a high-carbohydrate intake the days before prolonged intermittent exercise appears to have a positive effect on performance for the majority of players.

305

Replenishment of muscle glycogen stores

To establish if football players actually consume sufficient amounts of carbohydrate, Swedish and Danish football players were studied.

After a competitive match played on a Sunday, players in the Swedish team Malmö FF were monitored until the following Wednesday when they played a European Cup match. One light training session took place on the Tuesday. Immediately after the match on Sunday, and on the following two days, muscle samples were taken from a quadriceps muscle for determination of glycogen content (see Fig. NU 5). After the match the muscle glycogen content was found to be reduced to approximately 25% of the level before the match. Twenty-four hours (Monday) and forty-eight hours (Tuesday) later, the glycogen stores had only increased to 37% and 39% of the pre-match level, respectively. Muscle samples were not taken on the Wednesday because of

Figure NU 5
The figure shows the glycogen content of a quadriceps muscle for players from the Swedish top-class team, Malmö FF, before and just after a league match (Sunday). The figure also gives muscle glycogen values at 24 and 48 hours after the match, and an estimate of the level before a European Cup match on the following Wednesday (dotted bar). The values are expressed in relation to the level before the league match (100%). It appears that the muscle glycogen stores were only restored to about 50% of »normal« level before the European Cup match.

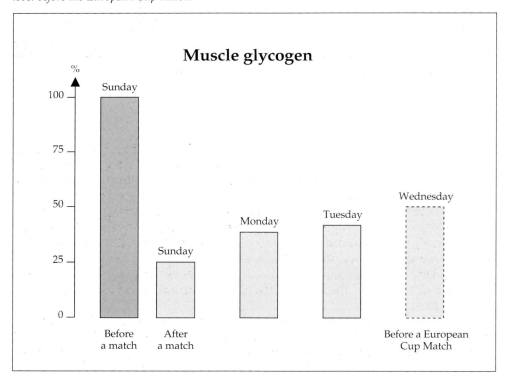

It is important for a football player to consume large amounts of carbohydrate in the diet.

the European Cup match, but it can be assumed that the glycogen stores were less than 50% of the pre-match levels. Thus, the players started the European Cup match with only about half of their normal muscle glycogen stores, which most likely reduced their physical performance potential.

The food intake of each player was analysed during the same period (Sunday – Wednesday). The average energy intake per day was 20.7 MJ (approximately 4700 kcal), with a variation between players from 10.5 to 26.8 MJ (see Table NU 1). By use of the activity profile and body weight of each player, it was calculated that most of the players should have had an intake of at least 20 MJ. Therefore, for some of the players the total energy consumption was much lower than required.

It is not only the energy content of the food that is important. The quality of the diet must also be considered, e.g. the proportion of protein, fat, and carbohydrate. The players' diet contained on average 14% protein (which lies within the recommended range), 47% carbohydrate, and 39% fat. If these percentages are compared with those recommended of at least 60% carbo-hydrate and no more than 25% fat, it is evident that the carbohydrate intake by the players from Malmö FF was too low on the days before the European Cup match. This factor, together with the relatively low total energy consumption of some players after the Sunday match, can explain the low muscle glycogen stores found on the days prior to the European Cup match.

A similar study assessing food intake was performed with Danish top-class players. The players completed food intake questionnaires over a 10-day period. Based on this information and an individual interview, the consumed amount of carbohydrate (CHO), fat (F), and protein (P) was calculated (see Scheme NU 1)

	Energy distribution in %			Total energy
	CHO	F	P	MJ
Football players (males)				
Danish	46	38	16	15.7
Malmö FF	47	39	14	20.7
National average (18-34 years)				
Males	43	43	14	12.5
Females	46	39	15	9.2
Recommended				
Males	50-60	20-30	10-20	11.9
Females	50-60	20-30	10-20	8.6
Recommended in football				
Males	60-70	10-20	10-20	15-25
Females	60-70	10-20	10-20	10-20

Scheme NU 1

The study revealed that the carbohydrate content in the diet of Danish top-class players does not differ significantly from the national average for individuals in the same age group and that the intake of carbohydrate for the players was lower than recommended. Thus, as with the Malmö FF team, the diet of the elite Danish players was inadequate for optimal physical perform-ance.

Practical applications

It is clear that eating a carbohydrate rich diet on the days before a match is of importance for performance. To consume a significant amount of carbohydrate in the everyday diet is also beneficial, as it promotes a high training efficiency as well as good health. Figure NU 6 illustrates how the muscle glycogen stores may vary during a week of training for a player that consumed either a high-carbohydrate diet or a »normal« diet. During training some of the glycogen is used, and between training sessions the stores are slowly replenished. If the diet contains large amounts of carbohydrate it is possible to restore glycogen throughout the week. This may not be achieved if the diet is low in carbohydrates. In the example shown in Fig. NU 6, it can be seen that keeping a diet rich in carbohydrate results in higher pre-training and pre-match muscle glycogen levels than does intake of a normal diet.

Figure NU 6
The figure depicts a hypothetical example of how muscle glycogen stores can vary during a week with a high-carbohydrate and a »normal« diet. There is a match on Sunday, a light training session on Monday, an intensive training session on Tuesday and Thursday, and a light training session on Saturday. The filled symbols indicate the values after the match and after training. The glycogen stores are replenished at a faster rate with the high-carbohydrate diet, thus allowing for proper preparation for training and the subsequent match. In contrast, consuming a »normal« diet may result in reduced training efficiency and the muscle glycogen stores may be lowered before the next match.

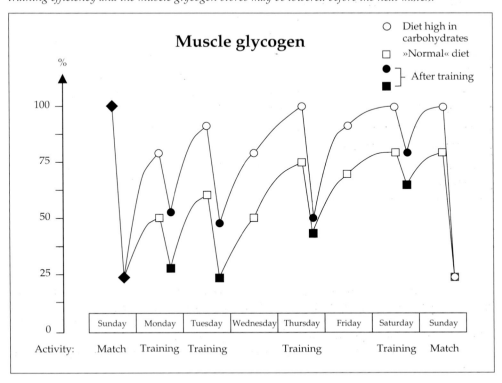

It is important to choose a well-balanced diet.

The highest potential for storing glycogen in the muscles is immediately after exercise. It is therefore advisable to consume carbohydrate, either in solid or liquid form, shortly after a match or training session. This is particularly important if the players are training twice on the same day.

What should a football player eat

Maintaining an adequate diet does not ensure good performance during a match, but it will improve the potential to reach a maximum level of performance. In this section, the types of foods a football player should ideally eat are discussed.

Food contains carbohydrate, protein, and fat as well as other important nutrients such as vitamins and minerals.

Carbohydrate

Carbohydrate can be divided into a simple and complex form. Examples of the two types of carbohydrate are shown below.

Simple carbohydrate	*Complex carbohydrate*
Low-fat confectionery (sweets/candy)	Potatoes
Cakes	Vegetables
White sugar	Grain (e.g. oatmeal)
Jam (fruit spread)	Bread
Soft drinks (e.g. Coca-Cola)	Spaghetti/Pasta/Rice
Fruit	

Both types of carbohydrate can be used for re-building of the muscle glycogen stores. In the first few hours following exercise, consumption of simple carbohydrates results in a faster storage of glycogen than intake of complex carbohydrates. However, after 24 hours there is no difference between simple and complex carbohydrates. The sources of complex carbohydrate have a higher nutritional value as they also contain minerals, vitamins, and fibre, and should therefore be preferred.

Fibre is an indigestible form of carbohydrate and can not function as a source of fuel. Fibre helps to prevent constipation and gives a feeling of fullness, but too much fibre can reduce the uptake of vitamins and actually induce constipation if water consumption is not increased at the same time.

It is important that a player's diet consists of a high proportion of carbohydrates. Below are some suggestions on how to increase the daily intake of carbohydrates.

Eat a large portion of potatoes, pasta, or rice with a hot meal

Eat large portions of vegetables
- boiled or raw vegetables with a hot meal
- raw vegetables as snacks between meals and as a supplement to lunch

Eat a lot of bread
- cut thick slices
- make sandwiches
- eat bread with a hot meal

Eat a lot of fruit
- as a snack between meals
- as dessert
- with cereals

Protein

Protein is found in foods such as egg, milk, meat, and fish (animal protein), as well as in vegetables and grain products (vegetable protein). Protein is used primarily for maintaining and building up tissues, such as muscles. The amount of protein required in the diet is a topic frequently discussed, particularly with respect to those sports where muscle strength is important or where muscle injuries often occur. Football can be included in both of these categories. The daily intake of protein by the Swedish players who were investigated was approximately 2 grams per kilogram of body weight, while the players from the Danish study consumed 2-3 grams per kilogram of body weight. This amount appears to be sufficient as the recommended daily intake for athletes is 1-2 grams per kilogram of body weight. In general, supplementing protein intake by tablets or protein powders is unnecessary for football players, even during an intensive strength training period.

Fat

Fat exists in two forms: *saturated* and *unsaturated* fat. The saturated fats are solid at room temperature (butter, margarine, and fat in meat) while unsaturated fats are liquid or soft at room temperature (vegetable oil, vegetable margarine, and fat in fish). Intake of unsaturated fats are essential for the body, and in contrast to saturated fats, unsaturated fats aid in lowering the amount of cholesterol in the blood, thereby reducing the risk of heart disease. The total content of fat in the average diet for a football player is often too high (see Scheme NU 1 – page 308) and a general lowering of fat intake is advisable. It is also important that saturated fats are replaced with unsaturated fats where possible. The following advice can help reduce the total amount of fat in the diet and also lower the ratio of saturated to unsaturated fat.

Limit the intake of french fries, potato crisps, etc.
  – replace with boiled or baked potatoes

Limit the use of butter
  – replace with vegetable margarine

Limit the intake of whipped cream, cream cheese, etc.
  – replace with a low-fat substitute, e.g. low-fat yoghurt

Limit the use of margarine for baking and frying
  – replace with vegetable oil

Limit the intake of meat, sauces, and other fatty foods

Limit the intake of whole fat milk
  – replace with low-fat or, preferably, skimmed milk

Minerals and vitamins

Food and drink supply the body with fluids, energy-producing substrates, and other important components, such as salt, minerals, and vitamins. In a well-balanced diet most nutrients are supplied in sufficient amounts. However, there may be exceptions.

In a study with top-class male Swedish players, it was found that the majority of players were iron deficient. A similar observation was made for the players of the Canadian National team immediately prior to competing in the 1984 Olympic Games in Los Angeles. Iron is an important element in hemoglobin, which binds to the red blood cells and aids in the transport of oxygen throughout the body (see page 22). Therefore, an adequate iron intake is essential for football players and especially for female players, who lose blood and, thus, hemoglobin during menstruation.

It is advisable to increase iron intake in periods when players are expected to increase their red blood cell production, e.g. during the re-building period of the pre-season or when training at a high altitude. As an example, the Danish players supplemented their diet with iron during a training camp in Columbia (2600 metres above sea level) before the 1986 World Cup in Mexico.

The recommended daily intake of iron for a football player is approximately 20 milligrams, which should be ingested via solid foods rather than in tablet form, as iron found in solid foods is more effectively absorbed from the intestine to the blood. Animal organs (liver, heart, and kidneys), dried fruits, bread, nuts, strawberries, and legumes are foods with a high content of iron. The most efficient way to absorb iron is by eating animal organs together with vitamin C from solid foods.

Pasta and vegetables have a high content of carbohydrates.
The food on the plate contains 70% carbohydrates, 15% fat and 15% protein.

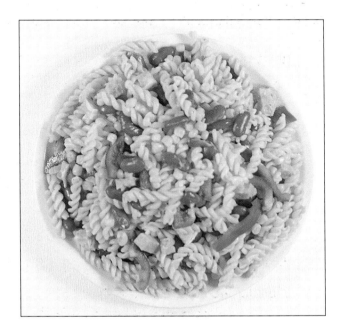

A question commonly asked is whether or not players should supplement their diet with vitamins. In general, vitamin supplementation is not necessary, but there are conditions where it might be beneficial. For example, it is advisable to enhance vitamin E intake when training at high altitudes, and to use vitamin C and multiple B-vitamin supplements in hot climates.

A diet of a football player

An example of a top-class football player's diet for one day is described here in detail. The diet was well-balanced, supplying sufficient amounts of carbohydrate, minerals, and vitamins. The total energy intake was approximately 20 MJ (about 5000 kcal).

Breakfast

Food: Four slices of white bread with jam, two wholemeal bread rolls with a little butter and jam, and two small tubs of yoghurt.
Fluid: Two cups of tea (without sugar).

Total: 66% carbohydrate, 24% fat, and 10% protein.
Carbohydrate intake: 194 grams; *energy provided:* 5 MJ.

Lunch

Food: Four slices of wholemeal bread with a small amount of butter, one egg, two tomatoes, two packets of raisins, two bananas, and a bowl of salad.
Fluid: Three glasses of skimmed milk and one cup of coffee (without sugar).

Total: 65% carbohydrate, 21% fat, and 14% protein.
Carbohydrate intake: 188 grams; *energy provided:* 5 MJ.

Dinner

Food: One bowl (large) of spaghetti with minced meat (beef), half an onion, one tin of skinned tomatoes, and a bowl of salad.
Fluid: Two glasses of skimmed milk.

Total: 61% carbohydrate, 20% fat, and 19% protein.
Carbohydrate intake: 220 grams; *energy provided:* 6.2 MJ.

These three main meals provided an energy intake of approximately 16.2 MJ (about 80% of the daily intake) of which 63% was from carbohydrate. The remaining energy was obtained from snacks between meals.

Snacks

Food: One apple, one packet of raisins, and one bag of sweets.
Fluid: Two cups of coffee (without sugar) and one litre of juice.

Total: 90% carbohydrates, 4% fat, and 6% protein.
Carbohydrate intake: 201 grams: *energy provided:* 3.8 MJ.

Total for the whole day: 70% carbohydrate, 17% fat, and 13% protein.
Carbohydrate intake: 803 grams; *energy provided:* 20 MJ.

Changing dietary habits

The studies mentioned earlier in this chapter showed that the normal diet of a football player is often too low in carbohydrate (see Scheme NU 1 – page 308). So, how can better eating habits be established?

In the study concerning the effect of a carbohydrate rich diet on intermittent exercise performance, 60% of the players' diet was controlled, whereas they, within given guidelines, could select the remaining 40% themselves. Using this procedure the average carbohydrate intake was increased from about 45% in the normal diet to 65% in the high-carbohydrate diet. The foods that were consumed in the carbohydrate rich diet are found in most households. This means that it is not necessary to drastically change dietary habits in order to obtain a better diet.

The first step towards better eating habits is to make the players aware of the content of their normal diet. It is advisable that players, or the individuals who prepare the food for the players, read the information labels on food packaging where nutritional composition and energy content of the food is given.

Meal times during the week

In general, a football player should eat three main meals per day – one in the morning, one in the middle of the day, and one in the evening. Each meal should constitute about 25% of the total energy intake, but on training days the meal after training should have a larger energy content than the other meals. The remaining 25% of the total energy intake should come from two or three snacks between meals.

The amount of carbohydrate in the diet should be increased a couple of days before a match. For example, if the match is on a Sunday, a carbohydrate intake of 55-65% of the total intake at the beginning of the week could increase to 65-75% after the training on Thursday. In order to get a sufficient amount of minerals and vitamins it is advisable that the intake of carbohydrate is mainly in the form of complex carbohydrates (see page 311).

The match-day meal

Undigested food in the stomach and the intestine can cause problems during exercise. Blood is diverted to the stomach region and exercising muscles, resulting in a reduced supply of blood to the brain. This is the cause of the common experience of feeling dizzy when running or cycling immediately after eating. Other possible side-effects caused by the digestion of food during exercise include upset stomach and diarrhoea.

On the day of a match the intake of fat and protein (especially derived from meat) should be restricted, as these nutrients require a relatively long time to be digested. The supposed beneficial effects of eating a big steak are mythical. Such a meal may in fact have a detrimental effect on performance. On the day of the match, food should in essence not differ from the food consumed in the normal diet, but meat and strong spices should be avoided.

315

The last meal prior to a match should be eaten 3-4 hours before kick-off. If too much food is ingested after this time, there still may be undigested food in the stomach and intestine when the match begins. The pre-match meal should contain a high proportion of carbohydrates. A snack high in carbohydrate, e.g. bread with jam, may be eaten about 1.5 hours before the match. However, the time references given are only guidelines. There are great individual differences in the ability to digest food. It is a good idea for players to experiment with a variation of foods at different times before training sessions.

In theory, it would seem beneficial to consume large amounts of carbohydrate during the hour before a match in order to increase the size of the carbohydrate stores. However, doing so appears to have a negative effect (see Fig. NU 7). An increased concentration of glucose in the stomach and intestine stimulates a greater release of the hormone insulin. Insulin slowly drains

Figure NU 7
The figure shows the effect of a large intake (70 grams) of carbohydrates 45 minutes before exercise. Length of time to exhaustion for the exercise was determined and blood glucose was measured before and during exercise, on one occasion with (A) and on another occasion without (B) carbohydrate intake prior to the exercise. The ingestion of carbohydrate caused the blood glucose to rise at rest and to drastically fall when the exercise began (A). The resultant effect was that exhaustion occurred at an earlier point. Thus, intake of large amounts of carbohydrate just before exercise can impair performance.

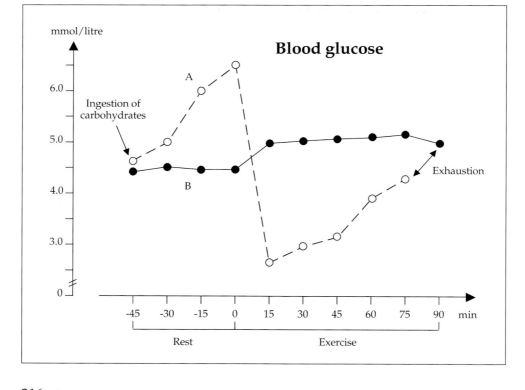

the blood of glucose, making surplus glucose disappear from the blood into various tissues such as the kidneys and liver. At rest insulin has a beneficial effect, but problems may arise if high insulin levels are combined with exercise. When exercising with a high insulin concentration there is an abnormally large loss of glucose from the blood resulting in a low blood glucose concentration. Consequently, the muscles and the brain gradually become starved of glucose, which eventually leads to fatigue (see Fig. NU 7). A large carbohydrate intake just before a match will also result in fluid from the blood passing into the stomach and intestine. Apart from the accompanying unpleasant feeling of having the stomach filled with water, there will be negative effects on physical performance due to the reduction in blood volume. In conclusion, one should avoid eating large amounts of carbohydrate during the hour before a match, and instead only consume fluids with a low content of sugar (see page 325).

Summary

The diet of a football player should contain large amounts of carbohydrate to allow for a high training efficiency and for optimal preparation for matches. Therefore, it is important for the players to be conscious of the nutritive value of the food that they consume.

On the day of a match the last meal should be ingested no later than three hours before kick-off, and it should consist of simple carbohydrates that can be rapidly absorbed. During the hour before a match, solid food or liquid with a high carbohydrate content should be avoided.

Fluid Intake

320

Fluid Intake

During exercise the body releases heat through the evaporation of sweat (see page 34). Sweat can also be absorbed by clothes or fall to the ground without any accompanying heat loss. Sweating leads to a loss of fluid, which may be 2-3 litres for a player during a football match. Under extreme conditions the reduction in body water can be higher, e.g. in a World Cup match in Mexico, one Danish player lost about 4.5 litres of fluid.

Loss of body fluids will result in a decrease in blood volume. Consequently, the heart will not be completely filled before each contraction and must beat more frequently to compensate. A decrease in body water will also cause the body temperature to increase more than normal during exercise, as there is less blood transporting the excess heat to the skin (see Fig. FL 1 – page 322). As illustrated on Fig. FL 2 (see page 323) these changes inhibit performance. For example, a 70 kilogram player who loses one litre of sweat during the first half of a match (1.4% of body weight) may have a 15% lower physical performance capacity in the second half.

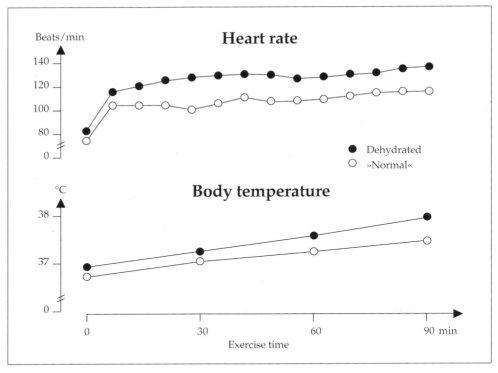

Figure FL 1
The figure shows how dehydration affects heart rate and body temperature. A player performed the same exercise on two occasions, once with normal water balance and once in a state of dehydration. Both heart rate and body temperature increased more when the player was dehydrated.

What to drink

A player should drink frequently during a game in order to replace the lost fluid. Before discussing the different types of drinks that can be used, some important aspects of fluid absorption need to be explained.

Fluid is absorbed into the blood in the small intestine through a relatively quick process (see FL 3). However, the fluid must first be emptied from the stomach into the small intestine. This is a much slower process that limits the rate at which fluid is absorbed by the blood. Fluid absorption is influenced by several factors including the quantity, temperature, and sugar content of the ingested fluid. The larger the fluid intake (to a limit of 800 ml), the higher the rate by which the fluid is emptied from the stomach. Warmer drinks appear to be emptied at a slower rate than colder ones, but drinking fluid that is too cold may result in stomach discomforts. A very low concentration of salt improves the rate of absorption, whereas the effect is reversed when the concentration is too high. These principles apply both at rest and during exercise.

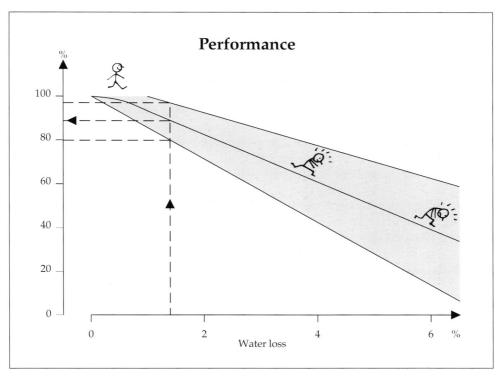

Figure FL 2

The figure shows how dehydration affects performance. Performance with normal levels of body water is presented as 100% and all other values are expressed in relation to this. On the horizontal axis, water loss (expressed per kilogram of body weight) is given. The reduction in performance for a given loss of fluid is expressed by a range (shaded area), as there is individual differences in how fluid loss affects performance. For instance, if a person had a water loss corresponding to 1.4% of body weight, the decrease in performance may be between 3% and 20% (indicated by the horizontal dotted-lines).

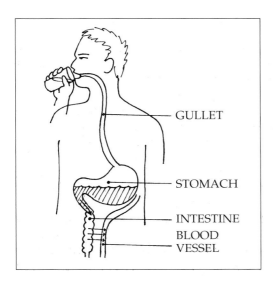

Figure FL 3

The figure shows how fluid after intake is absorbed into the blood. The rate limiting part of the absorption is the transport from the stomach into the intestine.

323

The most important constituent of a drink is the concentration of sugar, i.e. the amount of sugar per litre of fluid. Figure FL 4 shows the effect of drinking fluids with different sugar concentrations. A drink with a sugar concentration of 2.5% or less gives an optimal rate of emptying from the stomach, whereas a higher concentration of sugar reduces this rate. For example, more than half of the fluid with a sugar concentration of 5% was still in the stomach 20 minutes after drinking it. It should be noted however, that a 5% sugar drink can be absorbed faster if the sugar is of a special composition (a so-called polymer). Too much fluid in the stomach can cause an uncomfortable sensation during exercise and the excess fluid can not be used by the body.

During a match, the muscles gradually take up glucose (sugar) from the blood, which may lower the blood glucose concentration. Towards the end of a match this can be a contributing factor to fatigue. Drinks should therefore contain sugar in order to supply glucose to the muscles and to maintain a normal blood glucose level during a match.

Figure FL 4
The figure illustrates how the sugar content in a fluid effects the rate of transport from the stomach into the intestine. The values show how much fluid is left in the stomach after a given time when ingesting drinks with a sugar concentration of 0%, 2.5%, 5%, 10%, and 15%. After 20 minutes the fluid with a sugar concentration of 0% and 2.5% had disappeared from the stomach, whereas more than half of the other fluids remained in the stomach.

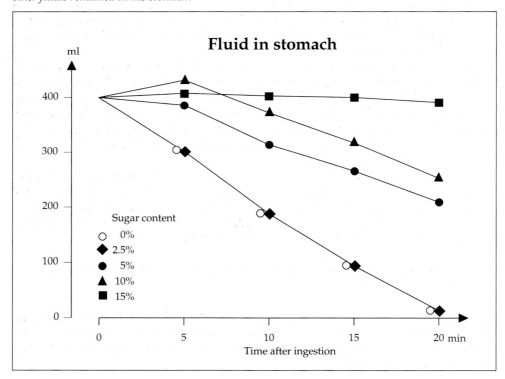

A player should drink both during a match and a training session in order to restore the lost fluid.

In a cold environment the need for water is minor, and a drink with a sugar concentration up to 10% can be used. Before using drinks with high sugar concentrations in a match however, the players should have tried these drinks during training to ensure that stomach upset does not occur.

Sweat contains salt, but in a concentration lower than what is found in the body. This means that relatively more fluid than salt is lost in sweat, so the concentration of salt in the body increases. For this reason, drinks should only contain little or no salt.

There are large individual differences in the ability to tolerate drinks and to empty fluid from the stomach. While some players are unaffected by large amounts of fluid in the stomach, others find it difficult to tolerate even small quantities of fluid. The players will benefit by experimenting with different drinks and drinking habits during training. By drinking frequently during training, a player who has difficulty in absorbing fluid during exercise will gradually be able to tolerate more.

There is no need to buy the »sport drink« products which are commercially available. These drinks are often expensive, and in many cases the sugar concentration is too high. If these products are used it may be necessary to dilute the drink more than is instructed. It is easy to make an appropriate drink. The recipe below gives a sugar concentration of 2.5%:

> *25 grams of sugar per litre of water with flavouring such as lemon juice or a little citric acid.*

Alternatively, hot or cold tea with added sugar at 2-3% concentration may be used. Carbonated drinks such as Coca-Cola are not recommended as the carbonation can cause discomfort in the stomach and the sugar content is too high (normally above 10%).

325

How much to drink

The body can only partially regulate water balance through the sensation of thirst as thirst is quenched before a sufficient amount of fluid has been drunk. In one study where subjects exercised in hot surroundings and were allowed to drink as much as they wanted, it was found that only 70% of the fluid needed to restore the loss was consumed. In another study, the fluid intake of three groups of soldiers marching in a temperature of 25 °C was monitored. The first group was not allowed to drink at all, the second group was allowed to drink as much as they wanted, and the third group was instructed to drink at regular intervals. When the performance of these groups was evaluated, it was found that the first group performed the worst; the third group, who also drank the most, performed better than the other two groups (see Fig. FL 5). These studies show that in order to maintain fluid balance, more fluid has to be drunk than just satisfies the sensation of thirst.

The colour of urine is a good indicator of the fluid balance and the need for water. If the body is dehydrated, the amount of water in the urine is reduced and the colour becomes a stronger yellow.

Figure FL 5
The figure shows the importance of drinking during exercise for the regulation of body temperature. Three groups of soldiers (A, B, and C) marched for six hours. The greatest increase in body temperature was observed in group C, which did not drink at all. Group A was requested to regularly replace the water loss and performed better than group B, which only drank when they were thirsty. Thus, in order to avoid a marked fluid deficit during exercise, one should drink more than just to quench one's thirst.

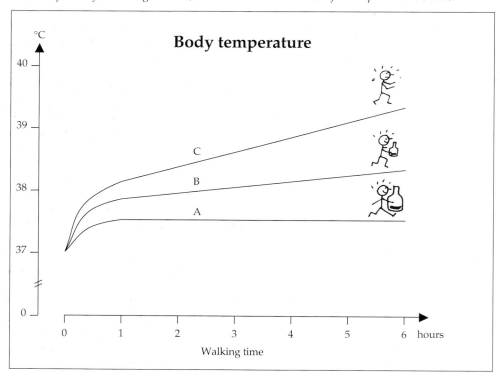

When to drink

Before a match

It is important that the players are not dehydrated before a match. The players should begin the process of »topping-up« with fluid already the day before a match. For example, an additional litre of juice can be drunk on the evening before a match, which will also provide an extra supply of sugar.

If more glycogen is stored in the muscles before a match than normally, the amount of water in the body is elevated, as glycogen binds water. An extra 200 grams of muscle glycogen, as a result of a high-carbohydrate diet (see page 311), will increase body fluids by more than half a litre. This will help to reduce the net loss of water during a match, so also in this aspect a high carbohydrate intake the days before a match is advantageous.

The intake of coffee should be limited as coffee contains caffeine, which has a diuretic effect and causes the body to lose a larger amount of water than is absorbed from the coffee.

On the match-day, the players should have plenty to drink and be encouraged to drink even when they are not feeling thirsty. However, during the last hour before the match the players should not have more than 300 ml (a large cup) to drink every 15 minutes.

During a match

During a match small amounts of fluid should be drunk frequently. It is optimal to drink between 100 and 300 ml with a 2-3% sugar concentration every 10 to 15 minutes. This will give a total fluid intake of between one and two litres, plus 30 to 50 grams of sugar during the match. This is sufficient to replace a significant amount of the water lost through sweat, and to satisfy some of the demand for sugar. Although fluid intake during a match is important, it should not interfere with the game. Ingesting fluid at a critical time during a match may disturb the playing rhythm, so players should only drink when there is a natural pause in the game. It is convenient to place small bottles of fluid at different positions around the field in order to avoid long runs to the team bench.

After a match

In a study the water balance of some players was measured after a match. Determinations of body weight before and after the match showed that the players had a fluid loss of 1.5-3.0 litres corresponding to 2-4% of body weight during the match. Although the players were advised to drink plenty of fluid after the match, only half of the lost water was replaced during the first four hours, and it took almost ten hours before the fluid balance was fully restored. Other studies have similarly demonstrated that restoration of fluid balance is a slow process. These observations show that it is not sufficient merely to increase fluid intake immediately after a match. It is not unusual that players are partially dehydrated on the day after a match.

Summary

The following recommendations regarding fluid intake may be helpful for a football player:

1. Drink plenty of fluid the day before a match and on the day of the match – more than just to quench thirst.

2. Drink frequently just before and during a match as well as at half-time, but only small amounts at a time – not more than 300 ml of fluid every 15 minutes.

3. Drinks consumed just before and during a match should have a sugar concentration lower than 3% and a temperature between 5 and 10 °C. The addition of salt or other substances is not necessary.

4. Drink a lot after a match – even several hours afterwards.

5. Use the colour of the urine as an indication of the need for fluid – the more yellow the urine, the greater the need for fluid intake.

6. Experiment with drinking habits during training so that any difficulties in absorbing fluid during exercise can be overcome.

During a match it is appropriate to take in fluid during natural breaks.

Word index

References and further reading

Books

Handbook of Sports Medicine and Science. Football (Soccer) (1994). Ed.: Ekblom B. Blackwell Scientific Publications, London/Boston.

Science and Football (1988). Eds.: Reilly T., Lees A., Davids K. & Murphy W.J. E. & F.N. Spon, London/New York.

Science and Football II (1993). Eds.: Reilly T., Clarys J. & Stibbe A. E. & F.N. Spon, London/New York.

Textbook of Work Physiology. Physiological Bases of Exercise (1986). Åstrand P.-O. & Rodahl K. McGraw-Hill inc., USA.

Papers

Bangsbo J. (1990). Usefulness of blood lactate measurements in soccer. Science and Football 3: 2-4.

Bangsbo J. (1992). Anaerobic energy yield in soccer - performance of young players. Science and Football 5: 24-28.

Bangsbo J. (1992). Time motion characteristics of competition soccer. Science and Football 6: 21-25.

Bangsbo J., (1994). The Physiology of Soccer – with Special Reference to Intense Intermittent Exercise. Acta Physiologica Scandinavica, Vol 150, Supplementum 615.

Bangsbo J., Nørregaard L. & Thorsøe F. (1991). Activity profile of competition soccer. Canadian Journal of Sport Sciences 16: 110-116.

Bangsbo J. & Lindquist F. (1992). Comparison of various exercise tests with endurance performance during soccer in professional players. International Journal of Sports Medicine 13: 125-132.

Bangsbo J., Nørregaard L. & Thorsøe F. (1992). The effect of carbohydrate diet on intermittent exercise performance. International Journal of Sports Medicine 13: 152-157.

Bangsbo J., Petersen A. & Michalsik L. (1992). Accumulated O_2 deficit during intense exercise and muscle characteristics of elite athletes. International Journal of Sports Medicine 14: 207-213.

Berg K.E., La Voie, J.C. & Latin, R.W. (1985). Physiological training effects of playing youth soccer. Medicine and Science in Sports and Exercise 17: 656-660.

Boobis L.H. (1987). Metabolic aspects of fatigue during sprinting. In: Macleod D., Maughan R., Nimmo M., Reilly T. & Williams T.C. (eds). Exercise; Benefits, Limits and Adaptations, pp. 116-143. E. & F.N. Spon, London/New York.

Brooks G.A. (1987). Lactate production during exercise: oxidizable substrate versus fatigue agent. In: Macleod D., Maughan R., Nimmo M., Reilly T. & Williams T.C. (eds). Exercise. Benefits, limits and adaptations, pp. 144-158. E. & F.N. Spon, London/New York.

Costill D.L. (1988). Carbohydrate for exercise: Dietary demands for optimal performance. International Journal of Sports Medicine 9: 1-18.

Ekblom B. (1986). Applied physiology of soccer. Sports Medicine 3: 50-60.

Ekstrand J. (1982). Soccer injuries and their prevention (thesis). Linköping University Medical Dissertation 130, Linköping, Sweden.

Jacobs I., Westlin N., Karlsson J., Rasmusson M. & Houghton B. (1982). Muscle glycogen and diet in elite soccer players. European Journal of Applied Physiology 48: 297-302.

Maughan R.J. & Noakes T.D. (1991). Fluid replacement and exercise stress. A brief review of studies on fluid replacement and some guidelines for the athlete. Sports Medicine 12: 16-31.

Öberg B., Ekstrand J., Möller M. & Gillquist J. (1984). Muscle strength and flexibility in different positions of soccer players. International Journal of Sports Medicine 5: 213-216.

Reilly T. (1990). Football. In: Reilly, T., Secher N., Snell P. & Williams C. (eds). Physiology of Sports, pp. 465-487. E.& F.N. Spon, London/New York.

Rhodes E.C., Mosher R.E., McKenzie D.C., Franks I.M. & Potts J.E. (1986). Physiological profiles of the Canadian olympic soccer team. Canadian Journal of Sport Sciences 11: 31-36.

Rico J. & Bangsbo J. (1993). Coding system to evaluate actions with the ball during a soccer match. Proceedings from the 1st World Congress of Notational Analysis of Sport. 22-25 November, 1992, Liverpool, England.

Saltin B. (1987). The physiological and biochemical basis for training and competition. In: Mæhlum S., Nilsson S. & Renström P. (eds). An Update on Sport Medicine, pp. 16-59. Astra-Syntex, Oslo.

Togari H. & Asami T. (1972). A study of throw-in training in soccer. Proceeding of the Department of Physical Education, College of General Education, University of Tokyo, 6: 33-38.